Dan Kieran and Ian Vince

Dan Kieran is the editor of the best-selling *Crap Towns*, *Crap Jobs* and *Crap Holidays*. He is deputy editor of *The Idler*, author of *I Fought the Law* and writes for numerous newspapers.

Ian Vince is the author of *Britain: What a State*, *The Little Black Book of Red Tape* and co-author of *The Myway Code* with Dan. He writes comedy sketches for radio and TV and is contributing editor of *The Idler*.

THREE MEN in a FLOAT

Across England at 15 mph

Dan Kieran and Ian Vince

JOHN MURRAY

First published in Great Britain in 2008 by John Murray (Publishers)
An Hachette UK Company

First published in paperback in 2009

2

© Dan Kieran and Ian Vince 2008

A CIP catalogue record for this title is available from the British Library

ISBN 978-1-84854-015-6

Typeset in Monotype Bembo by Servis Filmsetting Ltd, Stockport, Cheshire

Printed and bound by Clays Ltd, St Ives plc

John Murray policy is to use papers that are natural, renewable and recyclable products and made from wood grown in sustainable forests. The logging and manufacturing processes are expected to conform to the environmental regulations of the country of origin.

John Murray (Publishers)
338 Euston Road
London NW1 3BH

www.johnmurray.co.uk

To Pras, our third man, without whom we'd still be stuck in Lowestoft

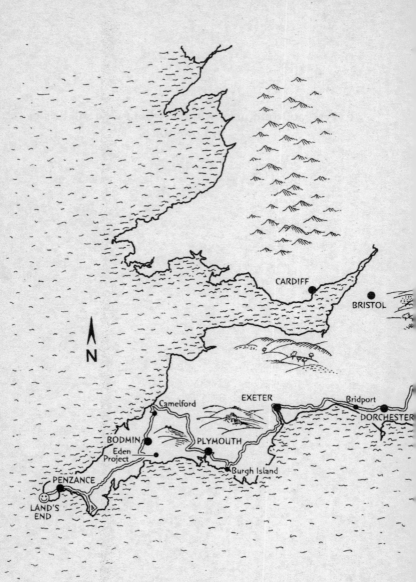

LOWESTOFT

Moulton

BURY ST EDMUNDS

CAMBRIDGE

Royston

OXFORD

LUTON

SWINDON

Princes Risborough

LONDON

Pewsey

SALISBURY

Shaftesbury

SOUTHAMPTON

PORTSMOUTH

BRIGHTON

OURNEMOUTH

Author's Note

Under no circumstances should anyone attempt to recreate the electrical chicanery performed throughout this book. Prasanth Visweswaran is uniquely acquainted with all kinds of power systems (13-amp, 16-amp, 20-amp, 32-amp single, two- and three-phase electrical supplies, not to mention lamp posts, garage lighting rigs, domestic and industrial fuse boxes and 50,000-volt electricity pylons). He has many certificates that qualify him to laugh in the face of death and poke serious injury squarely in the eye (just as long as he does so with his special electrician's red screwdriver).

See pictures from our epic journey across England at www.threemeninafloat.com

'When people moved slowly in their travel, there was time to establish proper communications with what was strange, to absorb, to adjust oneself. Now that we are whizzed about the world, there is no time for absorbing and adjusting. Perhaps it is for this reason that the world that the traveler knows is beginning to show less and less variety. By the time we can travel at four hundred miles an hour we shall probably move over a dead uniformity, so that the bit of reality we left at one end of the journey is twin to the bit of reality we step into at the other end. Indeed, by that time there will be movement, but strictly speaking, no more travel.'

J. B. Priestley, *English Journey*, (1934)

Introduction

The year 1958 is etched on people's minds for many different reasons. Relatives of the unfortunately named Sir Vivian Fuchs (pronounced Fucks) will remember 2 March fondly as the day their namesake crossed the Antarctic with caterpillar tractors and dog-sled teams in a mere ninety-nine days, giving hope to everyone who is seeking worldwide acclaim and has a family name that can be mistaken for a swear word. Fans of chess will remember 8 January of that year as the day Bobby Fischer astounded the citizens of America by winning their national championship at the tender age of fourteen. It was also, of course, the year when the Amirkabir University of Technology (Tehran Polytechnic) opened its doors for the very first time.

Snipers may be aggrieved that this brief list of memorable events that took place in 1958 glosses over the birth of Nik Kershaw on 1 March, and the fact that in May after a five-year flirtation with serrated edges, started so memorably back in 1953, the Japanese 10 Yen coin went back to having a smooth edge. But for the purposes of this adventure the most important thing to happen in 1958 took place on 2 September in the Morris car plant in Cowley, where a rather beautiful, if slightly timid, milk float was slowly and lovingly being crafted into the world.

Weighing in at 1,302kg she was an impressive sight, with her two-axle rigid body and flashy blue and white paint-work. However, a mere three months into life she could have rolled her headlamps in disbelief, wondering what the future held for a small electric milk float that could run at a maxi-mum speed of 15 miles per hour, when on 5 December the ribbon was cut on Britain's first motorway, the Preston Bypass. It was certainly a sign of the speed to come but, despite the inexorable pace of progress, she soon found her niche, delivering milk quietly and effectively to the residents of neighbouring Oxford.

As with many born on the cusp of the 1960s, her memory of that decade is something of a blur but she re-surfaced, with a rather buxom addition to her body – a cab fitted some time in the 1980s – at Birmingham Airport in 2001, having trundled the streets of Oxford throughout the sixties, seven-ties, eighties and nineties. It's probably not stretching the truth to say that during this time she delivered milk to many notable luminaries, including J. R. R. Tolkien – 1959 was his retirement year – and conveyed dairy goods along the cul-de-sac of time to Aldous Huxley, Harald V of Norway (who was very fond of pink milk), Hugh Grant (never left a tip at Christmas), Chogyam Trungpa (a Buddhist meditation master who always got very cross because she never carried Soya – well, who did in 1963?), so many bishops, cardinals and politicians it's too boring to list them all, not to mention His Royal Highness Philippe Duke of Brabant and Prince of Belgium, John Betjeman, Bill Clinton, Natasha Kaplinsky, Louis Theroux, Fox Mulder, Inspector Morse and the inim-itable Dudley Moore – all of whom would no doubt remem-ber her pottering along the road in the early hours of the morning while they stumbled back to their university digs after a night on the tiles. You can imagine them, at various

times over those four decades, taking a moment in between bouts of violent vomiting behind some bins to watch her purr serenely down the road as a new day dawned.

In 2001 her history comes much more into focus when, as I said, she was bought by Birmingham International Airport. We know, because we have *bona fide* evidence, that her new owners gave her a 'retrofit electric vehicle speed controller' and a '28-volt auxiliary circuit for aircraft lighting' (a speedo and flashing orange light to you and me), which cost the princely sum of £620. She began her new career shunting around people's bags when they went off on holiday – a bit of a comedown from her Oxonian heyday perhaps, but such is the indignity of retirement. It was towards the end of this period, however, that she began to show signs of a mid-life crisis (following a joy-riding episode involving a famous footballer in Nuneaton). So she was promptly sold on to a young man in Devon, who had read about peak oil and the imminent collapse of the global environment and decided an electric vehicle might be a good way to transport himself around in the future. But circumstances soon conspired against him and he, too, had to part company with her.

And so, one bright morning in the spring of 2007, a man in London frantically transferred the £1,400 he had agreed to pay for her via eBay into her current owner's bank account. She did not know it then but, at the age of forty-nine, our heroine was six days away from taking part in an attempt to deliver three men six hundred miles across England from east to west.

1
The Mighty One

DAN

It's fair to say that driving across England in a milk float is not something Ian, Prasanth and I have always dreamt of doing. It's certainly not one of those insane human conquests that rolls off the tongue like the number-one macho challenge facing the whole of mankind, 'climbing Everest'. It doesn't even equate to the second, and actually more dangerous, 'climbing K2' or the third, widely agreed to be suicidal, 'watching *Love, Actually* the whole way through'.

I can't imagine any of us ever attempting such perilous tasks as those. We'd be far too afraid of the long-term psychological damage such projects could induce, not to mention the long-term planning and safety systems you'd have to put in place before setting out. They would all require proper organization and that would be far too unrealistic, far too much like hard work, for amateur adventurers such as our-selves.

Our entire plan consisted of three things, written on the back of a beer mat:

1. *Buy a milk float*
2. *Get it to delivered (on a lorry?) to Lowestoft (farthest point east in England)*
3. *Spend a month driving to Land's End (farthest point west)*

A mere seven days from our planned departure, we had not even managed to acquire a milk float, more of which later, but first you're probably wondering why on earth we would we want to drive across England in a milk float at all. For the answer to that, we'll have to go back to the beer mat.

It was October 2006. Ian and I were in a pub celebrating the publication of *The Myway Code*, a book we'd written together, most of it in that very same pub. (It is, incidentally, the most hilarious driving parody that's ever been written). Keen to continue the driving theme, but also aware of the ecological impact on the planet caused by cars, we began to meander around the edges of an idea that might join two, apparently opposite, passions – is it really possible to love travel and the planet at the same time? A few pints later we'd settled on driving a milk float across England because we were both drunk and thought it would be an awesome adventure. It was at that point that Ian exclaimed, 'Three Men in a Float!'

After that things are a little hazy, although a woman did appear at some point and offer to show Ian her breasts (which we took as a portent of great things to come) before the pair of us ended up staggering off on our separate ways home.

For those familiar with Jerome K. Jerome's classic *Three Men in a Boat* but who may not know the author's history, I should point out that in 1892 Jerome was the editor of *The Idler*, a magazine that had been founded by Samuel Johnson back in 1758. I am deputy editor of the modern version and Ian is a contributing editor, so it's fair to say we felt entitled to take liberties with Jerome's comic masterpiece. I like to think that of all the attempts to modernize *Three Men in a Boat* since he wrote it in 1899, driving across England in a milk float is more in keeping with the spirit of the original than most. We had no pretensions to update it, though. We just saw it as an inspiration — well, more of an excuse, really, to go off on a silly journey of our own.

Over the next few weeks we talked about it with varying degrees of seriousness and, whichever way we began to look at it, a trip across England in a milk float began to make sense. Milk floats are electric vehicles so they are far better for the environment than your average petrol car, and it would be fascinating to see if such an eco-friendly journey was possible. Electricity is much cheaper than petrol, too. We calculated that the cost of a six-hundred-mile journey would be 2p a mile if you paid for the electricity in its most expensive form — from a domestic key meter — which meant it would cost us a grand total of £12 to drive from Lowestoft to Land's End. That was one-tenth of the cost in petrol to do the same journey in a car. But for me the most appealing thing about the trip was the chance of a slow travel adventure across England.

These days people seem to think you have to go to South East Asia to 'find yourself' or have an adventure, but surely you're likely to get more sense out of yourself by spending a bit of time travelling through your own country rather than dashing off to an alien one? The idea of frittering away a month travelling around Britain as opposed to somewhere exotic may seem rather quaint and absurd but that's only because our collective imagination has been hamstrung by an addiction to convenience and speed. These are not handicaps suffered by the slow traveller. If you're prepared to take your time, this country will soon start to morph into a place ten times its usual size.

So what is slow travel? My favourite way of explaining it has always been to use an analogy with food. We're all becoming more careful about what we put into our bodies these days and we should be equally careful about the kind of travel experience we shovel into our brains. In my view, conventional fast travel is becoming more and more akin to eating a supermarket ready meal. It's much cheaper to pick up a ready meal off the shelf than buy all the ingredients and make it yourself from scratch. It's much quicker to heat one up in the microwave when you get home when you compare it to making something magical by hand. And it's far easier to sling the half-eaten meal in the bin afterwards instead of having to tackle all the washing-up you created by assembling a culinary masterpiece. But ask yourself, which one would you rather eat? And so it is with travel. Taking your time, paying a bit more, learning something new and suffering a bit of inconvenience should be all part of the experience. Slow travel means you see the journey not as a chore to mutter about angrily under your breath, but as one of the main reasons for going somewhere in the first place. We certainly weren't going to drive six hundred miles across England because we were desperate to go to Land's End — our entire trip would be a celebration of the joys of the journey and the people we were sure to meet along the way.

So, idealism and intellectual armoury in place, we were all set. We just needed a third man, which is when I called my friend Prasanth, or Pras for short, whom I'd met one afternoon in Parliament Square while I was dressed up as a teddy bear (in an attempt to get arrested, but that's another story). Being one of those people whose life isn't cluttered up with a full time job, Pras answered with an immediate 'yes' when I asked him about it. 'When do we leave?' was the only thing he wanted to know. It wasn't long before lots of other people had become interested in the trip. We made promises, we signed things, but thanks to hectic family schedules, any motivation to do anything towards making the trip actually happen evaporated fairly rapidly.

The following spring I began to wake up in the middle of the night sweating about milk floats. That idea in the pub was getting closer and closer to reality. We had to leave on 26 May. My wife Rachel is a part-time teacher and our two-year-old son, Wilf, would need to be looked after if I wasn't around when she was at work – 26 May was the start of the two-week half-term. We'd managed to secure childcare (my mum) for the following two weeks, which gave me a four-week window to make the entire trip. So we were eight weeks from departure and still had no idea where to get a milk float, or whether, in reality, our trip was actually possible.

So when I got out of bed one bright April morning, after a night of milk-related terrors, I began making tentative enquiries, and it wasn't long before a sense of foreboding descended, the like of which I'd not felt since the night before my first shift working as a turkey beheader. It appeared, according to the experts at Dairy Crest and the Battery Vehicle Society, that the journey was just not practicable. Seeing as we'd given the impression to the people who had now put up money on the promise of our trip that all this research had been done and a milk float was already in the bag, this gave rise to certain levels of stress.

Dairy Crest were particularly negative about it. They own more milk floats than anyone else in Britain, so this was slightly dispiriting news. I'd imagined the PR value of being associated with our adventure would secure us a free milk float as soon as they heard of the idea. To be fair to them, they did offer us a diesel milk float, but then we would have had to call this book *Three Men in a Van*, which doesn't have quite the same ring to it, and would also go against our ecological principles. Lindsey from Dairy Crest was unmoved.

'Well, you won't do it in an electric one,' she said firmly. 'How will you charge it? You can't just charge it off a three-pin plug socket, you know.'

I had rather naively assumed that you could.

Ian, meanwhile, was reeling under the avalanche of exhaustion that faces anyone with a new baby – not to mention an imminent trip across England in a milk float. Despite such constraints, he pushed me in the direction of 'milk-float corner' on the internet. He'd had a few email conversations with various milk-float enthusiasts, who seemed far more optimistic than the 'professional' milk-float enthusiasts of Dairy Crest and the Battery Vehicle Society. The latter seemed to be plagued by the kind of infighting and back-stabbing you'd expect in the dark corridors of the KGB.

I called all the battery specialists and makers of electric vehicles I could track down over the internet, but every one of them was of the view that we wouldn't get very far. The man on whom Ian had pinned his hopes – he had at one stage offered to lend us his float for the trip – turned out to have exaggerated his own experience and the capacity of his vehicle, slightly. When I pushed him on a few details it emerged that he had actually only driven it a few yards, to a local car park, where it had promptly decided to set itself on fire. The burnt carcass of his vehicle had now taken up residence in his back garden, where it had remained for several months, much to the delight of the local rat population.

The man who appeared to be most qualified of all the people I'd contacted, after doing the Beaujolais run in a milk float with three different sets of pre-charged batteries the year before, was particularly damning.

'You're only hope is getting access to cooker sockets. They're 32 amps instead of your 13-amp domestic three-pin plug. A milk float needs to draw at least 32 amps. Plug a milk float into a 13-amp plug and the fuse will blow, simple as that. Now, see, every kitchen has its own ring main – that's an electricity supply separated from the one the rest of the house uses. So if you can persuade someone to let you take their cooker socket off the wall, take their cooker wires out of the socket and wire your milk float directly into the mains, and leave it there charging for eight hours with a huge cable hanging out the window and down to your milk float that's parked on their driveway, then you might get enough charge in your milk float to do twenty-five miles. That's if you've got a float with brand new batteries. Brand new batteries will set you back a couple of grand and you'll need them if your float's batteries are any more than five years old. If it's got batteries older than five years, then you can halve that distance to about twelve or maybe fifteen miles on a full charge, depending on the hills.' At this point I was feeling quite depressed, but then he delivered the fatal blow. 'Now you *might* find someone who'll let you re-wire directly into the mains via their cooker socket for eight hours if you've got an electrician with you, but to get all the way across England you'll have to persuade someone you've only just met to let you do that *twice a day*, *every day*, for a month.' He began laughing and continued for quite a while. I could only just make out, 'Now good luck with that,' between guffaws, before he hung up the phone. As you can imagine, by this point I was feeling rather dejected.

I rang Pras to see if he had any ideas about electrics and to my total astonishment he said, 'Yeah, I know a bit. I did a course in electrical engineering once.' I almost fell over Wilf's rocking snail.

'You're a bloody what?' I replied, seeing the slightest chink of light in the road of damning impossibility that lay ahead.

'Yeah, I thought that's why you asked me to come.'

But I'd had no idea at all. I just thought he'd find it fun. I knew Pras was a technical adviser, or something similar, at the Tate, but didn't have a clue about his electrical status. He was fairly convinced it would be possible to charge a milk float from 13-amp plug sockets and emailed me an indecipherable drawing that looked vaguely like something someone who knew about physics and electricity might understand. His argument was that while charging from one 13-amp plug socket *would* be impossible, we should, theoretically, be able to plug three conventional car battery chargers into three 13-amp plug sockets and plug those three car chargers directly into our battery. It sounded a bit unconventional but it was all we had to go on so I allowed myself to be convinced by his theory. The fact that he was the only person who thought it was possible seemed good news for the trip, or very bad news, depending on your level of cynicism and how much credence you give the 'experts' who seem to populate the world. However we were going to charge it, though, we still had to get ourselves a milk float with decent batteries, and fast.

When all seemed lost, we got a break. I made one final phone call to a chap who knew enough about milk floats to hold the milk-float land-speed record. (I'm not joking – he managed to go 73.93 miles per hour in a prototype model.) His reaction was what I'd hoped to hear from Dairy Crest.

'Brilliant, yeah, you can use one of ours, no problem. In fact, you might be able to use the one we broke the electric vehicle land-speed record in.' To say I was excited would be an understatement. I asked the big question.

'Can we charge it off a domestic plug socket, though?'

'Oh yeah,' he replied. 'It takes about five hours to get enough in the battery to go fifty miles.' We were home and dry.

I rang Ian and Pras excitedly. A futuristic high-speed milk float was, admittedly, not exactly what we'd had in mind – this was supposed to be about slow travel after all – but unless we were going to scrap the entire project, it appeared to be our only hope. He said he'd ring me when he got back from America in a few weeks' time. I was so relieved I forgot about milk floats again for another month.

Three weeks from departure I put in another call to our potential saviour, but it was another week before I managed to get hold of him. We arranged to meet in London to finalize everything another week later. This was just eight days from departure, but he seemed convinced that everything would be fine.

Ian and I stood waiting for him at our pre-arranged spot just off Regent Street for an hour and a half in fine drizzle but he never arrived. I got an apologetic email a day later. He still seemed convinced there was no problem with the float and tried to reorganize another meeting but we'd decided he would probably not deliver. So it was back to the drawing board, or rather eBay, with seven days to go. He finally contacted me the night before we were due to leave to say we wouldn't be able to borrow it for insurance reasons. (Another source alleged the real reason might be his imminent bankruptcy.)

I was on the verge of calling the whole thing off, and had even seriously proposed the idea of pretending the float had 'broken down' on day one, forcing us to walk the entire distance instead, which shows how far removed from reality I had become, when Stuart, a member of milk-float corner, decided to sell his 1958 vintage milk float (including the charger) on eBay. It had a full service history, and, he claimed, would easily manage thirty miles on a full eight-hour charge, despite having twenty-year-old batteries. It appeared the gods were on our side after all.

The previous Christmas about one usable milk float a month was being sold on eBay for about £1,000 a time, but the only one we'd found for sale in the weeks leading up to our departure was one that had been left outside in a back garden for so long that it was being drowned in a thicket of grass, assorted trees and stinging nettles. The asking price was £5. It didn't have any batteries or even any wheels.

Sensing that time was running out, Ian took matters into his own hands and emailed Stuart to see if he would take it off eBay immediately if we paid him £1,400 in cash there and then. Stuart immediately said yes, so we could probably have got it for half that, but we finally had a float, even if it was three hundred miles away in Plymouth. I set about trying to track down someone who would deliver it up to us, and had to cough up another £380, but at least then it would be in London.

Four days from departure the float arrived in the work yard we'd commandeered from Prasanth's friend Nitin in Tolworth, south London. We immediately named it 'The Mighty One' after Che Guevara's motorbike, as a joke originally, but the name seemed to stick. She was certainly a sight to behold. Pras and I walked around her, chuckling for a while, as the reality of the idea Ian and I had written on the back of a beer mat began to sink in.

It was then that I had the uncontrollable urge to drive her.

Driving duties for the whole trip had fallen to me. Ian can't drive and although Pras has a licence it's an Indian one, which he said, 'was slightly easier to get hold of than an

English one'. So I climbed in, sat on the bench seat that ran the width of the cab and began acquainting myself with the controls.

I don't know if you've ever drawn a stick man in a car but if you have, you'll be familiar with the kind of steering wheel I was now sitting behind. It comprised a long skinny trunk with a huge spindly dustbin lid of a wheel at the top. The dashboard in front of me consisted of a large, dented, orange metal box about two feet high and two feet wide with two keyholes and a variety of togs and switches on the top. It had two of those thin silver switches you get on mixing desks, which looked like they would break very easily, and a twisting knob on the right-hand side with three settings that read 'forwards', 'backwards' and 'neutral'. On the far side, another switch had '12V' written on it. That turned out to be for the electrics in the cab – the wipers and the lights. Next to that was a battery indicator, which consisted of ten lights with a plus sign at one end and a minus sign at the other. An enormous sticker that overshadowed the entire orange box displayed the warning words: 'TAKE CARE WHEN REVERSING'. None of it appeared to be very complicated but, for some reason, that made it all the more nerve-wracking.

I had called Stuart the day before to find out what driving a milk float was like and he'd given me an unforgettable reply – 'Have you ever driven a dodgem? You have one pedal for go and another one for stop. That's it.'

I flicked the starter switch. All ten of the battery indicator's lights glowed green but apart from that there was no indication that anything was actually 'on'. I turned the knob round to the 'forwards' setting and pressed the pedal gently. The float responded with a single faint click, lurched forward and immediately stopped again. Pras, who had come to check my progress, began laughing. I tried again. It lurched forwards once more and stopped fractionally later. Eventually, I managed to lurch my way around the yard's pot-hole-strewn car park. It felt like it could get up to quite a speed and I was feeling pretty good about it all. We had a milk float and it moved. So far so good. As soon as I got out of the cab I felt the uncontrollable urge to get back in it and drive around again. Stuart was right – it was just like driving a dodgem. When I got back in I noticed something that looked like a handbrake to the left-hand side of the driver's seat, and decided I should probably release that when I drove it this time.

I checked my mirrors, released the handbrake and pressed down the pedal, waiting for the click and the lurch. Nothing happened. It didn't move. I checked the key and it was turned on. I checked the battery lights and they were off. I turned the key on and off again. Nothing. A sudden sense of calamity came over me. It didn't work! Pras clambered in to take a look at the electrics but neither of us could work out what had gone wrong. I decided to try to push it over to Nitin's garage but was quickly overcome with common sense when I remembered it weighed two tons. Giant Haystacks would have had trouble moving it, even if each wheel hadn't managed to find its very own pothole to rest in.

I rang Ian who, to be honest, didn't really need to hear this piece of news at the precise moment that his daughter's pungent nappy needed changing. He suggested I rang Stuart, which had occurred to me but I thought I'd better calm down a little first. As it was, he didn't answer, so I left an irate and sarcastic message for him to call me back. Once again the prospect of doom enveloped me. Pras was unconcerned, pointing out, 'We've got four days.' I replied with the exact same sentence, but managed to turn the meaning of it on its head while spittle escaped from my mouth and I stamped around the yard manically. Pras suggested we go inside for a cup of tea and a biscuit and, let's face it, that's always a good idea.

Stuart rang back half an hour later and, with the air of a man leisurely swatting a fly away from his face, told me the connection cable by the seat was probably 'arcing'. That's the jump of electric charge you get if two electrical connectors are not touching properly. A similar, but more graphic, thing happens when you see a flash of electricity under a tube train. Pras, following his instructions, wiggled the cable under the bench for a while to the sound of cracks and the sight of a few sparks, and pretty soon the battery lights glowed green again and I could jerk my way around the car park once more.

At this point, to save the charge, we decided not to drive it any more until we got to Lowestoft, which I still hadn't managed to organize. Pras began dismantling the electrics to clean them and prevent further arcing. I decided to go home in case my nerves weren't able to take it.

I soon managed to track down someone to transport our milk float to Lowestoft (for another £300) and over the course of the next few days Pras, Nitin and I hung out in B&Q, buying all sorts of electrical gadgetry, some locks for the doors, solar panels for the roof — we were planning on using them to charge up laptops and mobile phones — bungee ropes, a few enormous sheets of tarpaulin for when it rained, and a roll of carpet and a bench seat for the flatbed at the back. We were now just one day away from leaving. I drove Pras back home that night and the excitement of our adventure began to take hold. Everything had been so last minute that neither of us had even thought about packing.

When I dropped Pras off outside his flat, near Peckham, I stared after him for a while, reflecting on what lay ahead. A lot was riding on Pras. His electrical knowledge would make the difference between total humiliation and the inevitable superstardom that would follow success.

The plan the following day was for me to wake up early and make my way to Nitin's house, do a few last things on the float to prepare it for transportation, get it loaded on the lorry that was coming at nine and ride up to Lowestoft with it. Ian and Pras were going up by train from Liverpool Street because there was only room for one passenger in the lorry. We would congregate at teatime outside the house of the people Ian had arranged for us to stay with.

It all sounded very simple, but of course it didn't happen like that. I was still twiddling my thumbs at Nitin's house at eleven when I got a call explaining that the driver with the lorry wasn't going to be able to get there by nine after all, something I'd managed to work out for myself. When he did eventually arrive at midday, he was so late that he'd been on the road for longer than his daily driving allowance, so he would not be able to drive to Lowestoft straightaway, and possibly not that day. He'd have to go for a sleep in a lay-by somewhere and make his delivery early the following morning. This scuppered my lift, unless I wanted to sleep in the cab of his lorry with him and his terrifying collection of tattoos, an offer that wasn't forthcoming anyway. By this stage, Ian and Pras would be well on their way to Lowestoft, or so I fondly thought. I rang Ian.

'Er, we've got a bit of a problem, mate,' I began, nervously.

'Oh,' he replied. 'You as well?'

Apparently, Pras had been late for three trains and, once he did arrive, it was a long time until the next one. So Ian

had been waiting with all his stuff, including a futon mattress, on the concourse of Liverpool Street station for the last
four hours.

'I've got so much stuff, I look like a fucking refugee,' he
complained. 'But enough of that. Where are you?'

I explained how my itinerary had not exactly gone to
plan, either. We had two options – go home and all go up to
Lowestoft the following morning, which, much as I love my
wife and son both of whom I was already missing terribly,
did feel like something of a defeat, or catch the next train,
wait for the float to arrive in the early hours of the morning
and set off on the road as soon as it did. We opted for the
second choice. All I had to do was get myself to Liverpool
Street and we could all get the train together.

Ian had one small question.

'You did get insurance, didn't you Dan? Otherwise we
can't go anywhere even if the float gets to Lowestoft. You
know it's the start of the bank holiday weekend tomorrow
don't you? Tell me you've got insurance. If you haven't, we
can't do anything till Tuesday and we'll be three days behind
schedule.'

'FUCK!' I replied. Of course I'd forgotten all about it.
'How the hell am I going to insure a milk float?' Ian didn't
know.

On the way to Clapham Junction I made frantic phone
calls to every insurance company I could get hold of but
none of them seemed to have a milk-float department. I
tried seventeen different brokers but couldn't get anywhere
with any of them, either. By the time I arrived at the station
I'd decided on a change of approach. Each time the person
on the end of the phone had asked what I was going to use
the milk float for I'd given an honest answer that was quickly
followed by an apologetic refusal. So when I got to company

number eighteen, I decided to fib a tiny bit. This company specialized in 'historic' vehicles, which The Mighty One certainly was. The man on the phone asked me what I was planning to use it for.

'Er, well, it's a charity thing.' I felt bad but we were desperate. 'Yeah, I've got three hundred children who'll be devastated if I can't get insurance in the next five hours.' I could sense him wavering and went for the killer blow. 'They've got £20,000 of sponsorship that under-privileged kids in Venezuela won't get if I can't get insurance for this bloody milk float. We're only driving a few hundred yards, up and down the road a few times.'

I got the cover for £70, and no doubt saved a space for myself in the warmest part of hell. But that wasn't the end of my problems. I now had to sign all the paperwork, which had to be faxed through to me, and fax it back for the insurance to be valid – not the easiest thing to do at lunchtime in a newsagent's the size of a broom cupboard on Clapham high street while carrying a rucksack with a month's worth of clothes and possessions on your back.

Ian, meanwhile, was discovering all sorts of problems of his own.

2

Lowestoft to Bungay

17 miles

IAN

As I dragged enough baggage to snap a mule in half out of the black cab and onto the concourse of Liverpool Street Station, I surrendered, like all bank holiday passengers, to whatever the railway network had in store for me. A Chinese proverb maintains that even a journey of a thousand miles starts with a single step, but in Britain it usually starts with a four-hour delay in a neo-brutalist transport hangar.

Liverpool Street was the seething tumult of commuters it usually is on a Friday afternoon, with the added ingredient of bank holiday panic. After a few missed trains, I eventually met up with Prasanth. When Dan first suggested Pras as our third man, he described him as having the demeanour of an Indian holy man – some kind of Peckham-based sadhu with preternatural IT and electronics skills, a photographer, guerrilla documentary film maker and the founder of an international environmental and sustainable development charity. We had met a couple of times and got on well enough. Pras turned out to be easy-going company while sitting around for several hours waiting for nothing to happen.

Sitting there on the concourse, I began to worry that I had got it all terribly, terribly wrong. I hadn't been paying close attention for about half a year – as a new dad, the rest of the world drifted past me for the first six months of my daughter's life. The result was that I had been kept both busy and befuddled right up to the last moment.

My bleary days had been punctuated by increasingly desperate calls from Prasanth or Dan as they wrestled with the technical side of the mission and I felt pretty guilty for not pulling my weight. But my absence from the business end had enabled me to cling on to what was beginning to seem like a delusion – that we could drive a milk float hundreds of miles across the country to Cornwall over the course of a month. For all intents and purposes, I had become the official cheerleader for the impossible.

Of course, it didn't help our cause that almost everyone Dan talked to about our mission seemed determined to dash his hopes. Fleet managers for dairies, electric vehicle experts and traction battery specialists were all certain that it couldn't and wouldn't be done. Yet I knew of at least half a dozen people who owned a milk float and could confirm what mileage they got out of their vehicles for what charge and in what terrain. Were the professionals lacking in imagination or were my electrically propelled friends and I fundamentally wrong?

There was something else on my mind, too, so when Dan phoned to say, 'I've just had a call from the guy who's picking up the float and he's not going to be able to deliver it today . . . ' I took the opportunity to remind him about the insurance. He replied in upper case, with a smattering of exclamation marks.

It was only the weight of my luggage and growing apathy that stopped me from going home right then. I'd been up all night making a five by three foot banner for the back of the float. True to my cheapskate, DIY ethos, I'd achieved this by tiling together sixteen A4 iron-on T-shirt transfers, produced on an inkjet printer, to make one large piece of Morphy Richards-ready artwork. The whole process had taken about eight hours, including a marathon five-hour ironing session complete with noxious fumes that, sadly, failed to get me high. That was just as well, really, as I'd spent the previous day driving to Cornwall to drop off my wife and daughter at her parents, where she would stay for the duration of our trip. I'd come back by train and didn't have time for hallucinations. My life was weird and disjointed enough already.

Dan finally arrived at Liverpool Street, complete with insurance all arranged. Never ones for much in the way of forward planning, we hadn't taken any long delays into account, so had decided more or less on the hoof to go to Lowestoft anyway, where the float would be delivered the following morning. Six hours after hauling my luggage from the cab and a good thirty-five hours since my last acquaintance with bed linen, I finally boarded a train with Dan and Prasanth, heading for the start of something we weren't sure we could finish.

Cold, windy and potentially disturbing for agoraphobics, Lowestoft is a town that seems to have borrowed its frontier look from a discoloured, clapped-out print of a spaghetti western. After travelling through the widescreen East Anglian countryside of open skies and far horizons, arriving at the shabby station was a little dispiriting. There was no grand eastern terminus designed by Victorian engineers, no Brunellian cathedral of transport, just a glum view back down a windswept platform – a view so reminiscent of a Latvian goods yard that it was a toss-up whether we would see tumbleweed rolling across the track or a detachment of the Red Army on reconnaissance.

Having lived in Lowestoft in the mid 1980s – which, to be fair, was not its finest moment – I struggled to overcome my negative feelings towards the town, particularly the sense that even on a good day it was the kind of place you felt you had seen in its worst light. Back then it was also economically depressed, having failed all the important tests that the twentieth century had set for it. A quick glance at the local newspaper hinted at an ongoing recovery that seemed to be taking longer than a mere quarter of a century.

We made our way to our digs for the night – the delightful home of John and Janet Myatt on the edge of a low cliff to the south of the town. I had 'met' John's son Paul – who is also the owner of a milk float – online after infiltrating the Milko mailing list, an internet group of dedicated followers of dairy vehicles. After I made a general appeal for information, Paul got in contact with me with offers of help, including the possibility of borrowing his float and accommodation at his dad's house.

John and Janet Myatt are a game couple, apparently ready not only to accept but embrace concepts of left-field lunacy. I'm not sure they would have treated us any differently if we'd turned up naked on unicycles or dressed to the nines as lawyers – they simply don't have a cynical thought between them. Completely unfazed by the situation, or the fact that our party of three suddenly grew to four with the impromptu appearance of Kim, our 'Lady From Radio 4', Janet cooked us a lovely meal of stuffed mushrooms and pasta and made sure we were all comfortable and content. John generally orbited the proceedings, conducting short conversations with each of his guests individually.

'It's nice to meet someone who is perhaps as mad as my son,' John told me. 'I thought it would be interesting to see just how mad you are and, well, here we all are.'

Dan's mobile rang. 'That was the guy with the float. He's on his way here — he's going to deliver it tonight after all!'

An hour later and the last member of the team had arrived. I finally got to see the two tons of 1950s technology we'd blown a heap of money on. Perched aloft on the back of a low loader, The Mighty One looked mighty indeed. Inclined slightly skywards as if it was about to be launched from the truck's ramp, and lit like a municipal sculpture by the lorry's working lights, it looked absolutely magnificent against the darkening sky. Ten minutes of delicate manoeuvring later and the float was parked up in John and Janet's driveway, ready for its first charge.

With the float delivered, connected to the mains and charging, or so we believed, our thoughts were turning to the journey ahead, when Dan let slip his evening bombshell.

'I'm still finding it hard to handle corners,' said our man, cheerfully. 'I haven't really driven round any — I've only driven around a car park.'

It occurred to me how utterly unprepared we were. Here we all were, three hapless amateurs and the Lady From Radio 4, imposing ourselves on lovely people, asking — as casually as the question would allow — to rewire their kitchen or take their fuse box apart, even though we hadn't tried out any of the charging kit. John even offered to let us charge the battery at his music shop in Hitchin, should we ever get that far. Now, it transpired, we hadn't even driven the float around a corner, any corner, or done anything more than orbit a car park in it. What utter buffoons.

'There are no flames leaping from the milk float,' said Dan, a little disconcertingly as he peered out of the window at The Mighty One. Pras had hooked up his three heavy duty DC battery chargers, bypassing the need to rewire John and Janet's cooker main, but he didn't seem entirely convinced that any charge was going into the float's battery.

Meanwhile, back in the house, the Lady From Radio 4 was conducting interviews and conversation turned to our arrangements for the big send-off the following morning. Needless to say, we hadn't made any arrangements. It was just a question of choosing an appropriate time to skulk away at low speed.

'It's probably a good idea to go through Lowestoft fairly early in the morning, because since they built the relief road, it has become very congested, especially on a Saturday,' said Janet, playfully.

'It would be good to set off around seven thirty,' Dan agreed, in a spasm of optimism.

After about forty-two hours without sleep, it was certainly time for turning in. Dan, Pras and I were sharing a room with two beds. Pras was happy to sleep on the floor between them, in my sleeping bag because, in the rush, he'd forgotten to bring his own. Adding to his holy man image, he used an enormous dictionary as a pillow.

'My dreads mean I can lie on anything, pillow, rocks, it doesn't matter,' he informed us.

Dan best describes what happened next.

'I took the camp bed – the previous occupant was an elephant if the mattress was anything to go by – and Ian took the bed by the window. Seeing as the curtains were open, he decided it would be a wise move to close them, but the second he touched the bottom of the curtain with one hand, the entire left curtain bracket and rail uncoupled itself from the wall and fell on the bed with a grating sound. Pras and I were helpless with laughter. Ian turned round giggling in that way you do when someone has shown you limitless kindness and you end up breaking something – the tension, guilt and hilarity of the situation are almost too much to bear. Ian went to close the other curtain and exactly the same thing happened. All of us were unable to stop laughing. It was the perfect release for all the strain of the first day.

Pras and I continued to giggle, and wheeze slightly, but Ian steeled himself and began the painstaking process of re-attaching the curtain rail to the wall and the curtain to the curtain rail. After five minutes of careful fixing it was all back in place.

"Now I'm not even going to fucking touch it again," he said, sitting back down on the bed. Unwittingly, though, Ian managed to sit on the corner of the curtain that had just draped itself on the bed, pulling the entire structure off the wall all over again. "Oh for fuck's sake!" he yelled as Pras and I both let out wails of uncontrolled laughter – the kind of helpless mirth that hits you once every few years if you're lucky. Ian joined in and we were all laughing so hard I felt as though I was going to have an asthma attack. When I said so, the two of them wailed even more. All three of us were like stranded asthmatic turtles lying on our backs clutching Ventolin inhalers.'

'We're going out into the unknown today,' said Dan, ominously, at just gone 10.15 in the morning. It was the first day of our epic sluggish journey across England. The weather was fair, if the wind a little gusty, but the forecast was rather grim for the next few days.

After an excellent breakfast of grapefruits, croissants and toast, and some early faffing and milling around, we packed up the float and got it out of Janet and John's driveway, ready to tootle into town and on to Ness Point, about two miles north. Just manoeuvring The Mighty One onto the road ate up a whopping 10 per cent of the charge, according to the battery meter, which seemed insane. Driving into town, we noticed that there didn't seem to be much oomph available, which was odd because this part of the journey was down a decent hill. Dan had to tickle the throttle continually to keep it moving down the mile-long incline. We were almost at the bottom when Dan realized that the handbrake was still on. This became something of a tradition.

The battery level continued to drop until it was down to 60 per cent as we reached Ness Point, and it began to occur to us that we'd bought a lemon – a lethargic, two-ton, skiffle-era, electric lemon at that. If the batteries could manage just two miles from a charge, we were totally shafted. Dan looked disconsolate.

'If that's the kind of mileage we can get from almost half the charge, it's going to take three hundred charges, A FUCKING YEAR, to get to Land's End.'

We all became very disappointed at the impossible prospect of obtaining ten eight-hour charges a day for the next month.

'That's totally shit, man,' Pras commented, not unreasonably.

I was so dumbfounded, I sought solace in distraction and went off to talk to a couple of cyclists who were setting out on the same journey as us but expected to cover sixty or seventy miles in a day and be at Land's End a week later. Fucking show-offs.

Lowestoft Ness is not the most promising of the nation's four cardinal points. Hidden away in the middle of an industrial estate of long sheds with off-white corrugated plastic roofs, the only way to reach it is by driving up a street with the less than glamorous name of Gas Works Road. The most striking feature of the area, however, is magnificent. Standing at well over 400 feet tall – higher than the Blackpool Tower – and capable of producing 2.75 megawatts of power, Gulliver is the largest wind turbine in Britain by a long way, and is only a stone's throw from the Ness.

Getting to the starting line of our journey at Ness Point was clearly an achievement, but leaving Lowestoft without looking like complete fools would be a greater triumph. At this point, we hadn't got into the swing of things yet. We milled around apologetically, not sure what to do with impending failure. John and Janet, who had followed us down in their car, offered us beds for the night, so that we could have another go at a charge, but that didn't feel right – we had to get going today, we had to leave Lowestoft.

As it turned out, John kept a boat at the Royal Suffolk and Norfolk Yacht Club in Lowestoft Marina and they had 32-amp charging points on the pontoons. That was the lure we needed to strike out from the Ness, actually to start the journey in earnest, even if only for the half mile to the Marina. Dan even hatched a faintly ridiculous plan to go along the coast from sailing club to sailing club. We felt distinctly nautical all of a sudden.

Boatyards and marinas are odd places. Despite the hi-tech nature of modern sailing, at most times of the day you'll find an assortment of (mostly) men in boiler suits tinkering, making things work and lashing stuff together, with an approach that could be described as Vorchsprung Durch 2×4. Arriving at the Marina, we hung around for a while and tried out this plug and that plug, but nothing seemed to work. The 32-amp plugs were indeed present on the pontoons, but not even our 25-metre cable was long enough to reach them. Having lost another 10 per cent of our charge getting there, it seemed as if we were stuck again. We found ourselves in another crisis of indecision, and a little wary of leaving the obliging presence of Janet and John in case we became marooned in the English countryside. What we needed was reassurance. Dan phoned Stuart to talk through our problems.

Once again, Stuart was the bearer of good news. According to him, the battery meter always showed the charge dropping off quickly at the start, but as it got lower, each 10 per cent bar of power took longer to disappear. He was confident that with 50 per cent charge remaining we would easily manage fifteen miles, which would be enough to get us to Bungay. It wasn't on our itinerary but our itinerary had been thrown out the window. Emboldened once more, we stopped being electric vehicle wallflowers and left the safety of failure behind. We struck out towards Bungay, while clinging on to the fact that another town, Beccles, was on the way.

The weather was beginning to close in. Rain started to fall, the windscreen began to mist and nobody had found out how to turn on the wipers. Three men and the Lady From Radio 4 ploughed onwards in a milk float that had a rakish air of impending collapse. It certainly wasn't a smooth ride – downhill in the rain felt like white water rafting and, even on the level, the mattress soft suspension meant that we bucked up and down like a neurotic horse on a trampoline. Up hills – even the comparatively gentle inclines of east Suffolk – we slowed to a crawl, the pitch of the electric motor dropping to a mournful, lethargic moan as we reached each crest.

The short journey was wearing. All of us were obsessed with the five remaining LEDs of the battery meter on the float's control box. One by one they winked out, but Stuart was right – the lower the charge went, the longer the LED lasted. By Beccles, nine miles down the road, we were on a roll, so much so that there was barely a debate about going the next six miles to Bungay. We were down to 40 per cent charge, but suddenly found the same kind of reckless confidence that made us dream up the whole thing in the first place. We were going to Bungay.

Three miles later and the meter showed its first red LED at 30 per cent. In the rule of thumb world of electric vehicles, there are only two hard and fast, black and white commandments and one of them is 'Thou Shalt Not Drive on the 20 per cent LED'. It had been drummed into us all. Although we were confident we could make it the last three miles to Bungay, it meant that we could not go any farther until we were fully charged again. This was the crunch, the guiding principle of the mission – we had to obtain electricity from people we'd never met in a town where we were complete strangers. We were utterly dependent on the milk of human kindness.

We arrived in Bungay a little after 2 p.m. A market town with a population of less than 5,000 situated in the valley of the River Waveney, Bungay is small. Parking the float in the town's pay and display, we set off on foot to find lunch and brace ourselves to hunt down a charge. A pub with a kitchen might be able to provide nourishment for all of us, including the float.

The Fleece Inn was nice enough, and Dan fetched the float to park for free in the patrons' car park. The beer and food hit the mark, but we were all nervous about making our bizarre request. It somehow just didn't feel right.

Dan disappeared outside on the pretext of getting better phone reception but, unbeknown to the rest of us, he was really on a mission to find a charge. Nervous and embarrassed by the task, he wanted to do it on his own. It didn't take long before he came across a likely looking target, the King's Head Hotel. Walking through the door, Dan said it looked a little grimy but was clearly well loved. Through the hallway and on the right was a little office that was almost fully occupied, in terms of volume, by a large man with a beaming smile. Dan saw immediately that this man's ample physique was dwarfed by an enormous personality.

'Er, hi,' Dan began, 'um, I've got a strange request.'

The man beamed. 'Oh good, I like strange requests . . .' From that moment, Dan knew that we wouldn't leave the King's Head without a full charge.

Matt, Dan's new friend and bar manager of the King's Head, was brimming with enthusiasm when we all got there a short while later. Dan had gone through the charging options open to us – the three domestic 13-amp plugs option, the 32-amp plug socket option (from any domestic cooker main) or even, at a push, a petrol generator with a 32-amp outlet – before bringing the good news back. He had pointed out that Pras was an 'electrician' to ease any fears Matt may have had.

'Well, you can try the three-plug option first,' Matt said, leading us to a function room out the back of the pub. 'It has its own power supply off the main pub circuit, so you can set up in here.' We followed him out into the car park. 'And you can park the float here,' he gestured to a space in front of a small white trailer (that Dan crashed into half an hour later). He opened double doors to a function room and we followed eagerly inside. 'After that there's a 16-amp plug upstairs you could try. We use it for the carvery, but you'll need a long lead. And if you're still stuck after that, my mum's got a generator and she lives about five miles away.'

We were awestruck.

'Can we try the plug upstairs first?' asked Pras. 'If that works then we're sorted.

Matt took up us a narrow staircase and led us into a large room, that was empty apart from a collection of stacked chairs by the far wall. The circuit was probably not strong enough for the current we would draw and Pras concluded that it would blow the fuse if we attempted it, so we decided to go back to the three domestic plugs option.

Before we started, Pras wanted to top up the batteries with distilled water, in case the levels were low. Low electrolyte levels could account for the failure of the three domestic plugs option at Janet and John's the night before. Pras and I went off in search of Matt, who had gone back to serve his customers, to ask directions to the nearest garage where we could buy distilled water. Apparently, it was miles away but that didn't matter because we had Matt, surely the most obliging bar manager in all England. He immediately went to his car and handed over a 1.5-litre bottle of distilled water with, of all things, an apology. 'Sorry it's not much,' he said, unnecessarily, but it was more than Pras could take.

'These people are so kind!' he said, a little confused. 'What is it about this milk float? Why are people so desperate to help us?'

But despite the water and the three 13-amp plug sockets and the three chargers we'd bought for this very purpose, after a pint or two in the bar (that were on the house) it became clear that the triple charger option was not going to work.

By 6 p.m., Pras and Dan were sitting at the bar wearing rather forlorn expressions. Matt came over to ask, 'How's it going?'

Pras shook his head. Dan said nothing. Matt filled the silence.

'So what do you need, in an ideal world?'

Just then someone wanted serving and Matt went off to attend to it. Pras looked at Dan, winked and called over to Matt, 'Just a socket with a 32-amp fuse on it. I can easily rewire the plug, it's no problem.' As he took the money for the round, Matt looked over and smiled. He cleared his throat and leant into the bar.

'There is something we could try . . . I think there's a 32-amp socket in the disco room. You could just wire into it directly, although we never had this conversation, or my publican will kill me.' He marched out from behind the bar and back in the direction of the function room.

Pras and Dan followed eagerly, like kids who'd been allowed in a surly neighbour's back garden to retrieve a lost Frisbee. By the time they caught up with Matt he had unlocked the door and climbed halfway up a ladder.

'This one,' he said, flicking a switch inside an enormous fuse box, 'is the plug at the end of the inside of the bar. I've turned the power off but if you take off the plug and rewire one of your blue ones in its place, you shouldn't have any problems. Put it all back carefully, though. I don't want anyone being able to tell what we've been up to.' And with that he scarpered.

I found Pras and Dan in the function room and couldn't help but smile when I saw the uncovered fuse box. All of a sudden we became animated – the game was on again.

Dan and I began to uncoil the armoured 25-metre cable while Pras took care of the plug socket. Half an hour later we had rewired the float's charger – a unit about the size of a small fridge that travelled with us on the back of the float – straight into the mains. We stood around it, preparing to flick the on switch. It was the first time we'd attempted to use the charger and had no idea what would happen next. Pras looked at us both, winced and flicked it. I expected an explosion, but for an agonizing split second there was no sound at all, then a confident 'whirr' as the charger sprang into life. Pras got out his multimeter and grinned.

'We have 10 amps going into the battery.'

'Is that good?' I asked.

'Fuck, yeah,' came the reply. 'The Mighty One was thirsty and is now drinking its fill.'

It was a great moment. Knowing it was actually possible to use the charger was a major boost. Now that we knew the three domestic plug system wasn't going to work it would make it easier to concentrate our efforts on what would. We needed 32-amp plug sockets – at least one a day for six hours, for the next twenty-eight days and then we might just make it to Land's End.

A few pints later, we found ourselves wandering around Bungay looking for food while The Mighty One continued to hum serenely in the King's Head car park. We ended up in a dingy basement trying to pass itself off as a kebab restaurant. It was certainly seedy enough, but lacked any charm whatsoever. The no-nonsense brusque service bordered on authoritarian and the basement featured tables with integrated benches – furniture of the sort often seen in Forestry Commission picnic areas and at beach cafés where you are compensated for the extreme discomfort by a stunning natural vista, or the rare chance to punch a seagull in the beak before it makes off with your pasty. Here there was only the glum reality of teenage life in a tiny town – cackling, drunk girls who are capable of integrating five uses of the word 'fuck' into every sentence, and boys beating the crap out of one another in order to secure the affections of these delightful, gorgeous beings.

I ordered a Margherita pizza, but received a seven-inch platter entirely covered in cheap melted cheese and nothing else. Dan opted for a chicken kebab, the Lady From Radio 4 had shish and Pras had the first of many veggie burgers he would consume on the trip.

Soon after, we were back in our beds at the King's Head for eight hours solid sleep. I reckon we deserved it.

3
Bungay to Beyton

41 miles

DAN

I woke up slowly, revelling in the fact that we'd managed to secure our first proper charge. It had been a tough first day but the excitement of the challenge now facing us was undeniable. As long as The Mighty One had ten green lights on the battery meter when we turned it on that morning, we knew the trip was possible. If it was down to us to persuade people to help us, I knew we had a chance, just as long as the technical aspects of the journey didn't trip us up too many times along the way.

Sure, we'd gone just fifteen miles but already the path ahead seemed less rocky somehow. I'd noticed a change at Ness Point, when all seemed lost before we'd even crossed the starting line. The three of us had sat in total despair at the challenge that lay ahead. Our worst fears had been confirmed when the battery appeared to be emptying fast. It seemed all the experts had been right – it just wasn't possible. We would just have to go home to the ignominy of hopeless defeat. But at that moment, a strange and wonderful thing had happened. I heard John Myatt talking on the phone. He'd seen a blue socket at his boatyard and was trying to see if we could use it to charge the float. So much for tactics and planning. Someone we barely knew was going out of his way to help us on our journey. I began to wonder whether we should relinquish control of the trip completely to coincidence and serendipity. Such a strategy would certainly involve less work. Perhaps our lack of planning and total disregard for organization might actually be our greatest hope for success. Both of these ideas appealed to me greatly. That's not to say we hadn't planned anything about our journey. We just hadn't planned any of the practical sides of the trip, focusing instead on the ideas behind it and the promise of adventure that would surely follow such a bold and hilarious plan. In that way, what we were doing was the antithesis of the modern holiday, for which you *only* plan the practical things and leave everything that matters, what you're actually going to do, to guide books and tour guides rather than allowing your own imagination and sense of adventure to lead you to interesting places. It seemed perfect to us to leave the 'hows' and 'wheres' to chance and spend our time luxuriating in the endless possibilities of meandering around with little or no idea of what we were actually doing.

It was time to get up and prepare for the day. Much as we were indebted to Matt for his electrical hospitality, the shower I had that morning left something to be desired. It required the kind of tantric positioning that just seemed silly. When I finally gave up, I discovered that most of the water had found its way onto the floor of the bathroom and my clothes were soaking wet.

Ian, meanwhile, found a little too much electrical hospitality in the shower, with water actually spraying through the shower unit's on-off switch. As our journey progressed, maybe there would be a whole series of electrical anomalies like this, as a way of balancing out the enormous force field of electrical luck that the float seemed to be creating for itself.

I went downstairs full of hope that breakfast would be jollier but the moment I sat down I knew where the rest of the water from my shower had gone – it seemed to be pouring down the wall behind the boxes of breakfast cereal.

Kim emerged looking bright and excited. We both ordered breakfast and began to chat about what lay ahead. Unburdened by the potential failure of our trip – even a total disaster would make for great radio – Kim was brimming over with all the enthusiasm the rest of us had spent the previous day ignoring in favour of being stressed. 'This is so brilliant!' she exclaimed over her cup of coffee. Hearing her explain back to me why this trip was going to be so wonderful rekindled my excitement. Day one had been traumatic but now we had let go of the experts' pessimism, we were surely about to race down the hill of joy and success – assuming, of course, that The Mighty One had a full battery and we weren't about to be stranded in Bungay.

Half an hour later we had dismantled the charging system and the four of us were huddled around the battery meter to see what would happen when I turned the key. Pras was the most positive, grinning widely. It seemed he too had woken in a more optimistic state of mind. We all cheered as those ten little green lights flashed on, which meant we should manage thirty miles that day. Ian looked so relieved I thought he was going to fall asleep instantly, such were the strains he'd placed upon himself during the first twenty-four hours, but he was soon leafing through the map excitedly. It felt like the real start of our grand adventure. It was time we got under way.

We said our goodbyes to Matt and thanked him for everything he'd done to help.

'It's been a pleasure to meet you and good luck in your quest,' he shouted as we drove away, adding finally, 'you mad, mad, mad, mad people!'

I waved animatedly, full of joy and excitement, and, perhaps, a touch of self-satisfaction. This was going to be a breeze I told myself, quickly becoming rather blasé about the whole idea of the trip. I was paying attention to the possibilities of the road that lay far ahead rather than the road that was immediately in front of me as I attempted to turn out of the car park. Kim screaming, 'STOP!' shocked me back to reality, and I realized I had nearly trundled right over a purposeful cyclist, who was peddling furiously in the rain. He wasn't expecting to see a milk float so he didn't, and I promptly almost killed him. Our two-ton contraption would make mincemeat of anyone, even if we were going at a snail's pace. We lurched to a stop and all our possessions tumbled over each other under the tarpaulin we'd methodically tied down on the flatbed behind the cab. I felt an icy sense of fear drift down my arms and over my fingers while Ian and Pras laughed nervously. It was only then that I began to realize what a bloody dangerous vehicle a milk float could be.

A sense of unease pervaded the float that had now spread over us, which I responded to by recommending to my companions that at no point should they feel embarrassed to mention their fear of impending death on account of my driving.

'Well done, Kim,' I said. 'It's probably a good time to say that if any of you think I haven't noticed something that could cause us to be killed or to kill anyone else, please feel free to mention it. Don't be English and embarrassed about it. I won't be offended.' They all began to laugh and we steeled ourselves for take off once again. This time everyone had their eyes firmly on the road and we shuddered out from the car park, drifted around a roundabout and down a small road heading in the direction of Diss, a town that lay twenty miles away.

Our brush with catastrophe left a certain sense of foreboding in the air for a few miles but once we realized the charge seemed to be holding, the nervous chatter gave way to laughter of a more uplifting kind. It was Bank Holiday Saturday so the roads were empty, apart from the rain that was showing the kind of constant defiance in the face of excitement that seemed strangely reminiscent of Gordon Brown.

Now that the pressure was off, Ian and Pras decided to play a game of Ventolin Top Trumps with their various asthma inhalers. While my occasional smoking habit is of the peer pressure variety, Ian and Pras take it far more seriously. Both have quite extreme lung problems, but rather than ever bother their GPs, Ian and Pras get their medication off the internet in bulk.

'This one's Fijian,' Ian said, full of pride, before breathing in hard to ease the loud wheezing of his lungs.

'Cool, man, mine's Indian,' responded Pras. Ian promptly raised the stakes.

'I've got some Lebanese Salbutomol in here somewhere, a *red* Lebanese Salbutomol no less,' he added with great satisfaction, brandishing a scarlet inhaler at Pras as though it was a bottle of Chateau Lafitte. I was listening in bewilderment.

'That should be some really strong shit,' Pras said admiringly. He took a lug of it with one hand and lit up another cigarette with the other. It seemed we were going to have another companion to add to coincidence and serendipity. Smoking.

Meanwhile, in a fug of cigarette smoke, I felt I was getting the hang of the driving. The two pedals were very simple to use but it wasn't long before I'd worked out how to drive in a way that would conserve our energy. It was almost exactly the same theory you would use when lazily riding a bicycle. Press the throttle (perhaps we should rename that the 'dawdle') to get a bit of speed up and then release it to freewheel for as long as possible while keeping a certain amount of momentum going at all times. The thing that ate up the charge most was getting the float moving from a stationary position, so driving became a matter of timing. I tried not to stop at all.

The other road users seemed intrigued rather than annoyed by our presence, tooting occasionally and waving a great deal more. A few people gave us a particularly zealous two-fingered gesture, which seemed to become more popular with our fellow road users the longer the trip went on, but no one screamed or shouted abuse as far as we could tell.

Inside the cab we were beginning to ease ourselves into our respective roles. Along with my responsibility for driving I'd also taken it upon myself to be continually stressed about whether or not we'd stowed all our stuff on the back of the float properly, and how quickly we were losing battery life. As chief navigator, Ian had his laptop open and was scrolling through the entire southern half of England on one-inch ordnance survey maps he'd got from a chap in Glasgow, in the hope that he could help us avoid any unnecessary battery draining hills. Pras, meanwhile, was smoking, filming and fiddling with wires and various unknown electrical gadgets. It was a curious mix of technologies, from the 1950s mechanics of the float to laptops, GPS positioning via mobile phones and even a 'To Let' sign Pras had commandeered late at night from outside a house in Peckham to act as a mount for the solar panels. Everyone seemed to have slipped effortlessly into a groove.

Bouncing gingerly along the road in the rain, I was reminded of something my friend Charlie had said before we set off. He'd been on various meditation retreats and apparently, when you go on these retreats, the sheer amount of meditation and doing literally 'nothing' drives you mad at first, but after a while the Zen-like side of things begins to take over and your mind becomes released from the chaos of the modern world. Charlie thought driving a milk float would provide me with a similar experience. After two days I was open to the possibility that after a month the quite staggering slowness of the float might begin to grate slightly.

On our way through the flat and rather unremarkable countryside, we came up with an ingenious plan. It was clear that the earlier we got a charge the better. Getting to Diss by lunchtime (we'd left Bungay at eleven) would mean we could either go twice as far by getting two charges, or that we would have all the rest of the day to find one charge, instead of arriving somewhere with no power at the end of each day. So it was that on the approach to Diss we began to steel ourselves for the embarrassment of trying to get powered up. Noticing our trepidation, the gods of coincidence decided to give us a shove in the right direction. Looming up ahead was a huge Morrisons hypermarket. The Mighty One is a Morrisons milk float. Coincidence? I don't think so.

Ian spotted it first and soon we were all convinced that these kinds of industrial units would be far more relaxed about us charging up, and far more likely to have easily accessible 32-amp sockets than your average domestic house. Surely they would have a 32-amp socket somewhere in a supermarket of that size? We parked up and ambled into the store. Ian asked to speak to the manager, a man called Peter according to the luridly branded 'Managers' sign, with a picture of his face beneath it. The sign said Peter was 'there to help', so we thought we'd take him at his word and, it must be said, he didn't disappoint.

He laughed when we explained our predicament and was soon waving us round to the delivery bay behind the store. It's fair to say none of us could believe our luck, and the gods wouldn't have that, so they decided to nudge us again and this time they really freaked us out. Peter introduced us to the delivery manager, Gordon, who was the chap with access to 32-amp charging equipment and, would you believe it, a former milkman.

'Where's your cable then?' he smiled. 'We'll soon have her humming,' as though a milk float turning up in the rain was the most natural thing in the world. The four of us stood there with open mouths, looking for secret cameras or some kind of explanation. Gordon, meanwhile, was clearly very pleased to see a milk float again.

'Blimey! It's . . . well, bloody hell . . . it's twenty-five years since I drove one of these beautiful machines! It certainly brings back memories,' he said, grinning. Ian, having regained his composure, wondered whether seeing The Mighty One made him feel nostalgic. 'I feel nostalgic about the machine and the time, yes, but it's a different world now. That system of delivering milk is dead, I'm afraid.' He ambled around The Mighty One, chuckling, and was soon reminiscing about life on the milk round. 'Oh God. I remember those pitch-black mornings very well. It was always raining and you couldn't really use your lights because they used up too much charge. People always tried to cut you up, too. You go so slowly that everyone thinks they can get past, even when it isn't safe.' He turned and pointed to me. 'You'll notice that on your travels. It's bloody terrifying.'

We'd already become completely paranoid about the

prospect of running out of power and getting stranded some-where, so we asked Gordon if he had ever come unstuck on his rounds.

'Oh no, you always used to manage to crawl back. Just. And I mean just. You could always tell if the batteries were getting really low. The lights would glow instead of working properly.' He laughed heartily. 'You'll find that when it starts getting close to empty, it begins to feel even *more* sluggish. That charger you've got looks a lot better than the ones we had, though. We used to have ones with mercury switches. They used to fuse together.' He raised his eyebrows. 'Those were the days!'

All Gordon's anecdotes seemed to be about how awful the experience of being a milkman was but a grin remained on his face for the entire time he reminisced about it. If anything, it seemed to get broader and broader the more uncomfortable and dangerous the stories became, which felt slightly ominous to me I must admit. But then he began describing the other, more human, side of the job and at that moment the smile began to leak away.

'Well, it's all long gone now,' he said somewhat wistfully, 'but you really used to get to know people in the old days. In some of the country areas the milkman was the only person they ever used to see. Every now and then the baker would turn up. The postman might come twice a week if you were lucky. It definitely made you feel part of a com-munity whereas now everyone's so insular, aren't they? You can be very lonely in a crowded room today. In those days it wasn't like that. Back then you got to know and look out for each other. But the milkman's days are over now.' He shook his head. 'I could tell you why . . .' he added sadly, taking a moment to stare up at the enormous hypermarket towering above us, 'but I suppose I'd better not.'

Once the charger was throbbing nicely, we left her out in the rain and went up to the staff café for a hot chocolate. I was curious about sneaking a peak behind the corporate curtain. It's fair to say I'm not a huge fan of supermarkets in general and was acutely aware of the irony that the very thing that had done most to kill off the humble milk float was one of the few places we had so far found to provide enough charge for us to continue our journey.

The 'back stage' area of the supermarket didn't disappoint my sense of curiosity. Out the back was like being in a rabbit warren full of food. I was amazed at how few people there were in the dark tunnels made up of Nik Naks, cans of Coca-Cola and huge haystacks of toilet roll as we were ushered through on our way to the staff canteen. When the population of this country finally take up arms against the Government for serving the interests of the people who want to make money in Britain rather than those of us who actually live here, I estimate it would take about ten people to take over each of the cathedral supermarkets that squat around the nation's towns and cities.

The stairwell we climbed up was lit by interrogation-style strip lighting and soon we found ourselves in the staff canteen, where a few glum-looking workers on their break sat by the school-dinneresque counter. At the back, a closed in smoking chamber was packed with fug and laughter. We immediately opted for the room full of smoke. After a hot chocolate and some stilted conversation with the spotty teenagers on their break, I ventured off to find a toilet. I found one next to a door that opened into the shop. The door was closed but I could tell it was the way into the store because it had a sign with a long mirror set into it. At the top of the sign it said: MORRISONS PEOPLE, ARE YOU LOOKING YOUR BEST? It was a nice thought, loads of young workers ready for a day in the aisles, decked out in their hippest clubbing gear or modish suits. But on the left and right-hand side of the floor-length mirror, two columns of orders seemed to contradict this idea completely. On the left-hand side the instructions read:

MEN

1. *Name badge – in position on left*
2. *Hair – neat, tidy and tied back if long*
3. *Clean-shaven – beards and moustaches neatly trimmed*
4. *No excessive jewellery – one pair of earrings only*
5. *Fresh food handlers – no jewellery*
6. *Pressed trousers – standard width, navy or black*
7. *Navy or black socks*
8. *Polished shoes – no trainers, soft or open shoes*
9. *Uniform – clean and pressed*

And on the right-hand side of the mirror, the list repeated the same things with a few amendments:

WOMEN

3. *Tasteful make-up – no nail varnish*
6. *Pressed trousers or skirt – standard length and width, navy or black*
7. *Navy or black socks or tights*

At the very bottom, a notice said: TAKE PRIDE IN YOUR APPEARANCE, although that seemed rather outlawed by everything that was written above it.

It may be rather impolite to accept the hospitality and electricity of Morrisons only to be rude about them afterwards but I don't care. That's my journalistic integrity for you. I'm even prepared to put my national characteristics of politeness, geniality and gratitude to one side in the name of investigatory reporting. So I also feel honour bound to say that all the staff members we saw that day looked totally miserable. Once in the canteen, even Gordon seemed to have lost the zest for life he'd shown earlier while talking about the numerous problems inherent in driving a milk float twenty-five years before. Perhaps it was because back then, despite the trials and tribulations he came up against every day, the fact that he was first and foremost a human being was not something his employers were desperate to squash out of him with their humourless, miserable corporate machine. I'm not sure if you've ever noticed but there's something inherent about the corporate structure that requires you to be inhuman. Stripping people of their humanity and common sense during working hours is the only way you can make them put up with the utter nonsense of management structure, targets and the mindlessly unsustainable pursuit of ever-expanding corporate profits. It reminded me of many bad memories I have of working in a vast array of crap jobs, and soon I became convinced that if I allowed myself to remain in such close proximity to it any longer, I might start coming out in hives.

A few minutes later we ventured inside the superstore to stock up on provisions. Despite the relentless rain and freezing cold we bought equipment for a barbecue, plus some sausages and grim-looking veggie burgers for Pras, bread, cheese, wine and a sleeping bag, also for Pras. It was remarkably cheap and, needless to say, turned out to be totally useless as a consequence, giving Pras many shivering nights throughout the remainder of our time on the road. I spent a while looking round the aisles for the holy grail of maize snacks, cheese balls, but couldn't find any. Ten minutes later we found ourselves back in the cab of The Mighty One eating spongy French bread. It may have been wet and cold, and the floor of the cab leaked, but we all felt it was preferable to squash ourselves in there rather than risk our collective sanity by going back to the staff canteen.

Sometime later, three hours after we'd arrived at Morrisons, we drove off in the energy-sapping rain you only get on a bank holiday weekend, and headed south for a campsite five miles east of Bury St Edmunds.

Despite the downpour and bad visibility, the journey was good road-wise. We kept clear of dual carriageways, opting instead for calm, meandering country lanes full of determined wildlife and empty fields. The wildlife was certainly not afraid of us as we trundled along, which was nice. Baffled rabbits and birds popped their heads up but showed no signs of the terrified panic you see when driving along in a conventional car, but the constant cold made it a battle towards the end. At one point I had to drive standing up because the right-hand side of my bottom became gripped with agonizing cramp – you've heard of tennis elbow, well by the end of the trip I'd christened this particular ailment 'milkman's arse'.

Milk floats are definitely summer vehicles. I began dreaming of what it would be like to drive it in the July sun, stopping occasionally for a brew and a fag. I was coming to think of the float as essentially a mobile hammock. Driving along with the doors open as a light breeze eased us along country lanes seemed much more alluring than the reality of constant shivering and milkman's arse.

It was getting dark as we neared the campsite. We didn't want to use our lights because it would drain the battery unevenly, something that affects the battery's ability to recharge. The rain was fairly lashing down when we finally

pulled up to a halt on the gravel entrance of an absurdly pretentious campsite. I was so relieved to get there. It felt like
we'd pushed ourselves almost too hard, covering over forty
miles in a single day. It did occur to me that it might have
been a good idea to ring up in advance to book a pitch, but
I quickly shook off the idea, reasoning that in such conditions as this, every campsite in Britain would surely have
plenty of vacancies. Besides, that wasn't the spirit in which
we were travelling. I must also admit to a twinge of apprehension that they might not want a milk float on their site.
I'm aware of how finicky caravan owners can be. Some caravan club sites will not even allow tents.

The office of the campsite was closed but a sign redirected
latecomers to the house itself. I left the others shivering in
the cab and jogged up the driveway. The house was like a
budget version of Southfork from Dallas. Before I'd even got
to the door a man came out shaking his head, which seemed
unfortunate seeing as I hadn't actually asked for anything.

'Sorry, we're full,' he said, without breaking his stride. 'It's
a bank holiday,' he continued, as though that in itself
was reason enough. On reflection, I suppose it was. I didn't
have the energy to argue, or even pitch our hilarious and
eccentric tale, which suddenly felt just a bit stupid.

I walked back to the float in the pouring rain and clambered back inside, slipping slightly as I got in. I told my
companions the bad news and we began laughing in that
slightly hysterical manner that takes hold of you when all is
seemingly lost. We started swearing wildly, doubting the
parentage of all caravan-site owners, and I soon managed to
wheel-spin out of the gravel driveway nearly taking out
a little ornamental tree by the entrance in the process. Pras
got out his film camera, sensing a moment of hilarious
misery.

'What was that place called?' he asked, in mock interview tone. Quick as a flash Ian piped up with 'Cunts Camping' and we all collapsed with mirth. I remember resting my head on the steering wheel and staying there for some time as my weakening frame began to ache. We were now totally screwed. It was 6 p.m. and we were miles from any large town. We had no money and no means of charging the float. It seemed our earlier optimism might have been misplaced.

We bounced along for a while towards a village called Beyton Green. Under the bridge that carried the huge A14, a large empty concrete area came to our notice. It would do in an extreme emergency if you were looking for somewhere to commit suicide but none of us fancied trying to sleep there. Charge-wise we were down to 40 per cent, so we knew it would be unwise to go much farther, or use our lights in the murky twilight.

Then just ahead we saw a pub, The Bear Inn, and decided to stop for a drink and worry about where to spend the night after we'd all had a few ales. The plan was that once I'd had a few drinks I'd have had too much to drive anywhere legally and we'd be 'forced' to spend the night in the car park. I was so desperate for a beer I didn't want to think beyond my third pint, by which point I was convinced everything would surely have taken care of itself. Then Ian spotted that The Bear Inn was a four-star bed and breakfast. Our eyebrows raised in unison and we stumbled through the rain in anticipation.

Behind the bar, a beautiful woman with thick black hair tied up in a bushy ponytail smiled when I came in, but told me that they were full for the night when I enquired about a room. She did seem intrigued about the milk float, though. Then her husband appeared with that wild and friendly look in his eye that instantly reminded me of Matt back in Bungay. He asked what the float was for, we told him about our adventure and the grin on his face grew even wider. He started pouring pints before we'd even ordered them and I could tell just by looking at him and his wife that we'd stopped at the right place. Johnny and Juliette were going to be on our side.

Sure enough, half an hour later we had managed to commandeer a free room for the night with two single beds, lots of floor space and an en suite bathroom along with access to Johnny and Juliette's cooker socket the following morning. We were living a charmed life and were soon waxing lyrical, talking a load of nonsense about the wonder of humanity and our new status as hoboes of the road.

The Bear Inn turned out to be split in two sections. One side soon became full of trendy young Hoxton types, while the other was already completely full of local men with thinning hair, even thinner cigarettes and broad hearty laughs. We looked at the two rooms carefully, wondering which one we should drink in, and settled for the corridor at first. We were not exactly young hipsters but not imminently approaching emphysema either. Then the younger crowd began pulling us towards them, once they'd clocked the milk float parked out in the howling wind and rain. When I told one guy what we were doing, his jaw dropped. 'We were talking about *Three Men in a Boat* in the car on the way here! That's so spooky . . . '

Much later, the four of us crammed ourselves into our room. Kim and I got a single bed each, hers was on account of our chivalric leanings while mine was to make up for getting milkman's arse, Pras got an inflatable mattress on the floor next to me and Ian put his futon mattress on the floor in the bathroom. Once all the power sockets were charging up God knows how many pieces of Prasanth's electrical treasure chest, we all fell asleep easily, snoring the night away in a contended haze. Another day and another generous stranger – so far things were going very well indeed.

4
Beyton to Moulton

22 miles

IAN

Whereas most vehicles of the twenty-first century do their best to insulate their occupants from the world beyond the windscreen, The Mighty One made it totally impossible to ignore the people and scenery we moved, exceedingly slowly, past. Our leisurely pace afforded us the opportunity to hear more than the usual truncated snatch of bird song, see more of the countryside at close quarters and, unfortunately, view road kill in a kind of ultra-lethargic bullet time. For the first few days of the trip, I was convinced that there had been some horrific upturn in animal slaughter on Britain's roads, but realized that this was the way things had been for a while, unnoticed by the rest of us, the occupants of those environmentally isolated boxes that we all speed around in.

Just as isolation was not an option in the float, neither was anonymity. A factory-built Ford Mundane-o leaves absolutely no impression on the world, save for a microscopic layer of exhaust emissions and the odd tread mark on a dead badger's duodenum, but a 1958 milk float changes the world around it in subtle ways. People who notice it, remember it. They wave, shout, jeer even, but it leaves a small soot-free mark on the world – not very big, not terribly important and just a little bit silly, but still an impact of sorts.

Three days into our journey and we were feeling the impact ourselves. The weather was shocking and our ride was rather high maintenance in the wet. Flapping tarpaulins had to be tautened continually, bungee ropes stretched and adjusted, while polythene sheets protecting the charger had to be gaffered down with tape, all in the pouring, relentless rain.

It was certainly not the kind of weather in which to conduct all-day missions in the open air and that, as we were finding, was the hard reality of moving any distance in a milk float. It was to the motoring experience what camping in a leaky tent is to staying in a well-appointed hotel. Slow Travel was all well and good, but I somehow doubted that Wet Travel would ever catch on. And then there was the steam. Everything misted up the windows, despite the fact that the float was, discounting the possibility of a fleet of wickerwork buses existing somewhere in the world, draftier than any vehicle on the road. The end result was that we all felt about as cold and deflated as a penguin's testicle.

So it was that we bade farewell to Kim, she would return midway through the trip and again at the end to keep up with our progress, before setting off from the warmth and hospitality Johnny and Juliette had provided at The Bear Inn in an attempt to get as close as possible to Newmarket. Beyton Green lies five miles or so east of Bury St Edmunds, a cathedral city that is, according to the 1911 eleventh edition of the *Encyclopædia Britannica*, 'pleasantly situated on a gentle eminence, in a fertile and richly cultivated district'. Almost a hundred years after that polite introduction was written, we descended into the town via its rather wind-swept eastern industrial estate. In common with almost every other industrial estate I have ever had the misfortune to visit, it had been developed entirely along straight roads punctu-ated by the odd token roundabout off which ran more roads, some straight, some featuring geometric curves as perfect as those drawn on the initial blueprints, long since filed away in a municipal planchest somewhere. The area reminded me of nothing so much as a soon to be re-purposed army camp, an in-fill development yet to be filled.

It was Bank Holiday Monday, so the impression that the place was deserted may be a little disingenuous and it certainly didn't fit with my memories of the town. Another place from my past, it had been twenty years since I had set foot in Bury St Edmunds and we had parted company as the best of friends. I adored the place because of its remarkable history and the inspiring buildings that had resulted. I'd fallen in love with the very idea of a small and not terribly urban city, where a certain amount of civic pride was more or less unavoidable and there was enough going on to fend off the deepest reaches of boredom. This particular cathedral city was blessed with a large park among the grounds of a ruined abbey, two colossi in the shape of the impressively large fourteenth-century Abbeygate and a chunky Norman tower about five lamp posts away in the same street. It also had the only surviving Regency theatre in the country, all sorts of half-timbered shenanigans and a direct link to the Magna Carta. How English do you need a place to be before you swoon under its influence? On our trip to find England, my expectations of discovering at least part of it here were high, which is all you really need to be roundly disappointed on all fronts.

Being English is a two-edged sword. The problem with many quintessentially English towns is that they could easily be accused of being just a little too prim and proper, a little chintzy. Indeed, you have to wonder whether Anglican cathedrals have little nozzles fitted into their spires and towers to spray some kind of gas that renders an air of genteel respectability over their small cities. But, given the overwhelming history of places such as Bury St Edmunds, it's inevitable that pretensions will surface, with lacy doilies, net curtains in the tutu style and frou-frou adornments displayed in abundance. It's what the English do in response to occupying modern properties in an historic area. We are quite tacky in that regard, swept along — as we sometimes are — on a wave of soft furnishings and starched linen.

I just hoped that I wasn't mistaken and that Bury was the real thing and not just a mausoleum full of young buildings already dead with frilly knickers pinned to the windows, or just as bad, perfectly preserved picturesque ruins artfully managed for the benefit of tourists and the commission of local estate agents.

Turning onto Angel Hill, we drove into one of the town's grand open spaces, rendered claustrophobic by our steamed-up cab as we were struck by yet another blustery squall. Gazing out of the front window as the rain battered against the screen put me in mind of those documentaries that follow the life of fishermen in old tubs on the open seas. All we needed was a few hundredweight of kippers on the back and the transformation from about-town dairy vehicle to wheelhouse of a trawler would have been complete.

Up on our right was that 'gentle eminence', a shallow hummock on which the old town had been built in a tight grid of narrow streets. To our left, stood the Abbeygate and the Norman tower. Even after the four years I'd spent living in central London, which does monolithic architecture rather well, they still appeared substantial and ponderous to me. Just looking at these buildings reminds you of Kubrick's obelisk in *2001: A Space Odyssey*. They are so forbidding in scale and power that they seem to possess their own pre-ternatural gravitational field. They were, however, once dwarfed by the Abbey itself, which was the largest in Europe. It must have scared the willies out of country folk arriving here on a pilgrimage to honour the East Anglian hero-king and one time patron saint of England, Edmund the Martyr, whose remains were interred − indeed buried − in a shrine in the Abbey.

We turned up into the town in an attempt to strike through to the other side. So far in the journey, we had managed to keep out of town centres − necessity had driven us around the relief roads and an interesting contradiction had emerged. We were so slow we didn't have time to stop unless there was electricity or food on offer. We soon found a convincing reason never to navigate a town centre again. The float steered like a cow − a three-legged arthritic cow that refused to accept the concept of turning left or right in favour of a dogged determination to go straight ahead. Whichever way it was pointing was, for all intents and purposes, the direction of the dairy.

Navigating Bury's bespoke one-way system was difficult, armed as I was with one-inch Ordnance Survey maps of southern England on my laptop − fine for rumbling about the countryside, but utterly useless when your path is obstructed by bollards every hundred yards. Squinting at the screen, it was hard to make sense of the over-magnified jumble of streets that was Bury St Edmunds. Prasanth leaned over to have a look. 'Fucking hell,' he said, with a little cackle. He had a point; it was a completely ridiculous exercise.

Bury's one-way system has something of the alimentary canal about it – a digestive tract that succeeds in shitting all vehicles out of the constipated town with laxative efficiency. Excreted with undue haste onto the ring road, we headed towards the more familiar territory of a retail estate – we were, after all, only trying to stop in Bury to get the charge we needed to reach Newmarket or thereabouts. East Anglia is meant to be flat but it isn't and here was the proof – we now faced a battery-busting incline that lay between us and the electrical potential of the retail park on its brow.

We crawled up the hill, The Mighty One's comfortable whine wound down to an agonizing whirr. Here we were, three days in, challenged by a 'gentle eminence' in Suffolk. If we ever got to the borders of brutally steep Cornwall, we were truly stuffed.

We made it to the top but we may as well not have bothered. None of the shops – Waitrose, PC World, Bennetts or Halfords – could help us because none had electric forklifts, which was our wheeze of the day, but worse than that, almost none of them seemed remotely impressed with our wacky mission. In Halfords, however, an assistant got into the spirit of things and racked his brains for somewhere he thought he might have seen forklifts operating. 'Have you tried B&Q?' he asked.

On the phone outside Halfords, I spoke to Lucy, the trading manager of the town's branch of B&Q. She started laughing almost immediately and I knew that we were on the home straight.

'We're outside Halfords, where are you?' I asked.

'We're only five minutes away,' she replied. 'You need to go down the hill and turn left at the roundabout.'

We went back down the hill. It's worth noting at this point that every hill has more than one side and we were heading down the wrong one. One more phone call to the B&Q manager's office from the bottom of the hill, some barely suppressed hysteria on the other end of the line, and the matter was cleared up. With new directions, I abandoned map reading in favour of some pointers from the manager of B&Q and my hazy memory of how the road system worked. After another orbit of the town we landed ourselves in a tight cul-de-sac that required a nine-point turn and an apology to Dan who, being of an *Idler* disposition, wasn't planning on spending three weeks working on his biceps. We finally arrived on the right side of the hill and pulled up in the B&Q car park at about 5 p.m.

It's a touching aspect of human nature that, when someone in gainful employment does you a weird favour on behalf of their employer and it starts to look a little more complex than just, say, turning up, plugging in, staying around for a while then going away quietly, they don't really want to know. So it was with Lucy. Prasanth gave me the look that says, 'It's not plug and play, it's kludge, plug and pray.'

We found a plug for a forklift charger, but it was the wrong plug entirely, so we were effectively in the same situation as we would be if we had to rewire a cooker point in somebody's kitchen. We had to fit our own socket to the wall temporarily while making everything appear perfectly normal. While Prasanth worked his electrical voodoo, I kept Lucy talking, which wasn't at all difficult as she was one of those people it's very easy to talk to if you go the extra mile, work a bit on the presentation and generally wave your arms around like a nutcase.

All hooked up and with the float buzzing away nicely, we hadn't been parked up for long when a man who could do with a couple of hours of a presentation skills workshop turned up in a white hatchback.

'What the fuck do you think you're up to?' he shouted.

'I'm sorry?' I was a little taken aback by the aggression. All sorts of things were running through my mind. Who was he? Why was he apparently so annoyed at three strangers in that most innocuous of vehicles – a vintage milk float? Was he something to do with B&Q? Was I about to be thumped to within an inch of my life in Britain's first dairy-related drive-by punishment beating?

'What's all this about, then?' he said, climbing down the stepladder of anger a rung or two.

So I told him all about slow travel, discovering England and the ecological angle, but he was still confused.

'It's for charity then is it?'

'No, it's just for the hell of it.'

'You're having a fucking laugh aren't you?' And with that, he wound up his window and sped off out of the car park into the miserable afternoon.

We sat in the B&Q car park for around two hours. The weather was just too nasty and our feet too wet and cold to go exploring what I remembered as a lovely town on the other side of the ring road. Where we were was just another bit of England, after all – not a pretty bit, though, more of a drab nook in a glum corner of a dull car park. We were parked on the public side of a tall white mesh gate that kept us out of the inner bowels of the B&Q loading bay, into which our 25-metre armoured charging cable was snaking its way. Health and safety – surely the greyest words in the English language – was responsible for the wedge driven between us and the good folk at the DIY superstore so, unlike Morrisons at Diss, where the management kept us entertained with free coffee in a warm room, there was no real possibility of getting an inside view of the B&Q machine. We elected to brew up on the back of the float in the car park, like a family of vagrants, and drink our tea in the steamed-up cab. I tried to imagine being in the same position in my retirement, parked in a warm car on the god-forsaken esplanade of a failed seaside resort, moaning about the weather and the state of the nation. The situation we found ourselves in was just as 'English' as that, but, ridiculous as it may seem, appeared to be far more normal.

Eventually, with the light fading quickly, Dan became restless about driving in such appalling weather and we disconnected, said our thank-yous and left, heading west towards Newmarket. Bury was behind us at last. It was a shame not to look at it with new eyes, but travelling through a place, no matter how slowly, is no replacement for stopping altogether.

Traditional grumbles about the weather notwithstanding, we got to see wider panoramas on this part of the journey than we had so far. The western half of Suffolk is gently undulating chalk downland set on the edge of the meres and fields of the Fenlands of Norfolk to the north. Under a wide sky flattened to dull white by the low cloud and drizzle, my eye was drawn to a long, low hedge with a large oak tree at the start of it. It looked for all the world like a line in a book, perhaps the head of a chapter of some country almanac where the oak formed an illustrated capital T. The sentence trailed off towards the west, punctuated by the odd tree here and there. I was still mentally rebuking myself for such an absurdly poetic moment when we spotted a hare – an animal that, after forty-two years of living in England, I had never seen before. The country almanac was complete – all we needed now was an old man with a pipe and a squint, leaning over a gate and dispensing aphorisms and rural folklore by the bushel.

'You see that,' said Dan, focusing on the hare, 'it's faster than us.'

'Everything's faster than us, Dan,' I responded, unhelp-
fully. Not just an oversized, souped-up rabbit, the hare ran
up the road in front of the float more in the manner of an
antelope or small deer than the carrot-crunching cousin of
rats we are used to seeing in this country. It was magnificent
not only for its rarity value but also for its absolute wildness.
I remember looking through a hedge some years ago, to find
a fox peering back at me. Its eyes were those of an intelligent
wild animal with certain understanding of the situation in
which it had found itself. I felt pampered and tame by com-
parison. At such close quarters, behind the hedge, the fox
was absolutely nothing like a small dog. We weren't lucky
enough to get that close to the hare, but its whole manner
had the same unpredictable single-mindedness about it.

'I told you it was the size of a lion,' remarked Dan, clearly
over-excited and out of control now.

The A14 between Bury and Newmarket is a very busy
road. It carries all the east coast ferry and freight port
traffic from Harwich and Felixstowe to and from the West
Midlands and is a motorway in all but name, so wasn't suitable for us in the slightest. Unlike most motorway schemes,
however, when they built this road in the 1970s, they simply
widened the corridor of the existing road without leaving an
alternative route for drivers who didn't fancy dicing with
death on a regular basis. So when we came to plan the route
to Newmarket, we were diverted far out into the sticks and
we managed to try out most points of the compass on the
way.

There were so many twists and turns that progress was
even slower than anticipated, and as the light was hurtling
towards twilight, we eventually conceded that we might
not get all the way to Newmarket. Gazeley, on the map an
interesting-looking village, could have been the answer, but

turning up at the only pub, the enormous Chequers Inn, hoping to check in got us nowhere.

There were no rooms at the inn – it was a food pub and a very recently refurbished food pub at that. Pristine and clean in a well-clipped village, it was set on an open crossroads and there was something not quite right about it. The local beer was lovely, the seating was of the Clerkenwell persuasion – big comfy leather sofas for holding court on the features of your latest iPod – and ceiling beams on which were displayed, curiously, a selection of rat-pack era Hollywood stills of the great and good, artfully hung in self-conscious clusters. Normally, you'd spend some time enquiring what the relevance of the pictures was to a capacious and sadly empty pub in rural Suffolk, but I'll admit to being too tired and brassed off to bother with it.

The landlord did ring around to get us some bed and breakfast accommodation in Moulton, the next village along, which was kind of him, but knowing we still had a few more miles to go in the near darkness made us restless. What was Moulton like, we wondered. Were there any pubs there?

There's the King's Head, we were told, but our host would not be drawn on its quality, preferring instead to invoke the innkeeper's oath: 'Publicans don't really comment on other pubs, so I can't really say what it's like.' Oh Lordy!

He was more forthcoming on the route at least. There was a little stream that ran through Moulton, and our route in would take us over a ford. 'It's usually just a dribble and it's only in spate a few days a year, so it shouldn't be too much of a problem,' he assured us, but that assessment took no account of several days of pouring rain. After a couple of miles of driving in the darkness, what lay between us and the village was a raging torrent, a dirty swirl of coffee brown water, glinting in the headlights of the float. However, the flood gauge indicated that it was only a foot deep, so, reasoning that it looked worse than it actually was, we took deep breaths and ploughed on through and up the other side.

Our accommodation wasn't difficult to find and, after settling in, we set off to sample the comforts offered by the King's Head. I think it's fair to suggest that Shelley behind the bar was hoping for a quiet night. With just a smattering of well-known locals propping up the back bar – known in the sense that their movements were predictable and they all looked like they were about to slope off – we probably looked as though we might be hard work at the wrong stage of the night. She was, therefore, a little wary and a little weary when we arrived. After exchanging glances with one another and with the non-committal negativity of the Chequers landlord still ringing in our ears, we asked if food was being served. The firm, but polite 'no' was not unexpected.

Sure enough, the back bar emptied out and our host was all ours as long as we could persuade her to have us.

'What brings you to Moulton,' she asked when we ordered another pint. We told her.

'No!'

It turned out that there, in that rather isolated pub in the middle of nowhere, we had found one of a handful of people in almost 100,000 square miles of Britain who was contemplating the purchase of a milk float. It works both ways. Shelley had also found us, the only source of a milk-float test drive ever to have passed through Moulton. When Dan promised me that chance and serendipity would be our guides, I had thought we were talking in very general, non-specific terms – we would be jollying along on a wave of English eccentricity that would draw people to us and make the whole thing work to our advantage. In my weirdest, wildest dreams I never thought that serendipity could be so literal, so specific. This is the kind of thing that happens when you relax about the details and just let a good idea take care of itself.

If travelling is for anything beyond personal development and evading work, it's for swapping stories with other travellers along the way. It turned out that Shelley was no stranger to long journeys in historic vehicles.

'A friend and I drove to Italy in an old Ford Galaxy,' she told us. 'It was just like what you're doing.'

She cooked us some chips and we stood and looked agog at one another while we drank beer. Truly we were on a charmed mission. Shelley, it turned out, worked all around the village and was going to be our passport to an easy charge the next morning. We could relax, our day was done and more beer was on offer. We slept well in the arms of chance.

5

Moulton to Cambridge

23 miles

DAN

After a night of wild and violent nightmares, I was woken just before nine by the smell of breakfast cooking. Gradually, I remembered that we'd asked Sally, in whose B&B we had spent the night, for the full English and so, leaping out of bed, I dashed over to Ian and Prasanth's room and began thwacking their door. They were both dead to the world so I hissed them awake with the word 'BREAKFAST!' and then remembered I was wearing just a pair of pants. Half naked, I glanced sheepishly around the landing and didn't recognize it. The carpet was very deep and comfy between my toes, though. I nipped back into my room, ducking under the door's low beam, got dressed, picked up the savage hangover I'd left on my pillow having got up too quickly, and was soon staggering under the weight of a thundering headache as I hobbled down the stairs.

The smells led me past a large clock in the hall to the breakfast table in the kitchen, where I found Sally in full 'I don't really know you so I'll talk a lot of polite nonsense' mode while niftily frying some eggs. There was no way of evading the slings and arrows of polite conversation without being rude, so I grinned through the throbbing pain in my head and nodded with as much enthusiasm as I could muster. Sally was a pro, though. I quickly realized the unwritten rule to which she was adhering, namely that she would keep nattering but I was under no obligation to join in, apart from by nodding my head or saying, 'Oh really?' every now and then. The appearance of a large plate full of food heralded a break in her flow, and then Ian and Pras appeared. She smiled at them both and said, 'Good morning,' with a slight look of anguish on her face. They both looked hilariously awful, something that cheered me up no end. Pras began mainlining coffee and looked disdainfully at the food on my plate. He didn't seem to consume very much at all unless you count cigarettes, coffee and AC current.

Ian, meanwhile, was manfully taking responsibility for more non-conversation with Sally while I hid in the refuge of my breakfast. I peered up from my plate, keen not to be engaged in any way by anyone, and discovered I was sitting in a beautiful homely room. Pictures adorned the cupboards and the whole place was well kitted out with antiques and ornaments. You can tell a lot about someone by their kitchen, you know. Sally was a full-bodied chatty mum who was just about to bloom into the joyous role of a firm but fair grandma, or so it seemed to me.

Five minutes after devouring my breakfast I found myself thrashing around in the cab of The Mighty One looking for headache tablets, muttering, 'Help me, Ibuprofen, you're my only hope,' over and over again with increasing desperation. In a few moments I'd found my first-aid kit and gobbled down three tablets. All I needed now was a can of Coke and I might just make it back to full consciousness.

Pras and Ian hobbled out of Sally's house a few moments later, looking like a pair of opium-addled Nepalese mountain porters. Pras had, in fact, drunk just one small cafetière of coffee, which didn't bode well for the electrical challenges of the day because he requires much more than that to rouse him. Ian was still half asleep but had to go off to find the Post Office and a cash machine so we could pay Sally's bill. I sat in The Mighty One, shivering and waiting for the tablets to take effect.

My memory of the night before was decidedly hazy. At first all I could recall were lots of pints and plates of chips. Then I remembered Shelley and perked up. Of course! She wanted to buy a milk float! What kind of chance was that? She'd promised us a charge that morning from a stately home, and then I think the excitement of the day ahead finally managed to pull me back into the real world. If all went to plan, we'd be in Cambridge that night, staying with my mate Ed, who, before we left, had offered us an overnight charge. Cambridge had seemed a distant dream back in Lowestoft and the idea that we might get there felt very comforting indeed, although it has to be said, in terms of distance, it really wasn't very far. Even in a milk float.

We left in the continuing downpour ten minutes later and were soon bouncing down to the bottom of an enormous hill on our way to the stately home, while Ian called Shelley to make sure the plan was still going ahead. Just as we reached the bottom of the hill, she answered the phone. It turned out that the owners of the stately home were not in and it would probably be impolite to rewire their kitchen without their permission. But all was not lost. Apparently, Shelley had another friend who was away, and rewiring her kitchen without permission would not be considered such an imposition. This friend, Ali, lived in a converted chapel – the converted chapel right behind Sally's B&B.

The Mighty One limped back up the hill, round a few hairy corners and managed to squeeze off the road between two large hedges into the chapel's driveway. Shelley met us a few minutes later, clambering out of a dilapidated car that was full of unknowable junk. She was dressed from top to toe in Barbour, wearing one of their enormous coats, a pair of boots and a slightly floppy cowboy hat. If Billy Crystal ever does a remake of 'City Slickers' set in and around Newmarket, Shelley would be the gruff but beautiful, no-nonsense love interest.

The chapel was a wonderful, if slightly frightening place. It took Pras a while to clamber up through the old organ pipes through Shelob-style cobwebs to get to the fuse box. He started to grin, and I'm sure he was salivating as he said, 'This has monster current! I could charge a fleet of milk floats from this!'

Ali's house was full of paintings, wine boxes and animal footstools that she made to sell at craft and antique fairs. It was freezing cold inside, so cold in fact that when we opened the door I felt colder than you do standing outside on bonfire night. Ian suggested we all huddle together out in the rain, just to warm up a bit.

Despite the cold, Ali had managed to invest the chapel with a homely presence and, although made of stone, it seemed to be absorbing her like a sponge. We saw a few pictures of her around the place and she had a lively face. You could imagine her bringing life into almost any situation, just as she'd brought a bit of extra colour to an old and seemingly forgotten building. It was the kind of place where you'd have a political campaigner hiding in a dystopian nightmare flick. We were sorry she wasn't there and very grateful for her kindness, *in absentia*.

Ian and Pras went off to the King's Head again with

Shelley to find a man she hoped would be able to take a look at The Mighty One's steering, which seemed to have loosened a little. I sat down at the kitchen table, while outside the charger throbbed. Cat food trays filled the space underneath the table and a huge overflowing box of Marlborough Lights took up a seat behind it. This was the first time I'd been on my own, while not sleeping, since leaving Lowestoft and it felt rather nice. I got out my notebook and looked at its utterly empty and seemingly endless pages and felt myself sag slightly. I steeled myself and began to jot down my thoughts on the trip so far.

The first thing that struck me was the way the country seemed to have grown since the day we'd left Lowestoft. We were in horse country, just outside Newmarket, and it occurred to me that the daily distance you can get out of a milk float is probably similar to the distance you could manage on a horse before it gets worn out and needs to rest for the night. That being the case, England, to us, had now changed from a tiny nation where, as Will Self once quipped, 'the only way to do a road movie would be to film it in real time', into a country as huge as it would have seemed to someone living back in medieval England, or any time, in fact, before the invention of the train or motor car. The excitement and wonder that dripped off that idea seemed to drown me for a while. I was overcome with questions. It's certainly true that our ability to travel all over the country at will has stripped away the sense of magic and mystery that was once contained within it, and if you give back a nation its magic, what kind of unexplained wonder might you awaken? Were coincidence and serendipity its gifts to us in return? And surely if you can make a nation 'grow' like that, our lackadaisical journey would be like watching the country through the lens of a microscope!

Maybe this was what people originally meant when they said 'travel broadens the mind'? It doesn't mean you broaden your mind by travelling longer distances to places that are farther and farther away, but by travelling slower and, therefore, closer to reality, which in turn alters the way travel makes you *think* – hence broadening the mind. Perhaps the truth is that now we can travel anywhere we please across the globe, the new 'frontiers' are not exotic foreign climes but the places right under your nose.

I felt as though I'd stumbled on the tip of an iceberg of an idea. I just hoped the rest of the trip would reveal everything relating to it that was now happily minding its own business deep under the surface.

The only other thing I jotted down in my notebook was that if I ever got stuck and needed a 'regular' job, I could now probably be pretty confident about getting one as a milkman.

Before I could get lost in another shivering reverie, a sprightly man wearing a boiler suit and a hearing aid appeared in the kitchen.

'Excuse me, can I look under your milk float?' he asked, politely.

This turned out to be Bob, or in Shelley's words 'Bobbledy Bob', the local mechanic and all-round nice chap on whom everyone in the village seemed to rely to keep their vehicles moving.

'I heard you wanted someone to take a look at the steering,' he explained. He looked the age of a man who had retired for long enough to be calm and relaxed about it, but was still a long, long way from the clutches of dementia.

I followed him outside and he began to clamber under The Mighty One's front wheels. I was rather concerned he might not make it back out again but he soon emerged, pulling himself up on his left knee and rubbing the water and mud from his boiler suit. Bouncing perhaps a tad too fast down some serious hills had affected the steering but Bob was not fazed.

'Yeah, I think it's fine, but bring it over to my place and we'll get her up on a jack and take a proper look. You've got a long way to go and we'll see if we can't help make sure you get there.' With that he sauntered off.

I went back into the chapel, sat down again, yawning, and promptly dozed off with my head on the table.

I woke, finally free of my hangover, what must have been a couple of hours later because Ian and Pras had returned and were rolling up the armoured cable and preparing to leave. The first thing Ian said to me was, 'Dan, we said Shelley could drive The Mighty One to Bob's place. Is that OK?' Shelley appeared at his shoulder, grinning slightly manically. I guess milk floats just have that effect on people.

I would like to claim that driving a milk float is much harder than it looks and it takes a good hundred miles before you really get the hang of it but that would be utter rubbish. After a hundred yards Shelley was driving far more confidently than I had and The Mighty One was responding well to her no-nonsense approach. I don't want to patronize Shelley by saying that while driving The Mighty One she looked like a little girl having her first ride on a horse, because she could easily deck me with one punch, but she really did. I've rarely seen such joy behind the wheel of a vehicle outside an episode of *Top Gear*. She loved it and thought it was exactly the kind of thing she needed for her job – while also allowing her plenty of space for her numerous dogs. She seemed slightly deflated when we arrived at Bob's house, Rose Cottage, a few moments later, and suggested I take over for the daunting prospect of parking up in the driveway.

She dismounted from the cab and began gesturing for Ian and Pras to hurry up as they walked slowly up the road, but I could see they were still far enough away to smoke at least two, if not three, cigarettes each.

The hedge separating Rose Cottage from Bob's neighbour's house looked like one of those thousand-year-old countryside heirlooms, with a million bits of wildlife happily cocooned in their own little world. Unfortunately, I managed to disturb their peace by ripping off a large chunk of it as I bounded the float up the driveway. Bob kindly commented that the hedge needed a bit of a trim as he retrieved armfuls of foliage and dragged it away to a compost heap. I parked near a slightly mournful and battered car that, it transpired, had long since been evicted from Bob's enormous garage. That useful outhouse was filled from top to bottom with bits of machinery, tins of paint, chunks of wood, bits of metal, engines and tarpaulin. I'm sure I even spotted a trailer in there somewhere before he emerged, carrying two rather dainty looking jacks.

'They won't be big enough. It weighs two tons,' I said, forgetting for a moment that I didn't have the slightest clue what I was talking about. Unsurprisingly, I turned out to be completely wrong and soon the front of The Mighty One was up in the air and Bob was underneath it, fiddling about with the wheels.

Ian and Pras finally arrived, wheezing in unison, just as Bob's wife Fran appeared, carrying a tray with the largest teapot I've ever seen and an equally huge tin of rock cakes. I wasn't actually hungry but when it turned out that Fran was vice president of the WI, I made damn sure I grabbed the largest cake in the tin. Well, it doesn't do to turn down a cake made by a member of the WI, let alone the vice president. And then, just when I didn't think anything could top a free service for The Mighty One, a cup of tea and a cake made by the VP of the WI, something completely unexpected happened. Even thinking about it now makes my eyes water with joy. For the first time since leaving Lowestoft the sun actually came out. I couldn't believe it. We all stared up at the sky, re-acquainting ourselves with what warmth felt like.

When Bob emerged from underneath The Mighty One, he was grinning.

'This is proper mechanics, none of that modern rubbish,' he informed us, disappearing straight back under it again. He began turning the wheels by hand, and called out, 'Yeah, it's a bit loose, but that's 'cause it's fifty years old. There's nothing wrong with it. You should be fine. Just don't get it wet underneath. So avoid the ford or Moulton will be the end of your journey. Whatever you do, don't leave the village that way.'

We told him, nonchalantly, that we'd already been through the ford the night before and he poked his head out from under the wheels with a look of total disbelief on his face, eventually stuttering, 'That's . . . that's impossible.' He went through the slightly painful process of getting up before adding, 'Last night it was even higher than it is now! You've got bare electrics down where the battery connects to the motor, and if they get wet, you're finished.' He shook his head and looked at us sharply. 'That amazes me,' he said, raising his eyebrows. 'You must have someone or something helping you.' I told him that the sign by the ford had said the water was only a foot deep and he laughed. 'That sign is on the bank two foot above the bed of the river. You went through three feet of water!'

It was no more than the three of us had come to expect. It was really no surprise at all to discover that the laws of physics didn't apply to us. The Mighty One was clearly blessed. It wasn't the last time she performed feats of magic on our trip, either.

Before we left Rose Cottage, Bob gave us one of his cards and offered us a free breakdown service for the next forty-eight hours, however far we managed to get. We gave him one of the enormous car chargers we'd brought in return, not that he wanted or expected any money, but the charger had turned out to be nothing more than ballast and we thought he'd find a use for it somehow. We said our good-byes to our three new friends and headed off in the direction of Newmarket and Cambridge.

To be honest, we should have gone much farther, but Ed's offer of an overnight charge was too good to miss. With the sun shining at last, this was the most relaxed leg of the journey so far, and rather fun. In the warmth the countryside seemed to glow, released from the relentless grey that had accompanied us up until now.

That afternoon is a blur of lush green fields drying in the sun. We whined along beside hedges and on gravel roads that didn't appear to offer much in terms of destination, but were banked either side by the magic of the unknown. It reminded me of the never-ending fields and trees of child-hood and the glorious patience of those too young to demand horizons farther than the one they can see with their own eyes – and too young to have been hoodwinked into thinking magic, adventure and happiness are to be found anywhere other than right under your nose.

Down neglected lanes lined with chest-high hedges we trundled, as the grey clouds were driven west by the batter-ing wind. The Mighty One made hard work of the gradual inclines but relished zooming down the other sides with a satisfying whine. To get to Newmarket and on to Cambridge meant joining main roads for a few miles where we experienced the unsettling overtaking manoeuvres Gordon had warned us about. The cars seemed to pass in smaller and smaller gaps until a juggernaut missed us by a whisker, cutting across our path as it fought its way up a hill. I looked at Ian in terror. 'I know, I know . . .' he replied, 'don't worry, I'll get us off it and find another route.' Ian had already become co-pilot extraordinaire. Despite our slow speed, we required dauntingly swift map-reading skills to keep us on track while avoiding major roads and hideous hills.

After a few attractive sidetracks, we came upon Newmarket, which proved to be much easier to navigate than Bury. We sailed down a straight road that cut its way through the heart of the town. Beyond it, the roads became busier and steeper, leaving us at the mercy of the hard shoulder as we dawdled through potholes in order to give the cars behind space to overtake on the single-lane carriageway.

An hour or so later we trundled into Cambridge and, having negotiated the ring road, found the entrance to Clare College. It was absurdly grand and posh. We all felt rather silly in a milk float and rang Ed to find out where he wanted us to park up, assuming we'd be sent off somewhere round the back.

'Oh no, I've cleared it with the college. Just park out by the entrance. I'll come down now,' Ed said. It must be the first time three slightly stinky travellers have alighted from a milk float covered in blue tarpaulin outside the grandeur of a Cambridge college. We did have to move the float, but not for aesthetic reasons. It was just because we had to get closer to Ed's communal kitchen window so we could rewire his small hob unit to get a charge. We did have permission to charge up but only because Ed had insinuated to the porters (he didn't actually lie) that we could use a normal three-pin plug. Therefore, because we couldn't turn off the power to the entire halls of residence, Pras would have to 'hot-wire' the cooker for us to get anything out of it. That meant taking the cooker plug socket off the wall, disconnecting the wires and wiring our charger directly into the mains, without turning the power off first. Pras was typically relaxed and began explaining his rules when it comes to electrics. I'm sure he said it in the hope of reassurance.

'It's simple, really. There's the English way and the Indian way. The English way is safer but the Indian way will get us to Land's End.' Ian and I looked at him aghast.

'But Pras,' I pleaded, 'yes, we want to get to Land's End but we don't want you to fucking *die* in the process.'

'It's cool, man.' He just shrugged, pulled back his dreads, tugged his electrician's red screwdriver out of his back pocket and wandered off in the direction of the kitchen.

In Ed's lounge, I reclined on his sofa, marvelling at how flash his university digs were, while simultaneously being utterly petrified that Pras was about to electrocute himself. At Clare College, we gave Prasanth's level of death risk a mark of five out of ten, but in retrospect it was probably closer to eight. This was when I opted out of any involvement in the whole charging process, which seemed fair enough to me. I drove us somewhere and then collapsed in a haze of beer and fags while Ian and Pras set about securing the fuel to continue our journey. They both seemed content with this approach, having seen at first hand how utterly useless I am when it comes to anything practical.

Ed's friends, who shared his communal kitchen, seemed entertained by the prospect of us hot-wiring Clare College. We didn't actually charge up there and then but Pras wanted to do the hot-wiring when he wasn't pissed, so he just did the dangerous bit and then we left for the pub, planning to turn it all on when we got back later that night.

We had a great meal at the Eagle, where Crick and Watson had become the first people to unravel DNA. I don't know about DNA but the pub's invention of the Yorkshire Wrap was certainly memorable – loads of roast beef and gravy wrapped up in an enormous Yorkshire pudding. Afterwards, we made our way back to Ed's digs via another pub, small but excellent and worthy of mention, despite the very boring man with his own radio show who had drunk so much he didn't seem to care that he punctuated every excla- mation with dribble.

Ed had a kind of town 'back-stage pass' that let us through special walkways and down through one postcard college after another, over the river, through the park and finally back to his rooms. On the way, we stopped on a bridge that looked out towards one of the college gardens. It was won- derful and completely unreal in the moonlight.

The Oxbridge world is not one that I was, or ever will be, a part of. I don't even have a degree. It would be nice, though, if those who do get to go were more like Ed – fully aware of how lucky they are. A conversation I had with Ed earlier perhaps explains why some Oxbridge students have a slightly blinkered approach.

Ed had told me how most of his friends had been 'tapped- up' by management consultants, banking and legal firms. One of his friends had accepted the advances of one com- pany in return for the company paying his fees and giving him enough cash to live on throughout his degree. One day he received a memo informing him that his Facebook page wasn't at all suitable for one of their employees. He was eighteen and in his first few weeks of student life. I can't imagine anything worse hanging over you through your uni- versity years than that kind of tedious Big Brother, ticking you off at every opportunity.

Believe it or not, I was asked to write an article for the Oxbridge careers magazine a few years ago, which they've reprinted every year since. My contribution was the introduction to a section called 'Not the Nine to Five', which was buried at the back of the magazine. I'd written about the joys, and inevitable poverty, of a freelance life that requires you to reject the pursuit of money in order to remain master of your own time. The entire section stretched to a pitiful ten pages in a magazine consisting of 348 pages of careers advice. The other careers in the 'Not the Nine to Five' section included the Army, the Navy and the Police, being an Astronaut, a novelty entertainer (represented by an article written by Timmy Mallett), a celebrity chef or a stunt man, and even mentioned someone who'd run away to join the circus. To be polite, I didn't think it really did justice to the entire world outside of the usual corporate suspects. Meanwhile, the management consultants, banks and lawyers (who had paid for the publication if the amount of advertising in it was anything to go by) were represented in large numbers in wrist-slittingly tedious detail. But working for a merchant bank doesn't seem a very amazing end to a young life once filled with such promise. After sailing through the education system, and wallowing in the joys of learning in such an inspiring place, doing such a tedious job for the rest of your life must be a serious anti-climax. Perhaps this begins to expose the flaw in our education system – there isn't much room for imagination. All the targets of the corporate world, with their league tables and life-sucking monitoring, not to mention vast debt caused by tuition fees and student loans, have permeated even our most esteemed educational centres.

An anonymous, but very well-respected university lecturer (of over twenty years) wrote of this problem in *The*

Idler. He titled his piece 'University. Why bother?' It gives a very interesting insight into how things are changing in our top universities. The anonymous professor wrote:

'I like to daydream about the old times when scholars and students were left alone to get on with it themselves. No one questioned their importance to society, and consequently, unhindered by cloying bureaucracy and poncey governments, they were places of vigour, radicalism and creativity. Such sensibilities were out of step with the inexorable rise of twentieth-century capitalism, and slowly but surely our great learning institutions succumbed.

'What we see now is that entering a university is a leap onto the escalator that takes you down into the basement of capitalism. There are no windows down there: it is dark. Only by a supreme effort of the will can you find your own way out of this vast and impersonal space. People are on hand to promise you a way out, but in return you will have to work very hard at learning to say the same things as all those who went before you. You will need to pay lots of money for this privilege, and there are many people willing to lend. Finally, a graduate fast-track scheme offers a lift up to ground level, but in reality you're just shoved through the emergency exit amongst the rubbish bins to make way for new arrivals. Unless you run immediately, the rest of your life will be spent there.'

Ed confirmed this was the case when he explained about the number of parties hosted by large city firms in the first few weeks of his degree course. They were all on hand with gallons of free booze to tell the impressionable young students how wonderful and lucrative their lives could be if only they signed on the dotted line immediately.

It all seemed rather a tragic waste, gazing out across those hallowed colleges and perfectly manicured lawns in the moonlight. I doubted it would be Ed's fate, though. He began writing for *The Idler* when he was seventeen and almost got into the *Guinness Book of Records* at school for organizing the world's largest 'Heads Shoulders Knees and Toes' with his fellow classmates. He managed to get Norris McWhirter to turn up to verify the attempt but didn't make it in the end because of a 'technicality'. I couldn't imagine that someone with his humour, spirit and zest for life would be the kind of mindless drone the city corporations were really after.

Back at the float, we set about collecting the lead we'd rather foolishly left unfurled on the road, only to discover that some fucker in a Daewoo had parked on our armoured cable. After five minutes of trying to lift up the car and pull out the cable, we decided to 'bounce' it free, having concluded that this rickety model was unlikely to be alarmed. Pras was sitting on the bonnet and bouncing like a man possessed when we finally got the cable loose. He climbed onto the back of The Mighty One, tapped the top of the charger gently, plugged it in and turned it on. Electricity wasn't the only connection going on it seemed. I had a feeling this trip was having rather a positive impact on my good friend Pras.

When we'd decided to attempt the trip and Ian had asked if I knew a 'third man' who might be up for it, the first person who sprang to mind was Pras, despite the fact that I knew very little about him. We'd met in Parliament Square on various protests against the Government's decision to ban any spontaneous political demonstration within 1km of the House of Commons. Pras and our mutual friend Mark, along with an assortment of other campaigners, had already been arrested for protesting illegally in the square when I joined the campaign.

When I met Pras I was amazed at the way everyone around him totally reveres him, but in a very quiet and largely unspoken way. He's admired for being a man of passion and conviction, and someone who is motivated by a fierce moral code, which is quite impressive for someone who also finds time to be a technician for the Tate gallery in London, a documentary film maker, a photographer and co-director of a small international development charity that raises money for projects in Guatemala and India.

The other thing about him is his seemingly infinite capacity to help people. Every single time I've been round to his flat he's had someone crashing with him for an unspecified amount of time. One of these friends told me a story that really puts him in perspective. Apparently, Pras had advertised some camera equipment in a magazine. A man answered the advert and came round to his flat to see if the equipment was what he wanted. It turned out that this man was from Madras, where Pras grew up, and had fallen on hard times. He needed the equipment to get his working life back on track. Needless to say, he left Prasanth's flat with the equipment, but not having parted with any money for it. In fact, as well as the camera equipment, Pras had given him money to help him get back on his feet. The two remain firm friends to this day.

Getting Pras to talk about himself is like getting an ethically produced pint of milk (for which a dairy farmer gets paid properly) from a supermarket. He hides behind astonishing modesty and it wasn't until later in the trip that I managed to extract any information about his background.

With The Mighty One charging up nicely, we adjourned to Ed's room and had collapsed on our various makeshift beds when Ed got a call from the porter. Apparently, he was getting cold feet at the prospect of the milk float being on the premises now that we'd moved it to the staff car park. He asked us to disconnect and move it by 7 a.m. Pras agreed to get up and sort it all out in the morning.

The next day we were setting off for Hitchin to meet John Myatt, who had seen us on our way from Lowestoft, and had promised us a charge at his music shop. The journey that would take us out of Cambridgeshire and south towards the north-west edge of London. I fell asleep with a satisfied smile on my face. In the days to come we'd be visiting the burial place of our inspiration, Jerome K. Jerome, in the village of Ewelme. If we could make it to a landmark such as that, surely anything was possible.

6

Cambridge to Hitchin

33 miles

IAN

As the official map-reader, I had taken it upon myself to apologize for all the inconvenient topographic features and traffic management systems that we were unable to avoid. Hills were a blemish on my good standing, and an obstructive one-way system, like the one that Bury St Edmunds had thrown at us, a stain on my character. In short, for the duration of our journey, I felt it was my role to accept full responsibility for geography as a whole.

The upside was that I could bathe in the warm glow of crossing county boundaries, and right now we were feeling pretty chuffed about having actually made it to a different county from the one in which we had started. Having got this far on a generally west by south-west line – tacking here and there around the odd hillock – we were, however, suddenly forced to go north by north-east for a couple of miles to pick up some electrical spares. We needed one of the big blue 32-amp plugs, and its friend the big blue 32-amp socket, because we had lost at least one along the way – it was presumably bumped off the back of the float after a sluggish getaway from one of our charges – and the only place I could track one down was the Newey and Eyre warehouse a little way out of town. The trouble was that it was entirely in the wrong direction. One of the problems with slow travel is that you begin to horde the hard-won miles and resent having to drive them again. We wanted to cling on to all the progress we had, against insuperable odds, managed to make and those two miles to Newey and Eyre added up to a four-mile detour. When you're limited to twenty-five to thirty miles a charge, a slow bumble up to the bypass and back starts to become significant. It was with this unreasonable and undeserved feeling of failure that I guided us up the A1309 Ely road.

As soon as we were off Cambridge's ring road, the wide single carriageway quickly became a red-brick suburban street, lined with between the wars vernacular semis, the odd arcade of shops, some bed and breakfasts and a large Arts and Crafts-era pub or two. Once upon a time, this road would have seemed like a generously proportioned boulevard, but traffic has turned it into a narrow and spiteful transport corridor. Where once the idea of commuting fifteen or twenty miles alone in your own car to get to work would not only have seemed ridiculous but laughable, the term 'close to work' now covers an ever-expanding radius. So much so that those among us with the most liquid capital may choose to have two homes, one a country retreat on the edge of a village and the other a 'pied-à-terre' close to the office in the city, so that they can have the 'best of both worlds'. They then drive between them in a German car so ludicrously over-appointed and luxurious it is virtually a third home in its own right. On their way they drive along roads like this one, not only spraying everyone and everything with carcinogens as they go but, in places, helping to create a fault line between neighbours – communities where the front gardens are effectively dead space and the road itself repre-sents an unassailable wall to interaction with people who live less than one hundred feet away across on the other side. In the modern world, the fixation with speed is the mother of another obsession – that everyone is a stranger, nobody can be trusted, your neighbour is not your friend. If more people regarded the road with suspicion, rather than the rest of the community, we might come closer to finding a solution to the increasing distance between us and next door.

Newey and Eyre was on another one of those godfor-saken, geometrically drawn industrial estates seemingly mapped out on the plans with the aid of a protractor and compasses, without any regard for the landscape it was imposed upon. Enormous utilitarian corrugated sheds the size of tithe barns predominated, with concreted slabs for forecourts, each of them holding court to an audience of trucks, trailers, skips and cardboard compactors. Forklift trucks serviced the assembly of tin machines, fussing away backwards and forwards like waiters with a tray of vol-au-vents, but hospitality for anyone not invited to this party was in short supply. Each of the sheds was surrounded by a chain-link fence with 'do not' and 'keep out' signs fixed to them. Some of these signs featured a black line drawing of an Alsatian, slavering viciously from a red triangle, so there was no real need to go hunting for the subtext; the signs may just as well have read 'fuck off or we'll rip your throat out'.

We had developed a theory in the float that one of the rea-sons why we had been so successful so far was that the very act of driving around in something so absurd made us seem, at the very least, unthreatening, and may have actually endeared us to people. We could clearly laugh at ourselves, and letting down our guard in that way had peeled back one of the layers with which we all onion-skin ourselves in order to deal with the world in the normal circumspect manner. Every one of us performs a dance of manners and etiquette every time we meet someone new. Deeper down in our animal instincts, we write various verbal and physical gestures into our approach and read back what is written, almost without knowing it. All this is largely for our own protection and so that we can see where we fit in the pecking order. Our daft mode of transport made us a little vulnerable. We were telling people that we couldn't carry on without their help and, so far, everyone had responded to that. Until now.

Parked up at Newey and Eyre, I couldn't help noticing a couple of those forklift trucks moving pallets of stuff around in the yard next door. Forklifts meant electricity and, seeing as we had a shade under thirty miles to go today to get to Hitchin, where a sure charge awaited us, I thought I'd try my luck. I tried to attract the attention of a man in a high-visibility jacket – a supervisor of sorts, who had given away his status by marshalling some of his subordinates back inside after a crafty cigarette break.

'Excuse me,' I said, as convivially as I could through the chain-link fence, but it was instantly all wrong. He frowned at me as he came over, and I explained the story in its wackiest incarnation. I danced around a bit on my feet, became very dynamic and animated, used my hands a lot – in that florid way that road protestors do in an effort to communicate with a line of gittish jobsworth coppers – but it wasn't having any effect. Not the faintest glimmer of amusement or interest flickered across his still furrowed brow. The chain-link fence was the problem – it was a barrier to communication and I couldn't seem to work the magic of The Mighty One through it. The screen-intertwined wire was interfering with the message as if it was a faraday cage, specially constructed to deflect the influence of non-rational arguments.

'Health and safety,' said the supervisor, invoking a second-ary shield before he added the, 'Sorry,' he'd been instructed to pass on during his most recent Customer Courtesy Training Day at an Essex Travelodge, at which point I gave in.

We did eventually get a charge from Newey and Eyre, though. After we'd spent a small pot of money on bits of plastic with metal embedded in them and some bargain-basement bungees for tying down the tarps even more, Pras got out his camera for the occasion and Jason, the man in charge of the warehouse, though clearly bemused at first, leapt straight into our world. He agreed to help and, while the float was plugged in, was happy to chat.

Jason is Cambridge born and bred. 'I've been here all my life and I don't plan on moving out,' he told me in his strange-to-outsiders Fenland drawl, a London–rural accent that comes over as an interesting mix of Suffolk and Smoke. I asked him, with my mind still chewing over thoughts on artificial division, fences and the like, where the lines between town and gown were drawn in Cambridge. He didn't seem to think there were any. 'It's a good mix – people who live here understand that the colleges look after the city. It does work. It's a good turn around of people, and there's always a good buzz with all the nationalities of students who come here.'

At this point we were interrupted by a selection of sand-wiches. The leftovers from a meeting that had just finished deep within the bowels of Newey and Eyre were presented to us on a wide platter – a cheap and easy kindness of the sort that speeds your day along.

After two hours of charge, we felt the time was right to skulk off, so around the ring road of Cambridge we trundled once again, past the entrance to Clare College, and at about

2.30, we finally joined the Royston Road out of the city. Nothing much ever got going until the afternoon in our little bubble. Piloting a milk float is equal in many ways to rearing a small child in that there are dozens of tiny jobs that have to be done, little necessities that pile up into a roster of duties you have to perform before you can truly get on with the day. You accept each of these with good grace and humour and emerge into the daylight some time after lunch.

The rain came down and a certain weariness overtook. This was our fifth day on the road. The excitement of the start had long gone and, with a very long way still to go, I felt as though we were starting to build up personal boundaries. The cab of the float felt even smaller than usual. There wasn't much to look at outside to the left or right of the never-ending strip of tarmac, which was punctuated by the odd squashed animal. This part of Cambridgeshire was, how shall I put it, as dull as ditch water.

The mood continued to deepen for the next hour but, to our credit, we jointly channelled it into a deep loathing of whatever was outside the cab, which brought us to Royston. To be fair, had we driven into the Hanging Gardens of Babylon at that point we would have dismissed it as crap, bitched about its one-way system and complained that the other six wonders of the ancient world probably had better bypasses. That's how we felt in one of Royston's car parks, wrapped up in a spiteful mood that signals you are longing for a pound of carbohydrates followed by enough hot tea and cigarettes to bring about spiritual enlightenment. Just half an hour later, hypoglycaemic blues assuaged somewhat by necking chips and Twix bars, we drove through the town and Royston suddenly didn't seem that bad. In fact, it was really quite a pleasant place and had a surprising aspect you won't find in many guidebooks.

One of my interests on this trip was in discovering how the geography of an area affects the people who live there and things that happen. It's something of an amateur fixation and a strange interest to have, for which I make no apology. I've done a few pretty strange things to investigate – in a very shallow and unstructured fashion – some of the ideas that lie behind it. These include drawing straight lines on maps, visiting old monoliths, doing the occasional spot of dowsing, drinking an allegedly magical potion designed to open up the third eye and make one spiritually receptive – a potion that could best be described as cold sawdust and twig tea – and trying to sleep in a Bronze Age burial chamber. The point of all these activities was to uncover the hidden meaning of 'place'. What makes some locations seem magical or more special than others? Where that magic is a shared experience, is it written in some way into the landscape itself or into human consciousness – a universal constant, like the divine proportions of the golden mean? These questions have always intrigued me, and I wondered whether, in relation to our trip, fuelled by serendipity, there was something about the dots we were joining on the map as we made our way west that was significant in some way.

What was obvious to me, being something of a well-read yet credulous berk, was our route's close association with what is known as the St Michael ley line. This allegedly straight line runs from just south of Land's End to just north of Lowestoft and joins dozens of sites of ancient significance, including a host of churches, the monumental Avebury stone circle and the chapel at St Michael's Mount in Cornwall, from which it derives its name. A remarkable number of these churches, mostly perched at the top of a hill, are dedicated to St Michael, with a few dedicated to St George, Michael and George both being dragon-slaying saints. So even though there are a hundred and one reasons why I am not at all convinced that the ley line has any significance at all, there is enough there to keep my interest in it. From the age of fourteen until I moved to London, I've never lived very far from the line and – as I mentioned – being of a slightly credulous disposition, it has always loomed at the edge of my consciousness. Now we were weaving our way along it like the snake that wraps itself around the rod of Asclepius – the ancient Greek symbol of astrology. At various points along the journey, we had crossed the line and now in Royston, like in Bury St Edmunds, we came to rest on the rod itself.

One of the first clues to finding out about a location, discovering why it is where it is and what makes it tick, is to look at the place name itself. The name Royston, it turns out, has an interesting derivation and learning its root unlocked a treasure trove of interesting anomalies. The name is thought to come from Roisia's Town, which in turn comes from the name of an ancient stone at the centre of the modern town – Roisia's Cross. There is some evidence that links this cross, of which only a sad stump remains, to the original seventeenth-century Rosicrucians, but there are more interesting connections to be made than this. Royston was a settled and thriving community hundreds of years before the original Rosicrucian manifestos were issued from 1614 on, and tyre-levering an interesting feature of the town's geography into what may have been an elaborate early situationist prank is probably a step too far.

The stump of the cross stands at a crossroads – not an unusual state of affairs, except when you understand the precise nature of the crossroads concerned. Royston is at the junction of the A505 – the M11 to A1(M) link – and the A10, the 'Old North Road' from London. Scratch away those dull road-atlas classifications, however, and the town becomes the crossing point of Ermine Street, the old Roman road, and the Icknield Way, one of the oldest thoroughfares in Britain, the route of which we would be shadowing for the next several days.

In folklore, crossroads are meant to have mystical, even paranormal, qualities – more than just where two roads cross, they can symbolize an *axis mundi*, the intersection of different realities where the upperworld and the underworld meet. They are said to be powerful places, and if that's measured by the number of serendipitous events that happen, the junction formed by Ermine Street and the Icknield Way is a prime example. Less than fifty feet from the cross, directly under-neath the Icknield Way, lies Royston cave – a man-made, cir-cular, bell-shaped chamber, seventeen feet in diameter and twenty-six feet high, which was unearthed in the eighteenth century. Its walls are lined with medieval carvings, many of which depict symbols and icons that were used by the Knights Templar, the military-religious order that helped tear the Middle East apart during the Roman Catholic crusades – the same Knights Templar, indeed, who made Baldock, another town ten miles or so down the Icknield Way, their English headquarters and who held a weekly market in Royston. One of the carvings in the cave is of a sheela-na-gig, an early Christian grotesque figure of a woman bearing her genitals in as unpleasant a way as can be imagined with-out the benefit of the present-day internet. One of just a few dozen in England, and perhaps one of only two not found on a church in this country, I later discovered that we had already passed a sheela-na-gig in the village of Moulton and would pass two more on our way to Land's End.

In terms of boundaries, Royston has an interesting history. The extents of five parishes converge on the cross. Until the

1974 local government reorganization, the town north of the crossroads was in Cambridgeshire, while land to the south lay in Hertfordshire. The Anglo-Saxon boundaries of ancient shires proved to be highly durable, but gerrymandering and bureaucracy saw them off in the end.

It is perhaps not too far-fetched to suggest that a man-made circular cave, possibly used by the Knights Templar, under the crossroads of two ancient English trunk roads, marked by a cross that may have a connection to the Rosicrucians, distinguishes Royston as a rather special place. Indeed, there isn't another location like it between here and the Czech Republic. Psychogeographically, these features add up to a startling conclusion – that the cave, the cross and the intersection of ancient paths mark out Royston for special consideration as an omphalos, a navel of the world, like a Home Counties version of Delphi.

Before we get carried away, we are still talking about the Home Counties and, with the hand of disappointment never far from any English journey, Royston cave turned out to be closed. Unfortunately, it not being the weekend or Bank Holiday Monday, our wet Wednesday timing obliterated centuries of synchronicity and I can't actually tell you what it was like, but do stop by if you are in Royston at the right time between Easter and September.

Shortly after finding the cave closed, the sun came out. In this place of meaningful coincidences, you can't ignore a sign like that and, spirits lifted, we decided it was time to move on. Having speculated about the Icknield Way and built it up to be some kind of spiritual freeway, I was looking forward to travelling down it. After a couple of miles of dead-straight unclassified road leading towards the A505, the Royston bypass, our psychic motorway, turned into an actual motorway – or one in all but name.

Imagine, if you will, attempting to drive along a cramped two-lane dual carriageway, bumping up and down hidden hollows in the road, at anything between two and 12 miles per hour. Superimpose onto that hundreds of cars, trucks and vans blustering their way to the A1(M) at 90 miles per hour, swerving around, cutting us up and generally promoting the fear of God in us, and it will become apparent that it was far from our favourite strip of road. For about forty-five minutes we were pulled and pushed this way and that by a hurricane of storm-force slipstreams – turbulent vortices left in the wake of high-sided vehicles on their bull-headed mission to move with homicidal abandon through the English countryside. You have to wonder what has happened to one of the supposed hallmark traits of the English – our moderate and reasonable character – when you encounter recklessness on the A505 scale of things. You can't help but wonder also what Boudica, Queen of the Iceni people who gave their name to the original Icknield Way, would have made of the testosterone-fuelled petrolheads driving down her road like maniacs. Never one for messing around very much, she would probably have gone straight to the source and removed their testicles. It was more than a welcome relief when we saw the sign that told us – the non-motorway traffic – to leave the carriageway just East of Baldock.

Baldock was not only the headquarters of the Knights Templar – the Poor Fellow Soldiers of Christ and the Temple of Solomon – it was also founded by them in the twelfth century. Indeed, the name Baldock may have a Middle Eastern origin, either being Baalbec in the Lebanon or Baghdad in Iraq, depending on who you believe. However, as far as we were concerned, it was the place where we decided that it would be an absolute wheeze to attempt to get a speeding ticket in a milk float. Recently bypassed, Baldock seems to have suffered from an outbreak of GATSO cameras, their fluorescent yellow-green back panels illuminating the path through Letchworth and on to our destination at Hitchin.

The plan was to find a speed camera situated at the bottom of a long hill and to monitor the sound of the motor as it gradually increased in pitch and volume in order to get a rough idea of our actual speed. The float was fitted with a speedometer – one that looked suspiciously like the sort you would find on a bicycle – but its exact operation confounded us. We had poked this button, held in that button and thumped it a bit, but all we got was an LCD read-out that looked similar to the display you would expect on a scientific calculator that had been dropped down a well. And then run over by a speeding milk float. It was considerably less use than a chocolate fireguard and we soon learnt to ignore it as the work of the devil.

Monitoring the crescendo of the motor was, therefore, the only way of getting a rough idea of speed. A float has no clutch, so the motor always turns with the wheels, no matter what – even if you stop throttling or turn it off altogether. In a vehicle that sounds its best 'cruising' at around 10 miles per hour, the insistent rising whine involved in going at over 30 miles per hour was so alarming, it was as if the fabric of the universe was about to crack open and swallow the float whole, along with the road, any adjacent speed cameras, the verge and parts of the immediate area. It seemed that the fall-out from forcing a vintage instrument of slow travel to go at the speed of the modern world could tear time itself apart – to say it was an unpleasant racket doesn't really do it any justice at all. We found out later what would actually happen if you found a hill long and mean enough to continue accelerating into the high forties and beyond. At some point, the armatures of the motor will fly off, the whole thing will seize up and the wheels will lock in a very unsporting fashion. The exact sequence of events that follows will depend on local conditions, but if you can ignore the brain-boiling cacophony for long enough, it will be replaced by the silence that follows certain death.

Had we known any of this, we might not have been so keen on testing the limits of The Mighty One's endurance. As it was, we attacked each GATSO with what, in hindsight, turned out to be near suicidal gusto.

At last, we spotted a day-glo panel at the foot of a hill that was straight and hazard-free enough to measure the consequences of our actions. Coming off the brow of the hill, we set off with a communal whoop. As the float rolled down the hill, unfettered by brakes or any sense of responsibility, the whine started to climb the scale of speed, the stepladder of recklessness. By halfway down, the pitch had risen to a subdued scream. Without any load on the back, save for some tents, tarps, bungees and electrical bric-a-brac, the suspension reacted wildly to any slight imperfection in the road's surface. Bouncing up and down, it felt more dangerous than we'd imagined any vehicle could at a probable speed of 20 miles per hour. Laughter broke out in the cab. Pras tried manfully to film the event, but he may as well have just turned the camera on and thrown it into a spin-dryer.

For the best part of a week we'd been trundling along the road at the pace of a concussed koala pulling a lead sledge, so every extra mile per hour felt extraordinary. As we sped past the camera at what felt like 155 miles per hour, but was probably nearer to 24, we let out another cheer and braced ourselves for the flash that never came.

'It might be one of the new ones. They don't have flashes in them,' said Pras, trying not to shatter the mood of derring-do.

'Some of them don't have cameras in them at all,' I remarked tactlessly, not bothered about shattering the mood.

'Actually,' said Dan, 'we'd better not try this too often because if we succeed too many times, I'll be banned before we reach the end.'

We found one more hill, a much longer, straighter and smoother one, as we finally passed the town sign for Hitchin. Disappointingly, there was no camera at the bottom of it and we resigned ourselves to arriving at our destination without a penalty charge notice to our or, more appropriately, Dan's name. We rumbled into town via Cambridge Road and set about looking for the music shop that bore John Myatt's name.

Hitchin is a small town of roughly 30,000 souls on the River Hiz. Although the locals now pronounce this as 'His', the letter z was once a contraction of the dental sibilant 'tch' sound and so the real name is, phonetically, 'Hitch'. (This is rather like the 'y' in 'Ye Olde Worlde Pub'. Fifteenth century printers, such as Caxton, did not have the Anglo-Saxon letter 'thorn' – which looks like a lower-case b and p imposed upon one another and sounds like the 'th' in, well, 'thorn' – so they replaced it with a 'y'. 'Ye' was always meant to be pronounced 'the'.)

We were early to arrive in the town – possibly because of our reluctance to brake during our series of speed challenges – and immediately found John's shop on a street corner where two typical Victorian brick-built terraces met. By the time we parked up, our float had been on 30 per cent charge for quite a few miles – the lowest we had gone on the trip so far. We were, however, pretty relaxed about it. We reckoned we would be able to limp in one way or another and, having a pre-arranged charge with John, we were confident that we would get enough juice for the next day's mission no matter how flat the batteries had become.

The imperative of finding someone and somewhere to renew the charge having been sorted out in advance, we were at a little bit of a loose end, but we soon came upon the milk float owned by John's son Paul, which in a way had brought us all together in the first place via the Milko mailing list. Peering over a fence we saw the lovely old Electricar vehicle parked at the rear of John's shop. It featured the 'Marsden' cab design – which, for non-aficionados of such things, is what you think of when you imagine the classic suburban four-wheeler float. The front of a Marsden cab has a little ten degree incline in it, making it look like an upturned snout – a symbol of optimism that always manages, for some reason, to make me smile. Our vehicle, on the other hand – which is also an Electricar, albeit of an older design – was re-bodied with a more angular-looking cab made by M&M Electric Vehicles. Originally, it would have looked very different, with a smaller, heavily split windscreen and very rounded corners for the cab top – more in the style of a Silverstream caravan or a post-war truck than what we think of as a milk float. The consequence of all this otherwise worrying trainspotter enthusiasm is the fact that our cab had a good deal more room in it, which, when you're carrying three and occasionally four people in it, is a definite plus. There's still not quite enough, but just enough to stop us wanting to kill one another after three miles.

John came out to greet us and I finally got to meet his son. 'This is Paul. He's got two milk floats,' said John, as if it was something to be proud of. In normal conversation, ownership of any number of milk floats would be something you kept quite quiet.

He introduced us all first by name, then by sobriquet. 'Driver, film maker, idiot,' he said. I was disappointed for

Pras and Dan in that they were obviously more successful in masking their true nature from him than I was.

After the unpleasantries and some tea, we set about securing our charge. Since all of this was a done deal, we could spare the spiel. We only had to be shown the cooker in order to get the job under way.

But even if this had been the first time we'd met, things were getting easier because we had become a lot more confident and assured than we were on our first day back in Lowestoft. Five days on the road had made us far more relaxed with the journey. We had made significant progress and were now safely out of East Anglia and on an arc around the north-west of London. It really felt as if we were travelling, as opposed to holding on to the comforts of certainty. To go back to the analogy I made at the start of our journey from Cambridge about bringing up a child, there comes a time in all babies' lives when they stop crawling and begin to move around more freely. At first they cling on to whatever is to hand. Then, one magical day, they let go of the furniture and take their first unaided steps. On our journey, we were on the brink of toddling our way across England.

7

Hitchin to Princes Risborough

40 miles

DAN

For me, the day began on a camp bed in a large dusty room with no curtains. My night's sleep had been punctuated by the kind of alcoholic chaos that unleashes itself across Britain's towns and cities every single day of the week. I feared for The Mighty One parked outside. It was the first time we'd left her anywhere unsafe. No doubt the residents of Hitchin had confused her with an all-night urinal.

I looked around the room and felt the uncontrollable urge to leave immediately. The house was in the process of being renovated and it didn't feel ready for human habitation yet. I was getting a similar sensation from Hitchin itself. We were staying on the edge of the town and, from what I'd seen of the outskirts, I had no desire to venture any farther into it.

I'd managed to secure my own room for the night while Ian and Pras had opted to share the other. In a fit of paranoia I began to assume that this was because I'd developed chronic body odour so I quickly unzipped myself from my sleeping bag and staggered off in the direction of the bathroom for an early morning shower. But there was no shower and the bath seemed to have been commandeered as a paintbrush-cleaning depot. I was far too lazy to contemplate cleaning it so I decided to wash as best I could in the sink instead.

Maintaining basic levels of personal hygiene with such a small amount of water is no easy task. I decided to attempt washing my hair first so I filled the sink up with water and then leant over to put my head in as far as I could manage. It took a great deal of contortion but I got the back of my head under the water line eventually, which caused much of the water to slop out onto the floor. I looked up for my wash bag, trying hard not to drip any more water on the floor, and realized I'd left it in my room. Cursing under my breath, I groped for my towel and realized I'd left that in my room, too. Now what? Standing there dripping over the sink, it occurred to me that this was the second time in the trip I'd got up too quickly and was once again paying the consequences.

I squeezed my hair into a kind of pre-pubescent horn, opened the door slowly, ascertained that no one else was up, and dashed back to my room to collect my things. A second later I returned to find the door of the bathroom firmly locked shut. It was surely impossible for anyone to have gone in so silently and so quickly. Was there a ninja hiding in the house? I then heard what could only be described as a farting colossus on the other side of the door. It reverberated from the toilet and through the floorboards beneath my feet. I was left with no option but to head back to my dusty room, shivering and cursing my misfortune.

After gazing out the window at The Mighty One for a few minutes, while being heartened by the patches of inviting blue in the sky above, I heard the bathroom door creak open. I darted back but by the time I'd got to it, whoever had snuck in behind me had already vanished. It's a good job

I never found out who it was because I'd never be able to look them in the eye again. On the other side of the door the most gut-wrenching smell began to attack me. Excuse my lack of discretion, but someone had unleashed the kind of behemoth stool that resembled a transatlantic cable. The stench was positively medieval. Then, I swear, I heard the toilet burp.

I decided to breathe in through my mouth so I didn't have to endure the smell but then began to worry that this might cause catastrophic problems in my lungs (unlike the nasal passages, they don't have any kind of filter system). So I winced and subjected myself to the whiff of doom while resuming the attempt to wash in the sink.

Ten minutes or so later I emerged feeling nasally violated but I had at least managed to wash my hair and give myself a reasonable clean. It was fairly unsatisfying but felt like a victory of sorts. When I emerged, Ian and Pras were laughing heartily in their room amid a fug of cigarette smoke, and it dawned on me that being able to smoke, rather than my personal hygiene deficiencies, were probably the reason for their desire to co-habit whenever the chance arose. Ian stubbed out a cigarette, hopped up to go to the bathroom, only to exclaim when he got there, 'Bloody hell, Dan, it stinks in here. You could have warned me!'

Is there anything more humiliating for an English person than being associated with horrendously stinky poos? I attempted to distance myself from the blame but knew immediately it was pointless. Pras was already cackling, so I just shrugged it off in disbelief. I would no doubt be labelled 'fart-man' for the rest of the trip.

I went downstairs half an hour later to find Ian and John deep in conversation about euphoniums ('a small tuba of tenor pitch you often find in military brass bands' according to John). It was time to make myself scarce so I darted up the road to take sanctuary in my favourite guilty pleasure – a McDonald's breakfast.

Ah, the McDonald's breakfast. How unjustly maligned art thou? I'm fully aware of the many grievous crimes (allegedly) committed all over the planet by McDonald's, not to mention the fact that my life expectancy probably drops by an hour every time I eat one, but those sausage and egg McMuffins really hit the spot. I returned from the counter carrying my brown tray, McMuffin and Tropicana orange juice in place, and found an empty table with a copy of the *Sun* resting on it invitingly. What luck! Two guilty pleasures for the price of one. I felt my shoulders relax and unravelled the wrapper that was failing miserably to contain the congealed fat that was attempting to pass itself off as my breakfast.

An hour later, I returned to The Mighty One, suffering from indigestion but nevertheless feeling slightly more relaxed, to find Ian and Pras all packed up and ready to go. It would be fair to say that this was something of a novelty, even so early in the trip. The two of them seemed to have slipped into a symbiotically lackadaisical groove and I was normally relied upon to cajole us into action. It seemed they were also keen to get far away from Hitchin as soon as possible. Perhaps John had suggested a recital.

Our next stop was Dunstable, one of those nondescript towns, like Luton, Milton Keynes or, indeed, Hitchin, that seems to be entirely populated with people who never actually chose to live there in the first place – the sort of town you have to move to because of a new job, or remain in only because you lack the confidence to pack your bags and leave.

Hitchin was disappearing rapidly behind us as The Mighty One eased her way up slow inclines that were higher than anything we'd climbed so far. The steep chalk escarpments seemed to frighten her at first but she soon steadied herself and methodically hauled us up and over every one. Inside the cab, sunglasses appeared and relaxed chatter about our new daily routine began to emerge. We skirted rural communities and all agreed The Mighty One seemed more at home in the countryside than in chaotic towns and suburbs. In terms of scenery, we were beginning to discover the country of our dreams – quiet fields and hedgerows peppered with red telephone boxes, occasional sheep, cows and ramshackle pubs with the words 'Ye' and 'Olde' in their names. This was as middle of the road as Middle England got. Ian seemed to read my mind when he suddenly piped up with, 'If this carries on much longer, I'll be a card carrying *Daily Mail* reader by the time we finish,' but the collective relaxed sigh was undeniable as we gently meandered our way along.

Huge clouds the colour of dishcloths that have been left on the sink too long loomed overhead as we whined over the roads, but the stiff breeze chivvied them along, leaving pure blue sky to fend off the next cluster rolling in behind. Now and then our slow meandering pace gained momentum down winding hills lined with broad hedgerows. All three of us would break into childish laughter every time the pitch of The Mighty One's engine hit a top 'E' as we bounded and bombed down steep slopes only to judder to a virtual stop when we had to drag our way back up the other side.

This stretch of the journey gave us the first wild meadow filled with poppies that we'd seen since setting off, and the first of many single ornamental white gates that seemed to serve no purpose whatsoever. It was as though a large mockrural housing estate had been planned but only the tacky white gate and pots of pansies at the entrance had so far been granted planning permission. For a while, I was convinced that the meadow and the gate were portents of great or unexpected things, temporarily forgetting we were on our way to Dunstable. My dreams were duly shattered when we hit the outskirts of town.

The only other time I'd come across Dunstable was because it was home to a branch of a chain of shops I'd once worked for. The owner of the group of shops was two and a half feet tall and seemed convinced he was running a chain of cotton mills circa 1865. He and his business partner, who, allegedly, enjoyed masturbating furiously into carrier bags on his lunch hour, used to make the staff listen to 'The Glory of Gershwin' all day every day. If you were very lucky, you might get to listen to the Lighthouse Family after lunch.

Thankfully, we hadn't had to venture too far into the town before Ian had spotted a small forklift truck in an industrial unit next to a branch of Netto. A few minutes later, we'd met Graeme, a grinning Geordie in an oily blue boiler suit, who seemed convinced he would be able to help.

'Should be fine, mate. I'll 'ave to check with the boss, though. Hang on a minute.' He disappeared inside the office, reappearing a moment later with a slightly nervous-looking man wearing a suit, who relaxed sufficiently to agree to our strange request before leaving us in Graeme's capable hands. On the other side of the building, on the back wall, we found a socket. They'd stopped using it because they'd just bought a new forklift that ran on gas.

'If you'd come last week, we'd have plugged you into that,' said Graeme. 'We've put a normal socket on the wall now . . . but it should be OK.'

Unfortunately, it wasn't OK but Pras managed to do something highly illegal, which I'm not even allowed to write about because he's worried he might get retrospectively arrested. Suffice to say the cold plug became a warm plug and then a very, very hot plug. However, a few hours later we were charged up and ready to go.

In the meantime, I'd shuffled off to Netto to see what culinary delights I could find as lunchtime approached. I emerged twenty minutes later with six cheesy baps, half a kilo of ham, an industrial-sized sack of Mini Cheddars, two tins of luxury Amaretto Soffici biscuits and a very reasonably priced bottle of Sancerre, which tells you everything you need to know about the eclectic and frankly baffling nature of every branch of Netto. The shopping itself had taken me about five minutes to collect. I'd spent the other fifteen rooted in the crisps and snacks aisle, watching a small toddler gradually explode.

At first his mother wouldn't let him have any crisps, but, after he'd blown his first fuse for an impressive five minutes non-stop, she'd relented. Then she wouldn't allow him to choose the brand of said crisps, so he kicked off with gusto for another solid five minutes. She eventually relented again, letting him choose Monster Munch (which appeared to be being sold in extra value bags of 150), but then she wouldn't let him have a bag before they'd got back into the car. By this stage, I think she'd realized that everyone in the shop was watching her progress and her resolve suddenly seemed to steel. As I walked over to Ian and Pras, the tantrum had spilled from the checkout into the car park and the child methodically threw everything he could reach from the trolley down on to the tarmac. Shattered jars of American hotdogs in brine began rolling towards a drain while she stuffed the manic boy in the back of the car before driving away erratically. His feet were sticking out the window as they turned onto the dual carriageway – all of which was yet another perfect illustration of the eclectic and frankly baffling nature of every branch of Netto.

After our, frankly absurd, packed lunch, we pulled out of Dunstable in the early afternoon drizzle, aiming to cover the twenty-five miles that would take us on to Princes Risborough. Happily, the sun soon emerged.

Since leaving Lowestoft the counties had been ticking past and we were now striking out in the direction of Oxfordshire, edging closer and closer to Ewelme, the burial place of Jerome K. Jerome. All of us were aware that making it that far would be a huge psychological victory. Looking back, something definitely changed in my outlook that afternoon. I have to admit that the first section of the journey, Lowestoft to the borders of Oxfordshire, was not the stretch I'd been most looking forward to travelling through. That part of England is filed in my brain in the 'unimaginative and dull geography' section. No doubt this is doing it a huge disservice, and in retrospect it was probably the relentlessly awful nature of the weather in that first week that made it feel so grim, but once Princes Risborough beckoned, my spirits seemed to soar. We began to make joyful, but always meandering, progress through the countryside. As the temperature rose we were able to drive along with the doors open to get the proper milkman effect, which thrilled us all enormously. The Mighty One seemed to sense the change, making light of minor hills rather than wheezing up them, and generally rushing defiantly through the countryside (relatively speaking, of course).

This rather pleasing turn of events ended abruptly when we finally arrived in Princes Risborough. With just 25 per cent of the charge left, and rush hour rapidly approaching, we freewheeled down towards the high street with no idea of what to do next. We'd managed decent mileage that day but, since Dunstable, hadn't spotted any of the out-of-town shop-ping malls or industrial units we were beginning to rely on.

We tried a small branch of Tesco first but they didn't have the required amperage, so we ended up parking on a garage forecourt and sussing out our options on foot. It was at this point that I began to hallucinate. Well, I thought I had to be hallucinating at the time because up in the sky I could see *five* red kites. Yes, you read that right. Five. Red kites are one of the rarest birds you can find in Britain and there were five of them flying above our heads. Red kites are not the kind of bird you can be mistaken about. In the sky they are as unmistakable as a golden eagle. You know when you're look-ing at a golden eagle because it looks the size of a wardrobe and you can't believe something of that size could possibly fly. Red kites have equally distinctive bent wings and a tail in the shape of a 'V'. I suppose you could mistake one for a black kite, but if you think you've seen a black kite in Britain, you are almost certainly hallucinating, because you just don't get them here. Well not that I know of. Red kites are also red, which makes them easy to recognize.

If I seem slightly manic it's because a year earlier I'd spent a miserable wet weekend in Wales with a pair of binoculars failing to spot a single solitary red kite and here were five of them soaring over the town centre in Princes Risborough. It was a wonderful moment in the trip and an even better one if you have the slightest interest in British birds of prey. These raptors sit at the top of the food chain. Their very existence requires a healthy ecosystem to be in place. It would be fair to say that I am very enthusiastic when it comes to hawks and falcons. Most men lust after cars and gadgets and want to be racing drivers when they grow up. I lust after goshawks and my ambition is to be a falconer so I can stroll around forests with a huge great eagle on my fist.

Come to think of it, that would sort out all the ASBO kids and gangs of pissed-up teenagers who are out and about in the evenings in places such as Hitchin, and who enjoy urinating on the wheels of milk floats every night. Getting falconers like me to stroll around with eagles on our arms would get their attention pretty quickly. You'd have a whole new generation of Bill Oddies within half an hour. Birds of prey are nature's very own celebrities. Forget youth clubs – what you really need are falconry centres packed with eagles, hawks and other raptors, with falconers giving lessons on how to catch rats, in the middle of our most notorious problem estates.

In case you're thinking that falconry is just for poshos and I must therefore be one of those people who delights in shooting the crap out of pheasants with a 12-bore shotgun, here are two fascinating facts you probably didn't know about falconry.

One, it's not for rich people. Well, it never used to be, even if it appears that way today. Hawking – hunting with a falcon to catch rabbits or small deer for your dinner – was very popular among ordinary folk in the days before all the common land was enclosed between 1750 and 1860. After that, only rich people could afford the land needed to go hawking, which is why it's thought of as a sport reserved for the aristocracy. These days you have to be time-rich rather than cash-rich to have a falcon. So if you want to be a falconer, you'll have to go freelance and quit your job immediately.

Two, it's not like having a flying pet. Hawks flown by falconers remain utterly wild and stay with the falconer because he/she is a more efficient food source for the hawk than being out in the wild. The relationship between a falconer and a Harris hawk can last for up to thirty years; with

a golden eagle, it can last for up to eighty. This is why falconry is so inspiring. It's like being able to bridge the gulf
between human and wild life at will, giving you a totally new
relationship with the natural world.

Despite the red kites, Princes Risborough proved to be
pleasing to the eye but rather repellent to the soul. We tried
a couple of Indian restaurants because Pras was convinced
that asking for help in Urdu might get results, but they didn't
like the idea of unplugging one of their ovens so we could
wire in our float for three hours at their busiest time of
day, which was fair enough, I suppose. The only option left
appeared to be an all-you-can-eat Chinese called Top Wok.
Pras and I went in cautiously while Ian fumbled about with
the map and his mobile phone. We seemed to have sleep-
walked into potential catastrophe. Even if we got a charge we
had nowhere to spend the night and the nearest campsite was
ten miles away, a distance we'd be hard pressed to cover even
if it wasn't rapidly getting dark.

Happily for us, Shane, the owner of Top Wok, was
friendly and, as he listened, the familiar look of enthusiasm
appeared in his eyes. He very generously offered to let us
unplug his walk-in freezer for an hour and a half so we could
give our batteries a lift, just as long as we ate in his restaurant
first. We settled for a takeaway, eating it in The Mighty One
round the back while various confused chefs and kitchen
hands looked on.

The Mighty One was drinking greedily but our sleeping
arrangements were still looking rather desperate. If we
charged for ninety minutes, which would give us around 40
per cent on the battery charge, it would be ten o'clock
before we unplugged – not enough charge or time to make
it to Dorchester-on-Thames, our nearest bed for the night.
There was nothing for it but to find somewhere to sleep in

Princes Risborough. Funds were tight so a bed and break-fast was out of the question. Wild camping seemed to be our only hope, until my mum happened to ring to see how we were getting on.

'You're struck in Princes Risborough? Well, you should ring my friends Kath and Mac. They live just down the road. They'll probably know of a campsite nearby, and you never know, they might even let you pitch your tent in their back garden.'

They did better than that. An hour later we were all sipping cups of tea and munching our way through plates and plates of biscuits after they'd offered to put us up in comfy beds for the night. We didn't want to push things by asking for a charge but we needn't have worried – Kath already had a plan, which she mentioned casually while pouring the tea from an enormous teapot.

'Did you know the Hypnos bed factory's down the road? They make the Queen's beds. In the morning, I think you should go and try to charge up there.'

Three 'idle' men travelling across Britain in a milk float charging up at the Queen's bed factory? That sounded about right.

8

Princes Risborough to Wantage

39 miles

IAN

Arriving in Princes Risborough last night, everything seemed wrong. Tired, with our battery depleted, we turned up in a town operating on a kind of reverse serendipity principle. Had our natural gift for making useful discoveries, guided by the hand of some unseen force that looked kindly on our mad mission, been worn out through overuse? Princes Risborough, despite being in a perfectly enchanting area of the Chilterns an easy afternoon's drive from London, had nothing in the way of accommodation to offer us. There were no campsites within ten miles, most of the shops were shut and there was little in the way of a prospect for a charge. On top of all that, I had reached rock bottom in terms of blood sugar and I could feel my brow furrowing like gravy skin on its way to a leathery solid. I have to admit that the novelty of our quest was beginning to wear off and, to cap it all, as we pulled up in the centre of town, I received a call from one of the Milko milk-float group offering us a free charge and a bed for the night – in Tring, ten miles or so back where we had just come from. Here I was, brassed off in Middle England, in a town that appeared next to hopeless for our needs, having steered us around a town that had it all. Even the magnificent red kites wheeling over the town transmuted into circling vultures, capable of picking over the remains of all hope.

In my miserable stupor, I left the other two and wandered down the street in search of nothing in particular. When I returned, with my face consciously adjusted into an open-minded, blank-eyed smile – something that is, I believe, known as a shit-eating grin – I found Prasanth and Dan chatting cheerfully with the wonderful Shane at Top Wok and a place to sleep all arranged with friends of Dan's mum. My first effort at a negative mood was now a happy failure.

Dan was obviously feeling the strain himself. To be fair, bringing your mates along to stay with friends of your family is always something of a daunting prospect. In order to bridge the gap between relaxed conversation and respectability in the eyes of your family, you have to walk a tight-rope of etiquette and manners. There was always a danger, having crossed the divide between informality and not wishing to show up Dan as the farting oik we revered, that we would let the side down by forgetting how to use a soup spoon or simply unleashing a trail of expletives and corporeal gases into the sitting room while criticizing their digestive biscuits and taste in soft furnishings. All of this would leave Dan's nice intermediate class credentials blowing, as it were, in the wind – or so Dan apparently thought because he took it upon himself to remind us that Kath and Mac were friends of his mum and, by extension, we weren't to embarrass him. 'They're into cycling and healthy lifestyles,' he said, glancing at my cigarette. I didn't think this really needed saying, but took it as a sign of how stressed Dan was by the situation. I'm glad, however, that my ineptitude with a soup spoon is still a closely guarded secret.

Dan needn't have worried because it all went terribly well. Kath and Mac were the embodiment of loveliness and unconditional hospitality. Retiring to our shared quarters, Prasanth and I proceeded to channel our vagabond ways by using every available power socket to charge our cameras, phones and laptops.

The next morning, tea and a selection of preserves on toast were stylishly dispensed through a serving hatch into the dining room. I've always been deeply impressed with the idea of a serving hatch – it is a quintessentially English concept, demonstrating a certain order to the operation of meal times. Where our Continental friends would simply rip the door off between the steel-plated kitchen and the veneered dining areas in the name of efficient cuisine, the English knock a hole in the wall and fit a pair of tiny little doors into it – doors that are to be kept closed except at mealtimes. It also confirms my belief that the true mark of an English person is someone who wants to open either a bed and breakfast establishment or a village Post Office. Even though I count myself as a rather modern person, I too feel the call and have always secretly longed for a serving hatch of my own, albeit a remote-controlled one with silver sliding doors, behind which, at my command, an aluminium robot busies itself preparing meals and drinks. This *is* the future, after all.

Our free bed and breakfast over, it was time to say our thank-yous and leave. It wasn't very far to our next bed – it was, in fact, just a few hundred yards to a whole factory full of them.

Hypnos make beds. Thousands upon thousands of them leave their factory every year bound for furnishing stores up and down the country and abroad. Royal patronage is very impressive if you like that sort of thing, and does at least confirm the level of luxury available to you if you are able and willing to part with enough funds to obtain it. It's obviously also a mark of quality in these days of flat-pack furniture assembled with the aid of an Allen key and two or three hours of arguments with your partner over the exact meaning of a booklet of unspecific diagrams – you really can't imagine any self-respecting Highness or Majesty lowering themselves in this way. Whether or not you have blue blood, if you are going to have any luxury or quality in your life, it strikes me that a bed is a perfect place to start, and Dan and Prasanth would probably agree, given the fact that they are both so well acquainted with, and such fine exponents of, the sleeping arts.

Under a fluttering Union Jack, the factory's magnificent white and blue art deco frontage looked spectacular against the blue sky as we pulled up. We attracted attention almost immediately. Office staff leaned from the steel-framed windows above the showroom and it wasn't long before we saw the boss, Peter Keen. Normally, seeing the boss so quickly isn't necessarily a good omen. A short speech, the gist of which is 'Get off my land' often follows, but there was none of this with Peter.

'When you guys turned up on a milk float outside the factory,' he told us, 'my receptionist asked me what we should do with you, and I have to say, I looked out of my window and I told her that I wished I was with you. If I didn't have to go to Scotland for a wedding today, I'd get on a forklift truck and follow you, because I think what you're doing is absolutely amazing.'

Peter, who is the chairman and owner of Hypnos – like four generations of Keens before him – gave us a mattress for the back of the float and arranged for his graphics department to make up some signs for the front and sides to explain our mission succinctly. While The Mighty One underwent her graphic makeover, the addition of home comforts and a two-hour top-up charge courtesy of Hypnos technician Richard, we were treated to a tour of the factory with Stan.

Given that we would have just hung around smoking cigarettes, talking bollocks and interviewing one another like the media whores we are, a one-and-a-half-hour factory tour was something of a distraction, as well as a first for all of us. Stan, our guide and a seasoned pro in the world of bed manufacture, did as well as you can with the material, taking us through the whole process and leaving no stone unturned. We certainly left with the right impression – that the beds were made to a high standard by skilled workers – but the tour reminded me of nothing so much as an extended 'through the round window' section on a children's television programme. When I was a child, people actually made things in Britain – according to *Play School*. The film-clip mini documentaries of men in boiler suits were as much a part of the programme as Big and Little Ted, Brian Cant and those slightly disturbing rag dolls.

The whole factory had a certain charm because it was dealing with an old-fashioned process, concerned as it was with upholstery, carpentry and their attendant sensory impressions – the smell of cut wood, the acoustics smothered by cloth and foam. Entering an environment dedicated to manufacture was a nostalgic phenomenon.

Stan led us through various parts of the factory, each with its own distinct form of cacophony, linked only by the wallpaper of Radio 2, its dedications, news and travel flashes punctuated by a carefully selected playlist of easily forgettable music. On the shop floor, nail guns, industrial sewing machines and exotic species of power tools presumably unknown outside of the context of a bed factory, formed a barrage of noise, and we had to listen very hard to catch Stan's commentary. At the end of the tour, we were offered coffee in the Hypnos showroom, a placid retreat from the hubbub of industry. The beds were exceptionally comfortable and it appeared as though we had reached the idlers' spiritual home. Jerome would have been proud.

Jerome Klapka Jerome, author of *Three Men in a Boat*, *The Idle Thoughts of an Idle Fellow* and many others in the same vein, Freeman of the Borough of Walsall, a distinguished editor of *The Idler*, friend of Rudyard Kipling, Thomas Hardy and J. M. Barrie and all-round inspiration for *Three Men in a Float* rests in peace in the churchyard of Ewelme, which was the next stop on our journey.

Ewelme is an astonishing setting. Nestled in the folds of Oxfordshire's hills like a jewel secreted into a crumpled handkerchief, the village is the perfect embodiment of the rural idyll. Wobbly looking brick-built cottages tuck themselves into the hillside, lending the scene the warmth of their rust-red walls, while at the top of the village lies the church, massive and indomitable in a roughly round yard, looking as though it had run aground during some biblical flood. Built from knapped flint and stone and capped with an unusual crown of brick battlements, its most striking features are its wide gable ends, which are constructed in a deliberately decorative checkerboard pattern.

To a backdrop of cawing rooks and the tiny explosions of song from chiffchaffs, great tits, robins, dunnocks and wrens, we opened the gate and went into the churchyard in search of Jerome's final resting place. He has been hiding here since 1927, resting somewhere in idle peace among the buttercups and daisies. For some reason, we set off towards the almshouses, arranged around a little courtyard behind the church.

'God's house in Ewelme,' read the sign. 'You are welcome to visit the Cloisters, but please respect the privacy of the residents.'

'How on earth do you get to live in a place like this?' asked Dan, rhetorically.

He was right to wonder. The cloisters were arranged around a tiny courtyard under the broad church tower. Timbered arches carried an arcade canopy around an intimate quadrangle, thick with summer scents, where even the busiest minds would be forced to stall into contemplation. In the centre of the yard, a rusting Victorian implement of some kind that featured cogs and wheels – perhaps an old water pump – was the crowning glory of a tableau that could easily have been a shrine to retirement. Bestilled machinery, geraniums and pelargoniums growing with reckless ease, buttercups, bird song and a peaceful country graveyard to die for – Ewelme was turning into an epic homage to rustic England. It was the absolute genuine article.

We ambled aimlessly, stopped in our tracks by the place. It was one of the few times we explored somewhere so thoroughly simply out of idle curiosity and it was fitting that we came to this moment while seeking Jerome's grave. We almost forgot why we were there. At the end of a pathway, as with all such pathways in Britain, we found a skip and a white van, and, jolted back to the modern world, turned back to find something more restful. Dan suggested that Jerome was buried at the centre of the cloisters courtyard, which would place him under the water pump. Although apparently quite a callous thought, given his love of the Thames, it would not have been so inappropriate but his *Idler* credentials would surely be at odds with being laid to rest under machinery – which only goes to show that you shouldn't go around stamping your own motives and beliefs onto others because, after another short search, we found Jerome's grave out in the churchyard, with an epitaph that would make the nose of any idler wrinkle in irritation. The full inscription read:

In Loving Remembrance of Jerome Klapka Jerome
Died June 14 1927 aged 68 Years
'For we are Labourers, together with God'
Corinthians III, 9

'I wonder whether that epitaph was chosen by some well-meaning relative to make up for all his years of sloth,' said Dan – who, I think, was a little disappointed and unable to associate the quote with the man. 'It's not quite what I was expecting to read on Jerome's gravestone, that's for sure.'

'Well, maybe it's satire,' I suggested, choosing to follow this comforting observation with a misquote of Jesus Christ: 'By His works, ye shall know Him.' The real truth of the matter was that Jerome was a deeply spiritual man, albeit a terribly intelligent and witty one. He appears to have had that rare gift among the devout of not taking it so seriously that he cheated on God's ultimate purpose for us – to be happy.

Our respects paid and feeling uplifted by our exploration, we clambered back into the float to strike out towards what will inevitably be known sooner or later as 'Jerome Country' or 'Three Men in a Boat Land'. The valley of the River Thames beckoned and beyond that, the home of a friend of Dan's – a man I was very much looking forward to meeting, comedy genius John Lloyd. First, we needed to top up our batteries and, luckily, I knew someone who worked in a power station.

That might be a little misleading. We weren't planning on

uncoiling 'the snake' – our pet name for the 25-metre armoured charging cable that had a mind of its own – and plugging it into a huge, fuck-off socket at the base of a cooling tower at Didcot Power Station, even though I'm sure that Pras could make that happen somehow. Instead, we were heading for the home of Clive Burke, a Milko member, owner of a Smith's float and all-round boffin.

Clive lives in Dorchester, not the one in Dorset, but the one on the banks of the Thames, and a very agreeable spot it looked on the map too, in that way that lots of oxbow lakes and abandoned river meanders pep up an area devoid of contour on the Ordnance Survey map. I could practically taste the still water represented by the dusting of light blue fills, and was drawn to the cartographic depiction of fluid as surely as if I was a fish on a gravel path. Maybe it's just me who gets excited by a 30 per cent cyan tint and the word 'weir', but there is something English about the aesthetic appreciation of water features. You only have to look at landscape paintings created in the eighteenth century chocolate box period of art to see a meandering river gliding its way to the horizon, a babbling brook adding energy to a composition, or a placid lake that offers a moment to reflect.

After a short drive down off the Chilterns, past the monumentally noisy base at RAF Benson, we arrived in Dorchester-on-Thames. Over the long bridge that crosses the River Thame – the confusingly named tributary of the Thames, which is, officially in any case, known as the Isis upstream of here – the landscape of ebb and flow more than satisfied my cartographic expectations. Of course, it's OK when you just have to look at the water – it's quite a different matter to navigate it. It was on this stretch that Jerome made his observation about manners and bad language on the river. There was something about piloting a boat that brought out rage. 'When another boat gets in my way,' he wrote, 'I feel I want to take an oar and kill all the people in it.'

We didn't know the number of Clive's house, but after a couple of trips up and down the road, someone eventually noticed our toing and froing and Clive's son James came out to wave us in. Clive was excited to see us and, preliminary introductions over and hot-drink preferences noted, we were whisked around the garden and garage for a tour of what's best described as Clive's fascinating 'stuff'.

First up was the mowbot – an ingenious robot that guides itself around the garden as it cuts the grass. It lives in its own little kennel, where it recharges itself when not at work, and feels its way around with the aid of a trip line along the boundary of the lawn. That done, next up was an impressive array of solar panelling, both the kind that heats water directly and the sort that generates a current. These panels, along with the wind turbine mounted on his chimney, gave the impression that Clive is in the business of seriously reducing his reliance on the National Grid. Given that he works at Didcot Power Station, he is either being deeply ironic or he knows something that we don't.

It turned out to be the latter. Clive has developed an enlightened interest in the subject of 'peak oil'. If you haven't heard about it yet, you will very soon. Peak oil is the handy way to refer to the incontrovertible assertion that, at some point, the production of oil will begin to decline. The fortunes of the developed and developing world are closely intertwined with energy use. A steep decline in production allied with the current growth in use – developing Asian economies, such as China and India, continue to fuel their 'economic miracles' with millions of barrels of oil – could easily lead to a global depression the like of which we have never seen. For peak oilers such as Clive, it's now a question of how we manage the decline to prevent or mitigate the catastrophic consequences. As with all environmental issues, it's clear that something has to change and anyone who says otherwise is burying their head in the sand, merely putting off the inevitable. So inevitable, in fact, that it has already happened. According to the US Energy Information Agency, Energy Watch, oil barons and companies worldwide, global oil production started to drop at the tail end of 2006. It's impossible to say when this drop will start to accelerate until after the event, but even the most optimistic predictions say that by 2020 the downward slide will have begun to gather pace. We can't afford to wait twelve years to develop 2020 hindsight.

A couple of hours later, we followed Clive and James in their Smith's float to the Barley Mow pub at Clifton Hampden – the 'once upon a timeyfied' pub Jerome recommended so thoroughly, except for the drunken or tall. After the second charge of the day, time was running short and we wanted to get on, so we resisted the low beams and the unpredictable steps up and down duly noted by JKJ, bid Clive and James goodbye in the car park and set off west towards Wantage and John Lloyd's house.

Didcot Power Station dominates the landscape, its six cooling towers belching monstrous vapour clouds into the sky and making the view into an industrial panorama. In 2003, it was voted the third worst eyesore in the UK by readers of *Country Life*, who are obviously not a representative sample, but I'm with the Range Rover, gumboots and retriever crowd on this one. The power station is a massive installation and the fact that we accept it as normal indicates the level of human interference with the natural world. The very requirement for such an enormous plant is depressing, but to see it in the flesh fuels a sobering realization that something about the way our country is organized is terribly, dreadfully wrong. With fossil fuels of all kinds causing such devastation to the environment, surely time is up for non-renewable energy?

The roads around Didcot remind me of roads in Fenland, which tend to go straight for a mile, then suddenly confront you with a right-angled bend, then go straight for another half mile before another sharp bend takes you back in your original direction. The landscape is so flat that you have a distinct sense of never getting anywhere. In a car, that's bad enough, but at 15 miles per hour or less, it seems interminable. To make matters worse, what you are navigating around is the boundary fence of that blasted ugly power station. At least our route steered clear of Abingdon, which, according to Jerome, 'is a typical country town of the smaller order – quiet, eminently respectable, clean, and desperately dull'.

We eventually arrived at John Lloyd's, following his emailed directions. Though the directions were precise, the email itself was something of a circuitous affair, taking time to pour scorn on the maintenance department of Corpus Christi College, Oxford and ending with the words 'Stop. Knock on door. Ask for whisky and dainties.'

I hope he won't mind me describing him as a comedy writing genius, but his career leaves me no other option. His work constitutes a ribbon of almost continual excellence through the past thirty years of British radio and television. It has an endurance uncommon to the art of comedy, which tends to date very quickly because it is often based on contemporary social mores and events. On radio, his panel games *The News Quiz* and *Quote . . . Unquote* were first broadcast in the late 1970s and are both still airing, while on television he is responsible for bringing *Not the Nine O'Clock*

News and *Spitting Image* to the screen, as well as producing all four series of *Blackadder*. He also had a formative hand in his long-time friend Douglas Adams's *Hitch Hikers' Guide to the Galaxy* radio and television series, and collaborated with him on two books, *The Meaning of Liff* and its updated cousin, *The Deeper Meaning of Liff*.

Liff, like all the best ideas, is very simple. Imagine a dictionary of place names – all those useless words that do nothing but hang around on the pages of atlases – and ascribe them to more or less universal experiences or familiar things for which there has hitherto been no name. Thus Shoeburyness in Essex gets a new lease of life as 'The vague uncomfortable feeling you get when sitting on a seat which is still warm from somebody else's bottom' and Liff itself is transformed from a village in Tayside, famous only for its psychiatric hospital, to 'a book, the contents of which are totally belied by its cover. For instance, any book the dust jacket of which bears the words, "This book will change your life".' *The Meaning of Liff* has a sticker on it, promising the reader that 'This book will change your life'.

'Of all the things I've done,' John told Paul Hamilton in an interview for *The Idler* magazine in 2003, 'I think I'm most proud of that.'

When we arrived, no signs of whisky or dainties were evident, not that I'd know a dainty if it slapped me in the face, and no sign of John, either. It transpired he was recording an episode of *QI*, the cerebral panel game – his most recent creation – in London. However, John's wife Sarah and PA Liz were there to greet us.

Sooner than we knew it we were in the back garden drinking beer and parrying quips with Liz and Sarah, two of those rare people who are incredibly intelligent and funny but in a completely unintimidating way.

So, on the seventh day we eventually rested. Liz cooked a superb meal, which we consumed with some gusto since we hadn't tasted home-cooked food for some time. Afterwards, we adjourned to John's study for a family game of Balderdash. Dan immediately started to browse the bookshelves, which were filled with yards of books on every subject imaginable. After he had wandered around for some time, he declared, 'This is like being in John's brain.'

John's real brain, meanwhile, was on its way, with the rest of John, from London. Sometime just before midnight, he arrived, looking tired. It's every man's right to look tired in his own study and I suddenly felt rather guilty about being sat there, a virtual stranger, in his brain, at which point he produced a bottle of Glenfiddich — an open invitation to everyone to leave theirs on the table in the hall. We drank and talked deep into the night. It was almost light when we eventually went to bed, without any dainties.

9
Wantage to Pewsey

38 miles

DAN

Five hours sleep after drinking the best part of a quarter of a bottle of Glenfiddich on top of a few beers and a couple of bottles of wine may not sound like the best way to prepare for the day ahead, but if my body ached, my spirits were flying. Either that or I was still pissed. At any rate I decided to get up, even though I could have lain in bed for another five hours if I'd wanted to. I think I must have still been drunk, or perhaps it was because before I'd gone to bed I'd taken pre-emptive Ibuprofen, but whatever it was, when I got up I felt like I'd left my body dozing contentedly under the sheets.

On the table by the bed lay a copy of *Gulliver's Travels* that I hadn't noticed the night before. I read the first chapter and grinned to myself wondering whether coincidence or John had left it there. Looking out of the bedroom window was like discovering yourself in a perfect world. John and Sarah's house is huge and luxurious and every inch the family home, but that wasn't what was carrying me away that morning. No one else was up, or they'd long since woken and gone out for the day, so I took the opportunity, being careful not to wake anyone, to amble out into the enormous sun–drenched garden.

There are times in a trip such as the one we were undertaking when the symbolism and sheer luxury of it begin to make you feel that you have disconnected totally from the normal world. I don't mind admitting that at times it was quite an emotional experience. The modern reality of news, politics, commuter trains, childcare, the Inland Revenue, terrorism and bird flu – all of the things we wrestle to keep on top of on a daily basis – meant very little here.

I reconnected with this world momentarily by ringing Rachel. She had taken Wilf to see his cousins for a few days. They were the one part of reality that I found no joy in being parted from, but they were both well and having fun in my absence. I rung off and began to let my mind drift back from the south coast where they were staying, gradually making my way to John's slowly warming garden.

I sat on a bench, watching bees hover above the wild long grass that grew on the edges of the luscious green lawn. Up in the sky, a few dark specks that could well have been buzzards caught my attention as blackbirds drifted by. I was certainly miles away in more ways than one that morning. But there's something about such a detached perspective that can give you more insight into the very real conundrums you pose yourself when you find you're all alone.

John is one of my three wise men, one of the people I turn to when life becomes too baffling and confusing to comprehend. In the last few years he, along with my two other wise men, has got me out of many difficult practical and metaphysical scrapes by being generous enough to share with me his conversation. It was reassuring to see that what lay behind all his wealth, success, happiness and critical acclaim was a very warm, and very funny, loving family. When we'd arrived, I'd taken the chance to corner Sarah to mention Prasanth's rather unusual fear of fish – he can't even watch *Finding Nemo* without having a panic attack. She replied, 'Well, we did have a few fish actually but they died a few days ago. Just in time apparently . . . '

While drinking the bottle of whisky with John the night before, the subjects of our discussion ranged from quantum mechanics and neo-Platonists to power, greed, love and war. I think we all saw it as a night off, so we let our hair down accordingly. Consequently, none of us took any notes and we completely forgot to interview John, so I'm afraid I can't share any of his quite interesting insights.

I flicked up Rachel's number on my mobile phone with an urge to call her again while my mind skirted around the irony that being separated from my little family, the most important thing in my life, was making me realize the all-encompassing hold it held over me.

I remembered talking to John on the phone a few years before, when my life was facing a kind of legal and personal meltdown, and he mentioned a scientist he'd just been reading about who'd searched the great library of history for the answer to the ultimate question – what is the purpose of life? This man had spent decades immersing himself in all humanity's greatest and most celebrated minds. He'd gone on to interview countless scientists, philosophers, psychotherapists, teachers, children even – anyone he could think of who might help in his quest to discover the answer to (you'll forgive me) 'life, the universe and everything'. John explained that after all his deliberation and research, the scientist settled on five words – 'to love and be loved'.

In his garden on that bright and sunny morning those words sidled up to me again, brushing my cheeks with a grateful glow, before dabbing a little water in my eyes.

Over the kitchen table a few hours later, while drinking gallons of tea and scoffing pastries and toast, John assured us that we were under no pressure to leave but he and his son Harry would soon have to set off for a golf lesson. A few minutes later, Pras had negotiated the many different fuse boxes that were positioned all over the house, and the charger on The Mighty One was humming nicely. I went to sit on the back in the sun to keep an eye on things but soon ended up falling fast asleep on our brand new Hypnos mattress.

Having paid our respects to the grave of our inspiration and one of the pubs featured in *Three Men in a Boat* the day before, I had a feeling that from now on the journey was no longer a homage or a joke but something that we were beginning to own ourselves. Expectation had been exceeded, our rather inept beginnings had been survived and I was convinced that more surprises and excitement lay ahead.

An hour or so later, John and Harry re-appeared on the gravel driveway. After a short stroll through the countryside with them and one of John's daughters, Coco, it was time for us to be on our way. With a bit of luck we hoped to get as far as Pewsey in north Wiltshire around teatime. I'd spoken to the second of my 'wise men', the writer and angler Chris Yates, because we were heading for his house the next day, and he'd reminded me that his friend and our fellow Southampton FC fan John Berry used to live in Pewsey and would be worth ringing for some advice about where to go for help. I rang John Berry soon afterwards and it seemed the gods of chance were with us yet again. It turned out that he'd moved to Swindon the year before but when I asked if he had any ideas of where we could get a charge, he began laughing.

'Well, there's a pub called the Cooper's Arms in Pewsey that I think might help you out. The landlady has one night off a year and, as luck would have it, that night is tonight. The man covering her shift will probably let you charge up from the kitchen and camp out the back if you ask him nicely.' I asked for his name and number so I could make the call and I heard laughter coming down the line once again. 'Well, you already did. It's me, and yes you can. What time do you think you'll get here? I'm behind the bar right now.'

Such coincidences were no longer a surprise and I informed Pras and Ian that, as long as we could make it to Pewsey, our place for the night was sorted. John Lloyd seemed to think Pewsey was an optimistic destination. 'That's got to be forty miles from here, but you should be able to make it to Marlborough,' he said. So we decided to head for Marlborough first, in the hope of getting an hour's charge, before heading on to Pewsey.

Before leaving, we had to have a photograph taken in front of The Mighty One, and Harry wisely decided that the best place to sit for it was up on the roof. After a few attempts, Pras was happy with the result. We hugged John and Sarah, thanking them for their generous hospitality, and promised to let them know if and when we made it to the end.

The road to Marlborough took us up and over many daunting hills. On one occasion, Pras and Ian decided to get out to reduce the weight as The Mighty One's progress was reduced to a literal snail's pace. The terrain was becoming more intimidating but had a relaxed beauty draped over it too. The spring colours brought verdant smiles to our faces and the temperature began to suit T-shirts and shorts for the first time since setting off. Sadly for us our meandering pleasure was rather sullied by a pit stop in Hungerford for ice-creams where we began to attract verbal abuse from heavily tatooed motorists and their passengers. 'What the fuck do you look like!' 'Wankers!' and 'Piss off you cunts!' was shouted at us while we sat bemused, having parked up in the centre of town to eat mint Cornettos. We'd been abused on the roads a few times by this point but nowhere else on our travels did our appearance cause such venom.

A few hours later we'd reached the outskirts of Marlborough and parked with 40 per cent of the charge remaining. My delayed hangover had now taken a firm hold and I found myself trying to doze on the narrow seat inside the cab while Ian and Pras went looking for some electrical inspiration.

As a fan of our ancient myths and legends, I was more than a little intrigued by Marlborough's motto, *Ubi nunc sapientis ossa Merlini?* (Where are the bones of wise Merlin?). It hinted at the stories and spirit of the county of Wiltshire. A large burial mound in the grounds of nearby Marlborough College is said to be the final resting place of Merlin, the curious magician who, among many of his other appearances, inhabits the King Arthur tales. Some believe this reference to Merlin's barrow is where the name Marlborough came from.

Considering the impact Merlin has had on our national consciousness, you might imagine we'd be better versed in his life, or the myth of his life at any rate, than we are. At the very least you'd think as schoolchildren we'd all have giggled at the fact that originally his name was Myrddin but was changed to Myrllin because Myrddin was thought to resemble too closely the French word *merde*, meaning 'shit'. Perhaps that's indicative of the way French sensibilities have altered our memory of an historical figure who preceded their invasion of 1066 – but we'll come to that in a minute.

Merlin appears for the first time in the 'Welsh annals' of the tenth century, where it states that he took part in a battle in Cumbria in 573. His lord and many of his friends were killed in the battle and he supposedly went mad and decided to flee, becoming known as a wild man in the woods of Caledonia (Scotland). He makes another appearance in some poems from the Dark Ages contained in *The Black Book of Carmarthen*, in which, among many bizarre tales, he is found chatting away to an apple tree and a pig about Jesus Christ.

In Geoffrey of Monmouth's *History of the Kings of Britain*, published in the twelfth century (it was he who changed the 'dd' in Myrddin to the 'll' of Myrllin, so as not to offend the Francophiles of the new kingdom), Merlin and Arthur become inextricably linked to various popular Celtic and French myths. Monmouth's book is said to be a eulogy to the Norman conquerors for ridding Britain of the Anglo-Saxons, who had ravaged the nation of Boudica's ancient Britons. This perhaps explains why he adopted so many French legends, which have become entwined in Arthurian myths. Monmouth is said to have invented as much as he uncovered through research, but that didn't hinder the book's success, or prevent Merlin's enormous popularity from growing exponentially out in the country at large.

Malory is perhaps the most famous chronicler of the Arthurian stories, writing a large part of his *Morte d'Arthur* in a French prison in the fourteenth century. In this work the legend becomes a 'romance' and all semblance of historical fact vanishes completely. Yet it is Malory's tales of Arthur and Merlin that we've come to consider the 'correct' version, fiction well and truly taking hold. All of this is an example of how characters and stories from the dim and distant past may be adopted by writers from the slightly less dim and distant past and altered – names, characters, beliefs – for their own political and religious purposes, and how that doesn't stop us considering these fictional accounts to be true when we read them seven hundred years later.

According to recent research, it appears that Merlin and King Arthur could actually have been Scottish heroes who never set foot anywhere near Glastonbury or the south-west of England at all. In *Finding Merlin*, Adam Ardrey claims that the famous magician and Arthur came together in an attempt to preserve the ways of the ancient Druids in the face of Christianity, and to drive out the Angle armies which had originally been hired as mercenaries from Germania by the Britons themselves (to fight the ailing Roman occupation). Once the Roman armies had been pushed out, the Angles decided to take over the country from the Britons completely. Merlin and Arthur fought together in that great battle of 573, defeating the Angles. Arthur became a legendary leader of men, despite having no royal blood, and went on to beat the Angles in a series of astonishing battles. Of course, very little evidence from the sixth century survives and the documents that do relate to it were largely written years later when Christianity had taken a firm grip on the whole of Western Europe. It's fair to say that religious scholars of the time would have been very keen to paint historical events in the Church's rather than the Druids' favour – seeing as they were keen to banish ancient pagan ideas in favour of their own more modern ones. Generations later, the stories of the heroic Arthur could not be removed from history because he was still far too popular a figure among the population at large, so these Christian scholars decided to turn him into a Christian hero instead of a pagan one. This is why Arthur finds himself turning into a king and becoming involved in a story about the Holy Grail. When it came to the ancient traditions of this country, the elders of the emerging Christian Church were very quick to absorb and adapt them to their own ends whenever they could, so why not rewrite the myth of one of the Britons' most famous and revered military leaders?

The Christians had a habit of building churches on ancient holy sites, which is why in churchyards you often find yew trees that pre-date the churches themselves. To the Druids, the yew tree signified a sacred site, and if you were a Christian trying to stamp out the old traditions, while being pragmatic enough to absorb and rename elements of the old belief system (Christmas and Easter for example), could you think of a better place to build your brand new Christian church?

Of course, what really happened in the time of Merlin and Arthur is now impossible to determine without a great deal of supposition and guesswork. To borrow a phrase from the film of a book we'll come to in a moment, 'history became legend, legend became myth and some things that should not have been forgotten were lost.'

Today we rely on the written word to keep track of the events that took place in the distant past but in the Dark Ages our history and traditions were recorded orally through stories and tales passed down from one generation to the next. This is why great figures from this period are often referred to as 'the great poets' – a phrase often used to describe Merlin himself.

Most countries have myths that 'explain' a fantastical path through the mists of time that set history on a course eventually leading us to the present day. It might surprise some to discover that J.R.R. Tolkien was so distressed that the original oral myths of England had been wiped out after the Norman Conquest that he set about writing his own detailed mythology to replace them. Rejecting the legends of King Arthur as an amalgamation of Celtic, French and

European stories, he began his painstaking life's work, the tip of which iceberg was published as *The Hobbit* and *Lord of the Rings*. It is appropriate that a passionate linguist should try to recapture some of what was lost of our oral tradition. Tolkien certainly wasn't afraid to make use of the earliest figure to appear in most of these legends either – our old friend Merlin again – giving him a brand new legend to inhabit and changing his name to Gandalf the Grey.

Merlin the Druid (a word that translates today as a priest of science and astronomy) and Arthur, a brave but common Scottish military leader, rather than Merlin the magician and King Arthur, should, perhaps, be the real focus for anyone seeking the forgotten heroes of our ancient land. Seen in this context, the stories of King Arthur and the Knights of the Round Table that we all know and love become little more than a narrative invention to illustrate the battle between good and evil, rather like a medieval *Star Wars* you could say. So to go back to Marlborough's motto – where are the bones of wise Merlin? – the answer is probably in Scotland but almost certainly not in Marlborough.

Ian and Pras returned while I was dwelling on the whereabouts of Merlin's bones, and reminded me that Marlborough College was where the great travel writer Bruce Chatwin went to school. We reckoned he deserved a nod as we ambled back out of the town and down towards Pewsey. Despite not managing to get a charge, Pras and I were feeling gung-ho enough to attempt the distance anyway, even though it would exceed our previous best by about fifteen miles. Ian wasn't sure this was the correct decision so he began pouring over the map to make sure we got there with as little elevation as possible. It was soon after this that, having come through the ford at Moulton unscathed, The Mighty One performed her second miracle.

We doddered along towards Pewsey, our earlier optimism slowly evaporating, especially when enormous hills began to appear that looked far more understated on the map than they were in real life. Remnants of ancient forests tempted us with their stories as we trundled south, passing through the long forgotten imagination of the undisturbed, deep terrain, and I began to wonder what tales and stories now hid amongst the landscape that, thanks to fifteen centuries of Christian control, we no longer had any hope of being told.

And still the hills came. Ian kept warning us about one particular incline that threatened to finish us off a mere two miles from our destination. The indicator on the battery reached the first of the red bars with another five miles to go. The prospect of getting stuck made us giggle nervously. If you drive a milk float to the point where it can no longer move at all, you will have damaged the battery beyond repair. In that case, our journey would be over. We decided that if it got to two red bars we would stop and start randomly knocking on doors in desperation. Sadly, when the moment came, there were no doors to knock on – just pretty streams and yet more hills through the beautiful but empty countryside. Ian was disconsolate.

'This last hill's going to finish us off,' he moaned. 'I can't believe it. We're so close but it's a double V [the sign on a map that reveals the savagery of the incline]. There's no way we'll be able to climb it with so little charge.'

However, with barely enough charge to power a TV remote control let alone a milk float, it appeared that The Mighty One had decided to alter the geology of the landscape and make it a downhill run into Pewsey rather than the mountain detailed clearly on Ian's map. It's possible, of course, that the map was wrong, but by this stage I think it's fair to say that the magical properties of The Mighty One were far more plausible than a cartographical mistake by the gods of Ordnance Survey.

We freewheeled in disbelief, whooping all the way down into Pewsey, and had soon located the Cooper's Arms. It stood down a small side road in front of a huge field with a couple of tourist cottages, one of which, it turned out, was to be ours for the night. A man and his girlfriend were sitting outside, drinking pints, as we began to dismount from The Mighty One.

'Ah,' he said, 'the Three Men in a Float! We've heard all about you!'

John Berry appeared with a huge grin on his face. 'You've come to the right place. You have no idea what's in store for you tonight. I hope you've got your drinking boots on.'

The familiar sound of Pras cackling expressed our collective excitement and relief. A few minutes later we were inside the pub, surrounded by pints of beer and smiling faces. By eleven we were all feeling very well lubricated indeed when John appeared at our table with yet more drinks.

'Come on!' he urged. 'You've got another twelve pints behind the bar to get through yet.'

10

Pewsey to Tollard Royal

41 miles

IAN

We slept with the door of our holiday cottage open, not so much to let in the refreshing night air but because we were trailing a one-inch-thick armoured charging cable out to The Mighty One. The cottage, its electricity supply and parking space were all kindly supplied by the Cooper's Arms, the pub that opened its arms to us and thrust alcohol in our direction for hours on end last night. I did not spend one pound. Even when I went to the jukebox, someone tapped me on the shoulder and said, 'There's five tunes in there mate, help yourself.' Had I thought about it clearly, I would have ordered six hundred Marlboro and a widescreen television to see where that got me, but let's be clear about this, I was far too pissed.

So, for the second morning in a row, we were in a pretty sorry state. All we could do was sit around drinking coffee in the mid-morning sunshine, waiting for The Mighty One to finish her charge. Then, having perked up a bit, we said our thank-yous and goodbyes to our new friends, and went quietly on our way – and, boy, did we have a job on our hands. Emboldened by our impossible hill climbs the day before, we were going to try to make it to Tollard Royal, another forty miles or so to the south-west.

Heading south on the A345 through the pretty village of Upavon, through which, oddly enough, the River Avon runs, we made our way to Salisbury. By the way, if you've ever wondered why there are so many rivers called Avon in Britain – a casual glance at an atlas will reveal at least eight major watercourses – it is because Avon literally translates as 'river' in the ancient Brythonic language.

We were following the River River down towards Salisbury as part of my 'let's go downhill today' strategy, and stopped off for lunch at the Swan at Enford, an idea that had apparently also occurred to the whole of Wiltshire. It was packed and with good reason – its reputation for delicious food was richly deserved. While we were there, we bumped into some folk from Pewsey, who remembered us from the pub the night before, and who had, naturally, been there for hours already.

Lunch over, we continued on the back road that shadows the A345 along the opposite bank of the Avon. Noticing some Old English type on the map very close to our route, I suggested taking a look at the 'ancient dovecote' at Netheravon, but the only thing we could find looked like a derelict privy in a field. Having seen a picture of the dove-cote since, I can confirm that what we saw probably *was* a derelict privy and we obviously completely missed the dovecote – which just goes to show that even slow travel is sometimes too fast.

We were now on Salisbury Plain, which is home to two things – Druids and the British Army. Ignoring the Druids for one moment – which is certainly safer than ignoring the Army – the military presence can feel rather oppressive. Everywhere you care to look, there are abrupt signs alerting you to the unhealthy consequences of straying onto MoD property. Red triangle warning signs that feature the silhouette of a tank are in abundance, the odd swarm of evil-looking insectoid helicopters passes over from time to time and the roads carry anonymous moss and compost camouflaged trucks with military number plates. Suppliers of chain-link fences and barbed wire probably do well out of it, as do the villages where the squaddy pounds are spent, but row after row of barrack blocks with corrugated roofs, more checkpoints, secrecy and intrigue than Cold War Berlin, and the reckless use of concrete for almost everything that can't be built out of wood, take an aesthetic toll on a place. Mind you, if the Druids ran Salisbury Plain, it would probably end up as some kind of pagan Junta, where every conflict was solved through rituals – naked women dancing around the protagonists, sprinkling juniper berries, and goats being sacrificed until they settled their differences. (That really does sound awful, not least for the goats.)

So, one hundred and fifty square miles of Wiltshire are effectively closed to the public by the activities of the Army, but that does at least have rather an interesting, if unintended, consequence. We saw masses of poppies, wide expanses of wildflower meadows, natural and untouched by humans in every respect, except the odd unexploded howitzer shell. Isn't it strange that probably one of the most destructive forces on Earth is in a way responsible for the flourishing of wildlife and a reawakening of common land that has, by and large, been lost since the Enclosure Acts? I find that deeply ironic and it shows the contra-karmic nature of Salisbury Plain and Wiltshire as a whole. The place is dotted with monumental imaginings made real, such as Stonehenge, Silbury Hill and Avebury, now managed by corporate organizations that seem to present them in as clipped and sterile a fashion as possible. Rare butterflies basking on fragments of shrapnel, supposed enthusiasts for ancient Britain whose ad hoc spontaneous festivals would be nowhere without advanced electro-acoustic sound gear – all these things make Wiltshire a county of real contradiction.

So what about the modern Druids? Strictly speaking, they are not Druids in a literal sense, more neo-Druids, inspired by the mostly incorrect romanticized vision of Britain's Iron Age, a product itself of rose-tinted literature from the seventeenth to nineteenth centuries. Some official neo-Druid groups, as opposed to wannabes with beards and Stonehenge-sized home-audio solutions, accept this historic fissure in our understanding of their spiritual forebears, and have moved somewhat under the umbrella of Celtic Reconstructionism – broadly, a form of pagan worship with its roots in the pre-Roman Celtic world. Other neo-Druids reject altogether any religious overtones, which is odd because a Druid is a priest, and without a priesthood, it would seem little more than just a toga party.

Real Druids were an altogether different class. It may have taken twenty years to learn enough Druidic lore to become a priest, but this is supposition – not one scrap of verse or story has survived untarnished by the superimposition of Christian or Roman folklore. Looking at it another way, however, much of the Druidic tradition has survived – festivals and holidays, oral literature and customs are still flourishing, albeit as the seeds of later traditions. They are the nettles and brambles that grow from the long barrow graves of kings long gone.

One Druidic practice that should, perhaps, have remained buried has become something of a modern thorny issue. Druids had an unusual form of punishment for members of their society who fell short of exemplary behaviour –

excommunication. Miscreants were forbidden from attending all religious festivals, the social oil that held pre-Roman society together, effectively ousting them from society. These were the Iron Age ASBOs.

It's interesting, in our new age of moral absolutes and summary justice, that the last time anyone practised the widespread exclusion of troublemakers from society was when we all lived in roundhouses and pick-axed people to death. Before we left Pewsey, we spent a long time talking to John Berry at the Cooper's Arms about his extraordinary work with the ASBO generation of children in Britain, and it was clear that for all our modernity, our technology and progress over the last two thousand years, our leaders are still as fatally flawed as they have ever been. John teaches at a secondary school in nearby Swindon.

'I sort of drifted into it,' he told us. 'I can't provide any insight into why I've been able to work with these kids for the last ten years. I think that maybe being male and six foot four might have something to do with it. But I was quite confident at it and had a lot of empathy for these kids, so from my earliest days in the job, I was given the dodgy classes. It became a bit of a timetabling habit and has just continued to be the case ever since.

'I'm proud to say that I work with the kids that the *Daily Mail* gets outraged about. They are the ones who wear baseball caps, the joy riders, the ones with drug and alcohol problems, teenage pregnancies, crackhead mums and jailbird fathers. In particular, the school's catchment area includes the red-light district, so we have a number of kids who are the children of prostitutes. Their school life is actually the one stable part of a very bizarre existence. I teach children who are late into school because they're checking that mum's OK in the morning, that they're not nodding off into their cereal and not about to accidentally set the house on fire. So they get to school when they can.'

'I'm playing Playing Devil's advocate here,' I said, 'but some people say these children are monsters, that they're out of control and need locking up.'

'But I think you have to look at the context. In all the years I've been working with children in difficulties, I've never met a kid with a troubled background who hasn't been messed up by it. There's always an underlying reason. It may not be the whole story; there are always kids who have an element of mischief about them but, even then, there's always a root cause and it's usually dislocation of the family, exposure to drug and alcohol abuse at an early age or domestic violence. I go into homes as part of my job and there are homes where there are no books, where you sit on packing crates and there's a sea of torn-up Rizlas on the floor and that's what these kids go home to every day. No wonder they get into trouble or are a pain in the arse at school.'

Was one of the problems, Dan wondered, the absence not only of suitable role models, but also of a strong community?

'Communities evolve and change all the time but we've been here before – there were dislocated families and broken homes at the end of the Great War and also at the end of the Second World War. Society had to re-acquaint itself and find some equilibrium again and maybe that's where we are right now. We've had a couple of decades of political and religious upheaval. These are changing times and we're always in a state of flux. That's certainly the case in Pewsey, where we're not even sure if we're a village or a town any more, but the kids take their cues from the big towns all around – Salisbury, Bath and Swindon – rather than Pewsey. You visited our wonderful kebab shop last night and you probably found there was a group of harmless, but slightly intimidating, boys.

Now, I know most of them and they're delightful, but they do want to be "boys from the hood" when in fact they're more "boys in the wood". The best thing to do is just talk to them. They want to be streetwise but they're not. They are, like all teenagers, in a hurry to grow up. Childhood is getting shorter all the time.'

We turned to the subject of the nature of English villages and what it was about Pewsey that drew him there in the first place.

'I think Pewsey is unique – you can imagine people in villages up and down the country on a beautiful Sunday morning like this telling you their village is unique – but I think we're more unique than they are! There's a sense of local pride here. There's a certain defensiveness about English villages, which is why I think that there are so many competitions.'

'Too right,' agreed Dan. 'I've yet to visit a village that hasn't won or been a runner-up in Britain in Bloom. What is it about Pewsey that's unique then?'

'Well, I came here in 1991 on a long weekend with my girlfriend. My parents had moved here and as soon as we got here we thought, "What the hell have they done?" We lived in places that had Costa Coffees and McDonalds on their high streets and counted ourselves as quite cosmopolitan and streetwise, but on Pewsey high street there was just a man and his dog. Anyway, I went to the Cooper's Arms on the Friday night and I'm still here sixteen years later.'

Back on the road, we'd reached Amesbury. Heading over the hill that leads south out of the town, we were spotted by a group of young lads. As we slowed to a lethargic crawl, and perhaps mindful of a morning of ASBO talk, we braced ourselves for the humiliation of accepting the inevitable rude arm and finger gestures in good faith – the lot of any tragically underpowered vehicle on Britain's roads – but to our utter surprise, they started waving to us and cheering The Mighty One, a vehicle that would surely lose any hand of Top Trumps, even one entirely composed of milk floats.

Amesbury was the nearest we were going to get to Stonehenge, which lies a few miles to the west and which we had consciously decided to avoid – maybe because so much has been written on the subject and it is so thoroughly well known it has almost become a cliché. We didn't feel we could add anything of any substance to the discussions about the ancient monument, which have, in any case, become largely academic. The place is a tourist Mecca and, in the light of this and certainly in terms of our journey, it seemed largely redundant – like an attempt to discover the true nature of London by visiting Piccadilly Circus. Also, we were far too cheap to pay for the car park.

We eventually trundled into Salisbury past the car park for Old Sarum, and were too cheap to stop there as well. Another monument managed by English Heritage, the history of Old Sarum is widely understood. It is, to cut a long story short, the previous location of Salisbury – New Sarum. The more pretentious Salisbury residents are, the more likely they are to refer to themselves as Sarumites.

We didn't have much of an idea of where on earth we were going, so we took in the sights of the ring road as part of two unplanned complete circuits of the city. What was certain was that we were due to meet Dan's second wise man, famous angling supremo Chris Yates. What was also certain was that we desperately needed to get a charge before going any farther.

We eventually ended up in a large car park to the rear of Sainsbury's – our agreed meeting point – at around four o'clock, just as the supermarket closed. Dan dithered, the way that you do when faced with four hundred empty spaces, and just as he was executing a brilliant half-arsed three-point turn – the only kind possible in the float and only then with about five acres of uninterrupted tarmac at your disposal – a loud beeping of horns came from behind us. Dan lost his rag – something I've never seen him do before – leaned out of the door of the float and let loose a stream of invective at a car trying to pass him.

'What's the matter darling, can't I turn round in a car park?'

I hadn't realized that Dan, my friend and all-round rather lovely gent, was feeling the strain so much. To say it was an uncharacteristic outburst is playing it down and Dan was immediately mortified and a little shocked, especially when he found out that the beeping wasn't coming from the car trying to get past, which would explain the nonplussed bemusement of the lady driving it, but from the vehicle of Chris Yates, who was desperately trying to attract our attention.

Standing there in the car park with Prasanth's camera trained on me and Dan, be-headphoned and with a microphone pointing at Chris, I was just having a minor media whore moment – of the kind you'd expect to see if you teleported a film crew of Channel 4 gits to the centre of somewhere that really couldn't give a toss – when in cycled a man at great speed on a bicycle that appeared slightly too small for him. He appeared very excited to see us, breathless even, although that may have been the cycling.

His name was Pat Shelley and, he explained, he ran a guided tour company in Salisbury that specialized in taking tourists around Wiltshire's ancient monuments and other archaeological wonders. He'd stumbled across us and wanted to help. He said we could have charged at his house, if only there was a free parking space outside, which there wasn't. Nevertheless, that was the first time that anyone had volunteered their cooker socket without having our ludicrous mission carefully explained to them. Meanwhile, Chris Yates had stopped being interviewed for long enough to pop into the goods entrance of Sainsbury's to ask for a charge on our behalf. They said no, using the three-word pass phrase 'Health and Safety' as justification, but still, there we were in a car park, not taking any responsibility for ourselves, and the world was running around doing our business unbidden. We liked Salisbury.

Pat suggested a pub around the corner, which was run, apparently, by a colourful local character who would be willing to offer us electricity if we mentioned his name. As Pat cycled off home, we decide to take his advice, but were halted in our tracks by the impromptu appearance of Dan's mother and her partner, dressed from head to foot in Lycra and riding bicycles, Roger, surely the only wholesome reason to wear Lycra. No sooner had we posed for camera-phone photos in front of the float than who should appear but Pat, even more breathless than before.

'My wife's going out with the dogs in the car, there's a parking spot in front of the house. Do you want to come and charge your float?'

How could we refuse?

We had trouble keeping up with Pat on his bicycle, the ridiculousness of which led to more than a little compulsive giggling in the float cab. For all her mightiness and the sheer torque at her disposal, The Mighty One was rather crap, and Pat had committed the cardinal sin of living uphill from Sainsbury's, so he had to stop a few times so that we could keep up. Watching Pat's legs whiz around like sandcastle windmills, propelling him into the distance, I made a mental note to offer to raise his saddle by an inch or so once we got to his house.

His home was a three-bedroomed red-brick Victorian terraced house quite close to the city centre. As we arrived, Mrs Shelley was waiting to take the dogs out in the car and Dan executed a near perfect piece of parallel parking for The Mighty One in the empty space. Being a hopeless man-boy who cannot drive at all, I only know it was perfect because Dan seemed immensely proud of his manoeuvre and, in fact, wouldn't stop going on about it for at least five minutes. Pras immediately set about putting the float on charge and Pat immediately set about putting the kettle on. Despite a supreme lack of effort on our part, things were going rather well. The comforting buzz of the charger became the back-drop of a lovely relaxed cup of tea. Chris turned up presently, as did Pat's friend and neighbour, archaeologist Phil Harding, perhaps best known for his TV appearances on Channel 4's *Time Team*.

'What on earth are you doing?' Phil enquired.

'We're charging this milk float,' said Pat, knowing full well that it wasn't a complete answer.

'I can see that, but why?'

'Well, I found these guys in Sainsbury's car park. They're going to Land's End in that. Isn't it great? I thought I should help them out.'

Dan elucidated with our boilerplate explanation of slow travel and our attempt to discover England and the English, adding the bit about Che Guevara's motorbike for comic effect.

'We're led to believe that everyone in this country is so jaded and selfish these days, but people – Pat, for instance, who we've never met before – are bending over backwards to help us.'

'I can quite understand why people would lend you a hand, because it is just so eccentric, you've got to love it. If you can't have a laugh at something like that, you might just as well pack up and die. The only other person I can remember who owned a milk float,' he went on, 'was Keith Moon.'

'He used to drive it around Staines, trying to run people over,' Dan remembered.

'I've got a book at home with a picture of Moon and his float,' said Phil. 'Should I go home and get it?'

'I could scan it and they could pin it up in their cab,' offered Pat – which is how a TV archaeologist was instrumental in supplying a portrait of a revered drummer to the occupants of a milk float on their drive to Cornwall. You just can't make this stuff up.

We repaired to Pat's lovely back garden and drank even more tea, but eventually decided that Salisbury and Pat had been kind enough to us and we didn't want to outstay our welcome. Having charged up for a couple of hours, we were confident we had enough to complete the final leg of our journey to Chris Yates's place, so we said our goodbyes.

I had kind of given up on map reading for the day. Dan had been pretty vague about where we had needed to go and he seemed to know his way around the city, so I let him get on with it. And now it seemed as if I could completely relax as Chris Yates was going to lead us out of the city and on to the road back to his house near Tollard Royal, a village on the Wiltshire/Dorset border. As you head down this road, which eventually leads to the dull sounding town of Blandford Forum, almost immediately the countryside owes more to the Dorset landscape of buxom hills than to the wide plateau of Salisbury Plain. These are cartoon hills, unreasonably exaggerated bumps of green of the sort that a primary schoolchild would draw under a smiling sun, adding a flock of seagulls all with one wing longer than the other. For us, it meant a number of agonizing climbs, followed by a good deal of abandoned hurtling downhill. The road was quite busy and fast, but straight as a die in places on account of its Roman origins, and therefore it was reasonably easy for other vehicles to pass us.

As we turned off right onto the B road to Chris's house, that other England came into view – the country of tamed wilderness, landscaped estates, uniform fences and walls, and copses planted as cover for game birds. It was undeniably pretty – Capability Brown and his ilk, after all, brought their genius to bear on the English landscape for largely aesthetic ends, and here it was, still working after three hundred years of judicious management.

We eventually turned into Chris's drive, which is at such a steep bank you could launch rockets from it, and came to a rest on a relatively level bit at the top.

I can't describe Chris's house without drifting off into a reverie. It is utterly charming and I don't mean that in a twee, net curtain, frou-frou kind of way, but rather the original meaning of charmed – being under a magical spell. Here the country is not redolent of neatly clipped hedges and rosy-cheeked postmistresses, but is as elemental a force as you can imagine. I am not a particular fan of pastoral England, having lived in it for around twenty years, and have frequently railed against the 'cities are bad, the country is good' point of view often mouthed by the media. I like living in London because it is a real city, with all the convenience and energy that the word 'city' encapsulates, but if I wanted to live in the country, it would be here in the absolute countryside. It's the real deal.

Chris's house is not so much set in the countryside as almost submerged by it. Nestled in the nook of a steep hillside, wilderness engulfs it like a high wave rolling over a beach into the hinterland beyond. The idea of wilderness has crept within, and you get the feeling that Chris is not a man preoccupied by any system of organization, preferring an organic – and let's not mince words here – untidy approach to life. I sympathize. Filing is for pencil-faced bureaucrats, a procedural illusion of effectiveness that masks the utter futility of middle management.

Chris is an angler – actually, for many, he is *the* angler. A kindly genius of the art of fishing, his books and articles on the subject are the words of a guru. Given his speciality, and Prasanth's morbid phobia about all things piscatorial, I wondered how this was going to work, but there was no need to worry. Chris, warned in advance, had carefully removed all traces of fish from the lounge, kitchen and dining room of his home – no mean feat for a man whose entire life revolves around them.

After some chat over mugs of tea, we set off to climb the steep wooded slope that backs onto his house. We were going badger watching. At the top, we walked a short way along a ridge and came to a halt by some bushes. In there, apparently, were badgers. We adopted the slightly crouched stance favoured for observing wildlife as Chris threw some scraps through the foliage into the clearing beyond. Within a few minutes we were all enthralled, speaking in hushed Attenboresque whispers, at the sight of two badgers rooting around the clearing. They stayed for five minutes or so until something unseen spooked their attuned senses and we lost them to a nearby burrow.

Back at the house, Chris cooked up a lovely pasta dish, cracked open a bottle of wine and we chattered until the house charmed us towards slumber. I was honoured to sleep in the study on a sofa bed. I read the first couple of chapters of Chris's first book and had to pull myself away to do the sensible thing, which was to go to sleep. I dreamed of fish flitting around in bright sunlit water before their frenetic movements were halted by the appearance of some kind of species of aquatic badger.

11
Tollard Royal to Bere Regis

20 miles

DAN

This wasn't sleep; it was hibernation. I came to thirty-five years later on Chris's driveway to find the house completely reclaimed by nature. Where it once stood, an enormous bank of flowers and grass wallowed in the sound of bird song. Chris himself had apparently decided it was time to change from being a wiry nonagenarian into a mighty willow tree. Overnight, it appeared, he had grown out of his study, dismantling the foundations of the house and pulling all manner of new life up from the earth beneath his feet. His trunk had spread along through the kitchen and sturdy branches weaved out through the windows and front door. His leaves had extricated themselves through a few holes in the roof, pulling it asunder, and his new lush green flesh had enveloped the entire building. But he didn't weep, although those who knew and loved him did, when a goshawk landed in the roof of his canopy.

I woke from that bizarre dream somewhat bewildered, and went outside to resume my slumber on the enormous trampoline in the front garden. It felt as though time had slowed down to the faintest amble, even though the clock indicated that it was already nearly lunchtime. We were in no mood to rush. Chris came out smiling and with two mugs of tea in his hands, and we drank every drop through a strainer of relaxed laughter. Ian and Pras stumbled out into the light an hour later, looking joyously dozy with knowing grins on their faces. It seems so trashy to write but it's true – it was as though we'd woken in the home of Tolkien's elves, Rivendell.

I doubt whether elves spend much time firing rotting fruit at a distant telephone pylon with a three-man catapult, though, which is how we proceeded to spend the next half hour. Pras got closest, slicing a Satsuma on the telephone wire a few yards to the left. All mine seemed to arc away at the very last moment, like the deliveries from Steve Harmison's first Ashes over in Australia back in December 2006. Ian appeared to be going for raw power and took great glee in the moment of release, laughing hilariously when he fired one so low that it didn't quite manage to clear the hedge and we all got showered with orange juice.

After such absurd exertions, Chris suggested we go for a wander to see his favourite oak tree a mile or so away, but not before we'd hooked up The Mighty One to his cooker socket. Once that was done, we collected a few bits of food for lunch and set off up the hill behind the house. We clambered up a steep bank through some trees and made our way across a meadow until we stood looking down onto a lush green valley. Down at the bottom was an enormous ash tree, tired and grey among the early summer bloom.

'It's been leafing later and later every year,' Chris mentioned sadly. 'Perhaps it's finally gone. I think it's the water table drying up. It looks like an Ent. It's not of course. We won't see Treebeard until later on.'

We plodded down the slope, driving away a few stray

sheep with contorted lambs trying to feed beneath them, and as we got closer to the ash, you could see faint flecks of green sprouting from the remotest edges of its branches. Chris became quite animated on realizing his old friend was not finished, not yet at any rate. He chatted to it and tapped its trunk before smiling and leading us off on our way.

The sun bathed us in a satisfying glow and it certainly felt as though time had broken free from its normal routine; or perhaps re-established an older meandering one, distinct from the modern rigidity in which most of us find ourselves. I felt much more in tune with this leisurely pace than I had when visiting Chris so many times before. Perhaps it was because the three of us had slowed down so much, and the required acclimatization was less of a leap. Anyway, it was the day from the trip that I remember fondly for being the moment when we really seemed to have nailed the concept of slow travel. Despite the languid nature of the journey so far, we did always seem to have one chore or another to fulfil. This felt like the first time we'd stopped and breathed in the reality of our surroundings.

Chris seems to live his whole life in this state of mind. He's so immersed in his environment that going out for a ramble through the countryside with him is like walking round the National Gallery with an expert in art history. All of a sudden, things that were simply pleasing enough to my peripheral vision began to come into focus and proffer legends and conversations. The colours around us felt more vibrant, while smells and sounds disentangled themselves from the dilution of each other, and I began to get a totally different perspective on nature's ebullient design. Where, back in Cambridge, Ed had a town 'back-stage pass' that let you in on secret places, Chris seemed to have a metaphysical one that gained us privileged access to the natural world.

On one of my first visits to see him, fleeing from the chaos of the city, he'd collected me from a nearby train station and driven a roundabout way back to his house. We stopped in an unremarkable lay-by and I followed him curiously through a thick hedge and down a much-neglected path. After a few minutes he stopped ahead of me, pointed up at a tree and whispered, 'What can you see up there?' I followed his line of sight as he began screeching like an owl. Almost immediately, two barn owl chicks appeared at the opening of a hole in the trunk and peered over the edge, expecting to see their mother, only to find two humans, one laughing and the other with a look of total astonishment on his face.

Now, way off in the distance, you could see our way emerging from thick woodland and winding its way up the other side of the valley. Farther on still, you could make out a building that was apparently an old school. Strolling along a path that was indented with the pattern of a tractor's treads we came across numerous red cartridge cases. I was surprised that this was the kind of place you'd come to shoot pheasants. Such destruction seemed at odds with the tranquillity and beauty of the landscape, but Chris explained that these things are inextricably entwined.

'I can't imagine what enjoyment you'd get from blasting birds with shotguns, either, but if people didn't spend a fortune to come to places like this to do just that, the landscape simply wouldn't be preserved.'

Scrambling up a bank of wild grasses speckled with bright yellow buttercups, we chanced on a natural spring that fed a pond. Chris pointed out landmarks as though they were old friends, and every few yards he was moved to tell us stories of his children's toboggans, stalking pumas and moonlit close shaves with whatever beasts of the night happened to be roaming through at the time. A stumpy hill covered with trees to our left reminded Chris of a late night walk he'd shown Rachel and me, with baby Wilf in a carrier on my back, a few years earlier.

'Oh God,' I recalled. 'We were supposed to be out for just a few minutes . . . '

In fact, we'd ended up on the run through the woods from a local gamekeeper, who no doubt had us down as poachers. Darting into the woods had taken us far from the prying headlights of the Land Rover that followed us, but also farther than we'd imagined from Chris's house. We'd returned some hours later, sporting the kind of outdoor glow that seems to follow you throughout your childhood. I hadn't felt it for many years. We were breathless and excited when we finally collapsed beside his fireplace – except for Wilf, who'd managed to stay asleep on my back the entire time. That night I'd concluded that hanging out with Chris was like being able to roam around Roald Dahl's imagination.

All too soon we reached the wood where Chris's beloved oak tree stood. The wood was the size of a postage stamp compared with the scale it would have been when the mighty oak had first begun to grow, but it still had the atmosphere of quiet age. We were reasonably close to the New Forest and no doubt at one time this was the middle of a thick and impregnable ocean of trees rather than a small hiding place for soon to be lead-blasted pheasants.

We skulked through the undergrowth, sniffing fresh garlic leaves as we went, and soon came upon the fabled oak. It had the squatted look that descends on a tree once it's made it beyond a thousand years of age. It's as though it can't be bothered to impress you with its height, as a younger tree would, relying instead on girth and the unmistakable aura and power that accrues only when life has begun around the time of the Norman Conquest. It had to be eight foot wide, and was about twenty foot tall before it's branches reached up into the light. The entire trunk was mottled and covered with a beard of moss. Younger trees appeared to clamour around it. One branch that was far more substantial than most oak trees, and two more comparatively spindly arms, grew out to nowhere in particular, giving it had a weirdly upturned-tripod appearance. We tiptoed around the saplings and through the lush green carpet of vegetation that was thriving despite the lack of direct sunlight, and Chris began to climb the oak, finally taking a seat ten feet off the ground while munching an apple. I leant up against the trunk and found it impossible not to let my mind rewind through snatches of the history that had surrounded it. Before long I began to feel completely overwhelmed and alone. Over the years the wood had shrunk to a mere roundabout of foliage, but still the tree was preserved in all its timeless glory. Chris told us that the air quality of the wood had recently been tested and found to be among the cleanest in the entire country. We all greeted this news by inhaling as deeply as our lungs would allow.

It's probably trite to mention the pointlessness of mankind when compared to such a powerful oak – the speck of time we inhabited when compared to its languid lifetime – but the slow theme certainly seemed resonant while leaning on its strangely alluring trunk. I have always found it curious that on the occasions when I allow myself to ponder eternity, as I did leaning up against Treebeard that afternoon, my imagination and thought processes seem to slow right down rather than speed up. It's almost as though the simple act of thinking about time going on forever causes your own world to grind to a complete halt. Excessive speed would seem the logical manifestation for the concept of eternity, wouldn't you think? But languor seems to suit the never-ending idea so much more than haste, to me at any rate. I began to wonder whether I'd stumbled on another one of those idea icebergs that I couldn't quite translate. Whatever it was, there was something reassuring about the thought of Treebeard outliving us all by centuries.

Reluctantly, we started back, humbled by the quiet power of such a beautiful tree. As we emerged from the wood, a roe deer bounced out of the tall grass and darted away. It seemed fitting to snatch a glimpse of this other natural, eternal, world, but it also reminded me how lacking in grace human beings can be. We all seemed to feel the same thing and everyone began to walk with much more care – hoping not to disturb any other creature that might be near. Ian stopped and pointed to a fenced-off meadow to our right.

'Skylark. Listen.'

Chris grinned, while Pras and I strained our ears to pick up the sound. Sure enough, there it was, a pure song repeated over and over again.

To give us the excuse to sit down and just soak in the scene, Pras set up his film camera and began sweeping the valley with it. I mentioned the slow travel nature of our trip to Chris, while we relaxed in the meadow in the afternoon sun, and the perplexity of slow time I'd picked up from his favourite ancient oak. It was something he'd clearly pondered himself.

'Ah, well, what you've caught hold of there is that fact that there's no such thing as *time*, only memory,' he said.

I often find myself stumbling around noisily, looking for the tips of ideas only to find that Chris has been quietly and calmly charting what's going on under the surface of our lives for some time. In fact, this idea that time itself does not exist in any real sense outside of our own perception, appeared most famously in the *Confessions of St Augustine* in AD 354. Whether we believe time is entirely subjective or not, it certainly makes sense that what we mean by 'time' does depend on our memory of the events that make up our lives. That would explain why time during childhood seems to last forever. To a two year old, a single year is half a lifetime, practically an eternity. By the time that child is fifty, a year has become one fiftieth of a lifetime, so perception of time speeds up as the years tick by. If you accept these ideas to be true of your own life, time as we experience it might not be as rigidly defined as you might think, which leads us into quite interesting and, for most people, uncharted territory.

These days we have the world of work to thank for the well-known phrase 'time is money', and if time at work seems to drag, think about the Industrial Revolution. In the factories of the steam age, clocks were literally slowed down to make people work longer and longer hours. Few people had watches so it was hard to argue successfully that your time was being 'stolen' by your employer in this way. Living in a period where your perception of time shifted and you began to take cues from a machine (a clock) rather than the physical world around you, must have been traumatic to bear. Especially when coupled with the miserable conditions of working in the new industrial mills.

If time *is* about perception though, perhaps we can teach ourselves to think about it in a different way. It may seem utterly anarchic to us not to have time structured to the second, but things were not always so inflexible. Society as we know it would collapse without that rigidity, but the world itself, and the natural instinct of human beings in my view, is completely and utterly indifferent to it. Relying on the sun, the seasons, your environment, the memory of your life and instinct for your sense of perspective, instead of a watch, seems more in keeping with a happy way of life to me. It's a wonderful idle thought. Imagine living a life without regimented time! I'm sure we could all learn to live very differently, and much more happily once we'd got used to it, in a world without time.

My friend Tom told me once that in some parts of Africa the concept of time is not at all the same as what the people have come to call 'white man's time', which they find so ordered and confining. They rely instead on a totally different set of values to structure their lives. To Western minds, such cultures need to be 'saved' from backward thinking, and introduced to our more 'civilized' way of life, but the concept of 'linear time' – that time is like a train travelling in a straight line from the past, through the present and into the future – that prevails in the West is considered rather 'backward' in other cultures. In Buddhism and Hinduism, for example, time is thought of as cyclical rather than occurring in a straight line. The Inuit of Alaska think in the same way and, curiously, use the word *uvatiarru* to describe both the long-forgotten past and the distant future.

I very much like the idea that there is more than one way to think about time. I've become convinced that the concept of slow travel, and its many attractions, is simply a way for those of us in the world of rigid time to connect briefly to this alternative and timeless world. For me, that's why slow travel seems so logical and meaningful – it's the tip of an iceberg that could give you the ideas you need to live your entire life in a far more fulfilling and satisfying way.

Inevitably, when we returned to the world of watches, we ended up leaving Chris's house very late indeed; so late, in fact, that Pras and Ian had both run out of cigarettes. We managed a few more cups of Chris's favourite 'lover's leap' tea before saying goodbye, not to mention another three-man catapult firing session, this time with a bag of perfectly good oranges.

By the time we got to the nearby town of Blandford Forum the charge had dropped to a surprisingly low 60 per cent. Spotting a Tesco on the outskirts of the town, we decided to go in and try our luck. We got a charge there but I'm not sure whether it could be classed as luck, not good luck anyway.

I'm one of those people who consider Tesco to be a real-life version of a company from a conspiracy theory film that, despite carefully crafted marketing and advertising campaigns involving fluffy teddy bears and people who seem just like you and me, is actually – not. After glimpsing behind the scenes at Tesco in Blandford Forum, I am now able to say that without it being a joke. Obviously, this is a very unkind thing for me to say. After all, they helped us charge our milk float, but, as we learned at Morrisons in Diss on day two of our adventure, journalistic integrity requires the suspension of typically English character traits, such as gratitude and good manners. I think they thought we were going to try to steal some of the pallets of toilet roll wrapped up with acres of plastic Clingfilm beside the float, or perhaps the manager thought we were curiosities that might give Tesco some much-needed positive PR if he agreed to help us.

There's a great book called *Tescopoly* you can read if you want to hate Tesco as much as I do. It details all the business practices that have helped them conquer this country and decimate so many of our towns and cities, along with much of the infrastructure created to protect our domestic food industry. You can't imagine a book more opposed to everything Tesco represents. You'd think they would have sued the author the minute the book was published but they did something far worse than that when it was released. They did something that reveals the extent of their all-encompassing power. Rather than sue the author and the publisher, they decided to sell *Tescopoly* in their stores. You see, it doesn't matter what we do. They are far too powerful to be stopped. They don't care and can take the criticism. Even if that 'thing' is a book about how much better the world would be if Tesco was wiped off the face of the Earth. You'll be hard-pressed to find a better encapsulation of the modern commercial world than that.

While I'm ranting about Tesco, there's only one thing I hate more and that's the celebrities who take huge piles of cash to make adverts for them. Come to think of it, these days it's difficult to find celebrities who won't do adverts. What happened to the integrity of famous people? Has that battle already been lost? I saw Bill Nighy on one of those 'now I'm old I'm a right miserable sod' programmes, banging on about how awful computers are. Imagine my surprise a few weeks later when I heard his unmistakable voice telling me about the new processor in a Sun Microsystems computer! I also admit to feeling pretty disillusioned when all of a sudden Stephen Fry seemed to have decided to appear in all the adverts on TV he could get his hands on, but I felt even worse when Michael Gambon, greatest living actor, got into bed with HSBC. For me, though, the final nail in the coffin of celebrity integrity came when Victoria Wood, Terry Wogan, Alan Whicker and Timothy Spall all took pieces of silver to appear in adverts for supermarket giants. Who do up-and-coming celebrities look to for guidance now if these national treasures are happy to trade on their popularity to flog us endless crap on behalf of Asda and Tesco? I mean, you expect it from the Spice Girls and that woman who used to be married to a bloke in Westlife, but

Victoria Wood? Terry Wogan? Alan Whicker? And Timothy Spall? Jesus wept.

We left Tesco at dusk in middle-class disgust and headed on for a campsite in Bere Regis. On the outskirts of Blandford Forum we noticed a gypsy caravan standing on a patch of grass beyond the exit of a roundabout on the A354. It wasn't exactly a picturesque spot. A man in a grubby white jumper with slicked back grey hair sat on a fold-up chair in front of a roaring fire. He had a pick-up truck along with his traditional caravan, and two horses were tied up to a hedge. He was the first fellow traveller of the road we'd come across, so we decided to stop and say hello.

Gypsies seem to be the one section of society that it is still socially acceptable to abuse verbally. Now, at the risk of making myself appear like some kind of dangerous extremist, I suggest we reverse this trend and start shouting. 'Get some fucking integrity!' to every celebrity we see on the street who has done an advert for a supermarket giant, instead of shouting, 'Get a fucking job,' to gypsies minding their own business on the side of the road.

Gypsies certainly come in for more than their fair share of abuse and we hoped this man would consider our milk float a sign of kindred spirits rather than of trouble. He seemed at ease when we strolled up. He'd been cooking barbecue chicken legs and immediately offered them to us. I decided instantly, having gauged his physical strength to be far superior to mine, that I would prefer to get food poisoning than offend him, so I took one eagerly and began chomping on it with relish. It was delicious. He introduced himself as John and answered our fairly abrupt and intrusive questions much more politely that we deserved. It emerged that he travelled throughout the summer from his home in Portsmouth and this was one of the few spots where he was generally left alone. When we asked him if he got much trouble, he rubbed his knuckles, which were heavily tattooed with the kinds of designs that seem so popular with alcoholics and people in prison films, before admitting that he had a shot-gun in his van and if anyone gave him trouble, he would sooner shoot them and deal with the consequences than take any of their 'fucking shit'. We laughed nervously before making a few polite noises and darting off as quickly as The Mighty One would allow. (I'm keenly aware of how carica-tured this description seems, but every word of it is true.)

A sedate forty-five minutes later we pulled up at the campsite in Bere Regis on the fringes of Dorset. Thankfully, the owners were not prejudiced against milk floats and soon we were tucking into our first alfresco dinner – sausages and veggie burgers on a disposable barbecue. Pras surpassed even his own enviable electrical skills by getting the milk float to charge up from one of the 16-amp electricity supply posts, carefully position for caravans. Ian and I stood there open-mouthed. Charging up from caravan power supplies was something else deemed 'impossible' by the experts before we'd set out. Pras explained that 16-amp was OK as long as the wiring was substantial enough to handle the current The Mighty One drew out of it. He pointed to the small grey number 16 on the plug socket, with the letter B written next to it. Apparently, when it comes to charging milk floats, B wiring is very good indeed.

12

Bere Regis to Burton Bradstock

28 miles

IAN

The next morning we found ourselves at something of a milestone. We had now crossed from Wiltshire into Dorset and, although the boundaries can be disputed, it felt as though we were, at last, in the west country. Three or four counties, depending on your disposition and how argumentative you wish to be, officially make up the west country. Dorset is certainly part of the official English Region of the South West, but that also includes Gloucestershire and Wiltshire, so what do they know?

The moot points of regionalist pedantry aside, verdant greenery under an air-brushed azure sky convinced us – the stuff of 1960s postcards luring city folk away from the smoke and down to the country for a week of warm drizzle and the occasional gale. Of more relevance to our theme of slow travel was that two of the three West-Country counties we had to cross to get to Land's End – Dorset and Cornwall – don't have any motorways at all. We had finally hit our slow stride.

As a consequence of discovering that we could rely on campsites and their fabulous 'electric pitches' to charge our batteries, we felt that the second half of our trip was going to be a lot easier than the first. The tourist trap of the West Country, we fondly imagined, was bound to have a string of campsites right down to the very end, and although it struck us as a little unsporting to do the easy thing and effectively pay for these charges, we were a little tired of all-day conversations about amperages, batteries and exotic power sockets. In a word, we risked becoming deeply boring if we didn't relax and look for the bigger picture in all of this.

That pleasant Tuesday morning at the idyllic Rowland's Wait campsite, we were officially loafing around waiting to be photographed by the local press. I had grown a goatee beard, trying it out for size. I reckoned that in the wild outback of rural England in a milk float, I wouldn't be mistaken for an IT consultant, merely an idiot. In a rare moment of pre-emptive preparedness, we had all but packed up the float while we waited for someone from the *Bournemouth Echo*. Richard or Roger, for either of those may be his name, eventually turned up and started buzzing about to get his picture. When the local press arrive – anywhere in England – something strange must always happen because they want that shot that says 'wacky eccentrics', mostly to differentiate it from the hundreds of pictures of people holding enormous cheques that are the mainstay of the average local newspaper. As a consequence, many photographers stoop to taking self-consciously 'creative' photos, or try to get you in impossibly uncomfortable positions, waving your arms and gurning like a lunatic with a cough-medicine habit. Often, the position they require you to adopt would tax a teenaged Hungarian gymnast who has removed one of her legs and mailed it to an adjacent postcode. At other times, they fit their ultra-wide-angle lens and take a picture of you from around two inches away that renders your face as that of a human bank vole. Our man from the *Echo* started off proceedings by encouraging us to play a game of Twister in the cab, arranging us into anatomically impossible positions until either he got the shot he wanted or someone's lumbar vertebrae turned inside out. That out of the way, he wanted to capture us in full slothful flight in the float, which was a lot better and saved us from being breathed over in the manner that opticians do, shortly before climbing up one of your nostrils. In all of the excitement, we were so rushed out of the campsite, we completely missed our turn and ended up going towards what the signs described as Monkey World Tank Museum. I was a bit disappointed when this turned out to be two distinct tourist attractions rather than the fascinating and ground-breaking theme park that the signs hinted at.

The Purbeck district of Dorset, through which we were travelling, is beautiful. It's largely made of chalk, limestone, various clays and sandstones, which, if you know anything about geology, is likely to make you very excited indeed and for all sorts of different reasons. The presence of chalk and limestone is what makes the coast of Dorset − dubbed the 'Jurassic Coast' − a bountiful source of fossils. Many limestones as well as chalk, which is itself a type of limestone, are formed from the shells of dead marine animals that accumulated on the beds of warm shallow seas millions of years ago. So, in effect, these rocks are actually made of fossils, just very tiny ones. Meanwhile, geologists of a more materialistic disposition are interested in the sandstones, which happen to be full of high-quality oil. Dorset is the largest onshore oil well in Europe and has the world's oldest continuously operational pump − one of the 'nodding donkeys' at BP's Wytch Farm installation has been pumping oil since 1959. The place would probably look like Dallas if it wasn't for the screen of coniferous forest that hides the installations.

The other thing you may come across in the area is the

British Army. Again. On our way from Bere Regis, we passed to the north of Bovington Camp, the location of the Tank Museum, which, as previously noted, has nothing to do with monkeys. We passed what appeared to be some kind of tank training circuit that runs parallel to the road. Signs erected along the perimeter warn drivers not to stop there under any circumstances. We didn't fancy pitting The Mighty One against a brigade of Challenger 2s, so elected to heed the warning and carry on.

Eventually, we left the heathland behind and crawled along back lanes towards Dorchester, which is situated on a ridge overlooking the River Frome, a languid, senile affair, meandering its way across its own flood plain. Halted by a herd of cows – another sign that we were truly in the West Country – the irony of dairy versus dairy struck us, but the farmhands scarcely give us a second glance.

On the fringes of Dorchester, Dan homed in on the forecourt of a car dealership.

'Is that a 16-amp socket?' he spoke up, excitedly. 'I just saw a blue 16-amp socket.'

'It was,' I answered, 'and can I say that I'm a bit worried about you.'

The 16-amp blue socket, located on the forecourt of Dorchester's Peugeot dealership, ranks as the easiest charge we obtained. We asked. We got. No fight, no comical story telling required, no hard sell, nothing but blank acquiescence to our ridiculous demands. It was terribly disappointing, as was the socket itself. Dan and I left Pras in charge of the charge and went off into town in search of food. However, so feeble was the feed from the car showroom, which was being used to power an air pump responsible for keeping an inflatable doo-dah in the air, that The Mighty One's charger kept tripping it out, again and again.

Serendipity called again. Putting off shopping for the inevitable veggie burgers for Pras and bangers for Dan and me, I wandered into the first second-hand bookshop I found and made an interesting discovery. My mother-in-law, Anne, a retired librarian living in Cornwall, had recently recommended Arthur Mee's book on the county, published in his *King's England* series, and there it was, the first thing I saw in the shop. According to the owner of the shop, it had come in the day before. The book was waiting for me and I duly adopted it.

On our way from Dorchester to west Dorset, we passed through Poundbury – a new village based on Prince Charles's architectural principles and design ideas. I expected to be a little disappointed with Poundbury and, in this way, it did not leave me disappointed. Prince Charles is well known for being an outspoken critic of modernist architecture. In 1984 he famously described the proposed Sainsbury Wing extension to the National Gallery, which faces onto London's Trafalgar Square, as a 'monstrous carbuncle on the face of a much-loved and elegant friend', rather putting the cat among the square's pigeons.

In 1993, construction work began on land owned by the Duchy of Cornwall at Poundbury. The guiding principle was to create a vernacular village that featured mixed development, where shops, homes of the prosperous and social housing all rubbed shoulders. There were to be no out-of-town supermarkets, no ghettos of poverty. In short, the village was to be a settlement that rejected zoning in favour of a more sustainable alternative, which is bang on the money as far as I'm concerned. I have just one problem with it and that's its fuddy-duddy-ness. There's nothing wrong with harking back to values of community and social cohesion – to use that terrible New Labour phrase – but surely you can do that without making every building look like something off the film set for *Dick Turpin*. There seems to be a secret longing in Poundbury to Xerox old styles of building purely as a matter of style rather than letting form follow function, which is, after all, what the original builder did. For instance, you may wonder why Tudor houses frequently have tall chimneys. Ornate and rather grand as they sometimes are, their height was practical. Even if the roof is now slate hung, as many are, the tall chimney tells us that it was in all likelihood originally thatched and the chimney was built that way to prevent embers setting fire to the roof. To pick another example, this time from Poundbury, many properties in the village feature bricked-up windows purely for aesthetic reasons – mimicking their seventeenth and eighteenth century predecessors. But there was a simple motive for bricking up your windows in the seventeenth century and that was because William III introduced a Window Tax in 1696, a regressive tariff on property that meant only the rich had unlimited potential for bringing daylight into their homes. Somewhere in a dark corner of the fusty, cobwebbed mind of our heir to the throne, this pointless, blank ornamentation may be some kind of weird homage to the grandson of Charles I but, to me, it looks for all the world like his grasp of architecture is far too literal, a little feeble and lodged firmly in the past.

In Britain, we are in love with our history and nowhere can this be seen more clearly than in the buildings we erect – often cack-handed copies of Georgian and Regency town houses set in winding sprawls of cul-de-sacs. At least Poundbury is not full of these flimsy fakes with their bullshit colonnades and flatpack Grecian facades, but where it makes a leap forward in terms of social values, it does so with one foot in the past. On the one hand it rejects the suburban planning sprawl in favour of pedestrian-friendly communities, but on the other it recreates architectural styles that are as irrelevant to contemporary Britain as, say, the monarchy. The best I can say is that it looks perfectly pleasant, pretty even, but that's the English for you. Take an exciting idea and dress it up as anodyne, say-nothing regression.

We left Poundbury nonplussed and were immediately tossed into the modern world again. The A35 runs the width of the county and into Devon, forming part of the main arterial route between Dorset and Exeter. It's not terribly wide at this point, however, and Dan was getting increasingly edgy in rush-hour traffic. This was not what he signed up to do, so we looked for a detour.

Just past Winterbourne Abbas, we noted a likely turn, which led to a road that ran roughly parallel to the route we were planning to take down to the sea. Past a long barrow and some tumuli, a magnificent vista suddenly opened up before us. We knew we could rely on the beautiful landscape of the country to tell us about England, but here was something that spoke volumes about who we are and what we're all doing on this marooned rock. For one thing, the history of early man is written into this landscape and we were lucky enough to see it at dusk, when the light slants sideways on to the hill, revealing the furrows and ditches of ancient field systems and strip lynchets – the distinctive ridged terraces formed when ploughed earth slips downhill over hundreds of years. All of this was revealed to us in the evening light as surely as if we had commissioned a hi-tech geophysical survey. Barrows, tumuli, ancient copses on hilltops and the odd farmhouse were all bathed in numinous dusty light.

'This is it,' said Prasanth, a little lost for words. 'I don't think . . . I can't see . . . how it's going to get better than this. Looking down this amazing valley, I can just about see the sea . . . It's the most beautiful place I've ever seen.'

A blackbird warbled a rich, fruity melody, while chiff-chaffs chiff-chaffed. Dan walked off and, wearing a straw hat, cut an impressive figure silhouetted against the sunset. You just wanted to hand him a saxophone and the sheet music to 'Stranger on the Shore'.

We had to move on eventually — it was either then, at that moment, or an unspecified number of years later in a range of caskets and a very large cardboard box for the float. The lure of cheap camping and a barbecue by the sea on this wonderful evening was a little stronger than setting up our own village on the spot where we stood.

The road wound its way down to the sea, joining the coast road a couple of miles outside Burton Bradstock, a small village just south of Bridport. There was a holiday park the other side of Burton, which we thought might have a spare pitch or two.

Climbing the hill from the village, we were overtaken by some lout who wanted to floor his 4×4. It turned out to be James, Dan's brother-in-law, who later told us, playfully, that we 'looked like tramps' in our milk float.

At the entrance to the holiday park, James swerved across our path, cut us up one more time, and hurtled off down the hill. Dan, completely unfazed by this, helpfully read out the highlights of the site we were entering, as outlined in bullet points on the sign at the camp gate.

'Swimming pool, bar, private beach, fantastic,' said Dan.

'Hey man, caravans for sale,' said Pras, following the bullet points down.

Dan let off the brakes and we, in turn, hurtled down the steep hill, with all three of us cackling at the hysterical whine of the motor, into Freshwater Beach Holiday Park. My hopes of perhaps grabbing a couple of spare pitches on the site were borne out as the park appeared to be almost totally empty.

Following the instructions for late arrivals at the site's reception barracks, we pointed our float in the direction of a field and set off. Well, here we all were. The words 'holiday park' conjure up images of bucolic loveliness, I always think – perhaps it's something to do with the word 'park', as in 'cultivated garden' – but it turned out to be more like 'park' as in 'an enormous car park' for tents and tourers.

As we drove past reception, I noticed an amusement arcade the size of a supermarket, called 'The Fun Zone', which looked as far away from fun as it's possible to get without sawing your own hand off and playing badminton with it. There was also a chip shop (closed), a supermarket (closed) and a laundrette (open) with a hot drinks machine (closed). The most amusing thing to do here appeared to be the ironing.

'Jesus Christ,' said Prasanth. Quite.

As we drove through to 'Field H' – a misleading term as it hints at some kind of fence or hedge that separates you from 'Field G' – I was overcome with ennui. It was utterly featureless – a large, flat, treeless field, punctuated only by tarmacadamed roads and a lot of crows, dozens of them, promenading about the place like little funereal litter collectors, pecking at this, nipping at that. They were the only item of interest in a six-acre field of desperation.

The roads weaved around the site, part of a bijou one-way system that alerted you to the presence of a bureaucratic mindset. True to form, there were many, many rules, all of which could be safely disregarded as far too authoritarian for a campsite. NO Fires. NO all male or all female groups. NO clothes lines. NO ball games in the touring field. NO skateboarding. NOthing was open. NOthing would make me want to return to this godforsaken shithole ever again. NO kidding.

Seeing as we were trapped here in Stalagluft-by-Sea, Desperate-Super-Mare, for the night, we decided to get drunk – not an original thought by any means, but the best one we could come up with in the circumstances. Fortunately, with James here, one of us – in this case, Dan – could go off with him to collect the brews. The float wasn't going to make it up the hill we had just careered down without either a full charge or a Saturn V rocket strapped to the top. When they returned about twenty minutes later, Dan stepped out of the Chelsea tractor somewhat ashen faced.

'What's up, mate?' I enquired. 'You look terrible.'

It turned out that, after ambling along at an average of about 10 miles per hour, Dan was no longer used to the terrifying speed of road travel. He had become so accustomed to life in the slow lane that he had forgotten what it is to travel at the hair-raising velocity of 35 miles per hour.

'I'll never get used to going fast again,' he lamented.

We didn't do very well in the getting drunk stakes. We had our barbecue and when we finally got around to putting up our tents, it was late twilight. What I'm trying to say here is that we did it in the dark.

I explored the fascinating world of the laundrette. I turned the iron on, and then off again. I found a snack machine next to the defunct hot drinks machine and had just enough change for J-19, fancying the reckless promise of a Crunchie bar. I received a packet of salt and vinegar crisps and a bottle of Oasis Summer Fruits, neither of which I could face. I tried the iron one more time, but was interrupted by someone whose life was as empty as mine, and shuffled off back to my tent.

Turning in through despondency rather than tiredness, I clambered into my sleeping bag to smoke fags and write up notes before I became so brassed off, I went to sleep. The next thing I knew it was dawn and a crow was dancing on my tent.

13

Burton Bradstock to Sidmouth

29 miles

DAN

We woke to the incessant retching sound of a thousand crows taunting us tirelessly, mugging us of our sleep, at the devilled hour of 5.30 a.m. I clambered out of The Mighty One, where I had elected to sleep, rather than in the tent, intending to go to the toilet block, but I found myself battered by an icy wind that was hammering the empty (apart from us) and forlorn (including us) camping plateau.

The sign on the road had promised a four-star campsite with its own swimming pool, bar and restaurant. The reality was somewhat different. They hadn't lied exactly, but the desolate plateau, paddling pond and closed fish and chip shop seemed at odds with the description. The 'holiday village' also had its own horse-riding school but this was more like a glue factory doubling up as a scrapyard. Meanwhile, the no doubt once serene horizon had been peppered with a seemingly endless number of static caravan homes, no doubt soon to be populated by negative equity casualties of the noughties housing boom. I climbed back under the battered blue tarpaulin and wearily attempted to go back to sleep. A few hours later, having endured the kind of fitful cold and feverish torment one imagines must plague the miserable state of limbo, I gave up, climbed out again and got dressed, shivering all the while. Ian emerged soon afterwards and we agreed without speaking that this was the worst morning of the trip so far. At ten, we plugged in the charger and The Mighty One began to quaff electrical juice. A three-hour charge meant remaining where we were until one o'clock.

If you imagine our milk-float odyssey as the English dairy equivalent of the Tour de France, we were about to begin the King of the Mountains stage. Our destination at the end of the day was supposed to be Sidmouth, but that meant contending with three savage hills, one immediately on leaving Burton Bradstock on the way to Chideock, another on the outskirts of Axminster and then a particularly vicious one approaching Beer and Sidmouth from the coastal town of Seaton. Such gradients were a real double whammy. On the one side you had to contend with the grinding struggle of climbing the hills with the inevitable queue of increasingly irate motorists collecting behind, but going downhill on the other side was a great deal more dangerous than we had thought when we set off from Lowestoft. We'd discovered from Clive in Dorchester upon Thames that if you go over a certain undefined speed, the motor would catch, the wheels would simply lock and a disastrous crash would inevitably follow, which was rather troubling when you consider that our 1958 milk float didn't come with seatbelts or a working speedometer. We hadn't known that when we'd tried to get a speeding ticket in Baldock. Now, as Ian pointed out, 'The Mighty One is bloody heavy. If we lose control going down a hill at thirty-five and crash, then, well, we're simply going to die.' We would just have to carry on relying on the whine of the motor and not allow it to go any higher than the sound of a top 'E', which so far had worked OK.

I comforted myself from the risk of impending death by frying a few stray sausages from the night before and rolling them up inside an anaemic slice of white bread from the campsite shop, although I felt confident about recognizing the 'safe' pitch of the engine. I had taken violin lessons from the age of four, and my teacher, Mr Chittock, told me that I could play 'by ear', which means you are able to distinguish a note in any key simply by listening to it. This skill had come in useful at fifteen, when trying to work out how to play the introduction to 'Sweet Child O' Mine' on the guitar to try to impress girls, but I'd never imagined it would potentially save my life when driving across England in a milk float at the age of thirty-one.

By 11.30 we'd had enough of the holiday village and decided to make a break for it, even though we'd have little more than a three-quarters full battery. The hill leading out of the campsite was suitably steep but The Mighty One was so desperate to leave that place that she bounded up and out of it.

A mile or so later we came upon the first mountain of the day. Our collective sense of trepidation was fierce enough when we approached but in a lay-by up the hill we spotted two police cars, and policemen making spot checks on passing vehicles. We had seen a few police cars on the journey so far but, despite being rather conspicuous, we'd managed to keep a low profile. That would be hard to do when driving up a savage incline at a speed of one mile an hour with a half-mile tailback of angry car and lorry drivers behind us. We all gulped. We did have insurance and a tax disc but even so, The Mighty One was surely a strong candidate for being stopped. We weren't sure if we could legally carry three passengers in the cab and everything on the flatbed behind us was stowed in a rather lackadaisical manner. If we were stopped, as we were convinced we would be, we'd have to answer a lot of awkward questions.

In retrospect, I can see that we were probably the last thing the police wanted to deal with, and so it proved. They did their best to ignore us as we ground our way slowly up the hill, and Chideock appeared ten agonizingly slow minutes later. As it was lunchtime, we decided to stop at the first pub we saw to grab a bite to eat. The food was not particularly memorable but the 'England' condom machine in the men's toilet was, selling packs of condoms bearing the slogan, 'wear your nation's colours with pride'. I bought a pack for pure comedic reasons and began to wonder whether a world truly existed where people took national pride that seriously.

The landlord of the pub, originally from Essex, didn't mention the condoms when he came over for a chat, having spotted The Mighty One in the car park, but he did talk about the damage to the village caused by 'holiday homes' that had priced local people out of the market. Apparently, it had got so bad that out of the 650 who lived in the village you could count on two hands the number of people actually born in the area. This is the kind of place where the curse of 'holiday lets' is most keenly felt. Houses in Chideock were rented out for as much as £1,800 a week in the summer. At rates like that in high season, you could make more money from a house that was empty for half the year than if you rented it to a local family all year round. So for local people, not only was buying a home in the village where they grew up an indulgent fantasy, they couldn't even afford to rent there any more either. According to the landlord, the village was literally empty out of season. We heard that irritated refrain a great deal as we headed through the holiday counties of England's south-west corner.

As we limped up yet another hill, the countryside began to turn on its typically English charm. Before setting out, we had thought that our journey would be about the beauty of this landscape – the 'green and pleasant land' of 'Jerusalem'. What we'd actually found was something else entirely. Despite the undeniable beauty of the countryside, the 'landscape' that had made most of an impression on us was the one constructed by the characters we'd met along the way. We'd been to parts of the country that offered much less to look at than this coastal idyll but they nonetheless felt beautiful because of the sense of community fostered within. Chideock, by contrast, appeared to be dying, the life being sucked out of it by the leech of tourism. Now, having played havoc with the thriving community life that used to exist, tourism had become the village's last remaining source of income, and so had become the only interest left to preserve. In holiday towns you often get the impression that local people are considered far less important than tourists and Chideock seemed a case in point. Local people no longer appeared even to exist.

The road to Axminster meandered pleasantly through small country lanes that were like tunnels of foliage so that you felt as though you were almost underground. Occasionally a break appeared, usually because of a gate, and stunning Dorset vistas of the kind synonymous with Agatha Christie stories expanded before our eyes. This rural peace was not to last, though. A few miles later we emerged from one of these green wormholes to be spat out onto a hideous single carriageway blurred by juggernauts and double white lines. These were the moments I came to despise. These roads had no sense of humour and they gave no quarter to travellers such as us. They were arteries of chaos that run in strips all over the English landscape. Roads leading to places called 'hurry up!' and 'I've got better things to do!' and 'I'm very important, get out of my way!' They were the world of haste we'd done so much to evade. And then, just to make things worse, another horrendous hill loomed ahead.

Looking back, I can honestly say that I remember being called a 'wanker', 'selfish bastard' and a 'fucking cunt' (at least, I presumed they meant me because I was the one doing the driving) just a handful of times during the entire trip. Most of that verbal abuse (apart from the hectoring we received in Hungerford) was thrown my way that afternoon. Trundling along with a stream of irate motorists trailing in our wake was not a pleasurable experience. We stopped to let them pass as often as we could, and once counted forty-eight vehicles overtaking us, but the opportunities were scarce and you could feel the rage building behind us all the time. Until that day I didn't realize that tractors had horns. It also led to me going faster downhill than I probably should have. We screamed along, sounding more like a Spitfire than a milk float, while the overtaking manoeuvres of our hassled companions grew more and more absurd.

Finally, after yet another picturesque but bloody terrifying descent, we made it to Axminster. There we blagged a charge from the famous carpet factory. The mileage we'd hoped to clock up had been rather overwhelmed by the contours of the landscape and we were down to 40 per cent of the charge.

We caused a bit of a stir at the factory. The Mighty One was starting to appear in local newspapers, and items had been broadcast on local radio news. We were beginning to be recognized and were soon surrounded by a flurry of people, keen to tell us what to do. It was the first time Pras hadn't been responsible for getting us powered up and it proved to be a bit of a nightmare. A few humourless men in dirty boiler suits began lecturing us about the low levels of water in the cells of our batteries and proceeded to chide us gently for our lack of planning and total disregard for forethought. I don't want to imply that we considered ourselves experts by this point, but I think we'd come to understand the capabilities of The Mighty One and found our own way of looking after her. We'd already got farther than anyone had thought possible.

Pras sat on the back of the float, rolling his eyes as though his lover was flirting with another man, while a collection of people began telling us what kinds of cables and voltage we needed. They gradually disappeared and I began chatting to him about his feelings on the trip so far. Pras was, and still is in some ways, something of an enigma to me, but the facts of his life that I managed to extract from him that afternoon turned out to be rather surprising, even by his standards.

He was born in Wimbledon on 18 June 1975 (eight days after me) but his parents were concerned that raising him in England might turn him into a 'spoiled yob' so they relocated to India when he was two. His father died when he was fifteen and his brother left soon afterwards to work in America, leaving Pras the responsibility of looking after his mother, who had become housebound. After school, he did a diploma in electronics and began fixing broken TVs. He got bored with that after a few years and decided to start his own taxi company in Madras, which he ran for three years, but the hours were oppressive. He often worked for twelve hours a day, seven days a week. When that became too much, he began a new life as a used-car salesman. He had connections with people working for insurance companies, who would get expensive high-performance cars, scratch them slightly and then erroneously claim they'd been written off in accidents to get the insurance money before buying a duplicate car. Pras would buy the 'written off' cars at a greatly reduced rate. He would drive them around Madras for a month or so (he had numerous Mercedes, BMWs and at one time the only Mitsubishi Evo in the city) before selling them on for a small profit.

When his brother returned home to work, Pras decided he wanted to travel and remembered that, as he was born in Britain, he would be eligible for a British passport. He filled in the required forms, got his British passport and received a letter from the Indian Government pointing out that, despite having lived in India for twenty-four years, as a British passport holder without the required visa, he was now an illegal immigrant and would have to leave the country immediately. He was told he would have to apply for the visa in London before he could legally return 'home'.

So he moved to England and soon found himself helping out asylum seekers from Sri Lanka in a halfway house. 'Most of them had been tortured and had gunshot wounds. They were the kind of people the *Daily Mail* call "layabouts" and "scroungers", but I helped them fill out forms and get the advice they were entitled to, because they would have been killed if they were forced to return home.' After that, he worked in the infamous Notting Hill Music Exchange before it was closed down for tax reasons, and I met him a few years later while dressed as a teddy bear during an illegal picnic in Parliament Square. I know that there's plenty more to Prasanth than that brief synopsis of his life, but at least you now know as much as I do.

The trip was certainly affecting him and had changed his attitude to travel.

'I've never travelled *this* slowly before. It's such a different experience. It's like we're *really* seeing places. I'm definitely going to take more time travelling from now on. I'm not going to fly to anywhere in Europe, either,' he declared. The beauty of the scenery was making an impression on him, too. 'I've lived here for eight years now, and I was born here, so England feels like my home, but I've always lived in London. I've been to Birmingham, Manchester and Glastonbury but I've never really explored the countryside before. The views are so beautiful I'm actually finding it quite tiring. Every turn seems to have a different landscape. I'm glad I'm travelling with two other people because if I was on my own, I would be travelling forever. I'd be stopping at every place to take pictures and talk to people. That's one of the reasons why I've always travelled alone before – because people get really bored with my slow pace. But I'm now realizing that I didn't even know what "slow" meant.'

He seemed to be getting on well with The Mighty One. 'The best designs are always simple. The Mighty One is brilliant. Every vehicle I've travelled in for a while, I soon begin to communicate with it – even though it sounds stupid,' he laughed. 'The first car I had was an Ambassador, an Indian version of a Morris, and that was from 1958 as well. I would happily take it anywhere because it was so reliable. I used to drive a thousand miles a week in it without any problems, and The Mighty One is pretty much the same. It goes slowly but it's so reliable because it doesn't have any of the new technology to break down. The more things you put on vehicles, the more things can fail.'

At that point the electrical and mechanical experts from the Axminster carpet factory appeared and asked him if he could go and have a look at something. Ten minutes later the charger was humming nicely. Sadly, by this time, the factory was forty-five minutes from closing for the day, so our charge would still be rather depleted. This was not news that pleased Ian, because now rather than make it to Sidmouth, we would probably have to spend the night down the coast in Seaton, a small town that held a few bad memories for him.

As it was, he needn't have worried. We got as far as Seaton with 40 per cent of the charge remaining, which gave us a decent chance of making it to Sidmouth, ten miles or so along the coast. As we pulled slowly up the hill out of the town, relief took the place of the apprehension that had previously enveloped Ian's face. He told us the story, breaking into laughter every few words, building up to a crescendo of mirth by the time he got to the end. It involved an altercation with the police.

'God, it's so embarrassing now, but at the time . . . Me and a friend, Michael, used to go birdwatching when we were fourteen . . . I know . . . and anyway, one day we found this little storehouse the scouts used to keep provisions in. Well, to cut a long story short, we broke into it to make a cup of tea and have a biscuit, and I got caught and ended up being cautioned in the police station. Apparently, I'd left my bird book up there and it had my name and address on the inside page . . . Despite this incriminating evidence, it still took them three weeks to come and find me . . . '

The hills soon became laughably steep. Once again, Pras and Ian suggested getting out, so severe was the incline, but by now The Mighty One was taking the gradients in her stride and we were soon making our way along the coast to Beer, toiling along narrow roads lined with ancient walls and towering foxgloves. In one place, the road narrowed even more between trees and hedges and that was where a disgruntled-looking man in a beaten-up car came at us at breakneck speed, screeched to a halt at the sight of us and reversed back aggressively the way he had come. It must have taken us five minutes to reach the passing point he'd reversed to so we could pass, and when we finally went by we expected to find a frothing beast in the grip of road rage. But he was laughing heartily, mouth wide open beneath his tangled grey beard, as we nodded our heads in unison, hoping it might help us up the one in seven hill.

We finally made it to the Oakdown caravan park, a few miles east of Sidmouth, in the early evening, feeling worn out. The caravan and camping site was perfectly manicured and I began to feel a sense of unease. Although we hadn't encountered any campsite snobbery since stumbling across the Bear Inn on day two, I couldn't bear the thought of what might happen if they turned us away. With 20 per cent of the charge remaining, and vicious hills either side of us, our options had become rather limited. I wouldn't say I was embarrassed by The Mighty One's appearance but it occurred to me that a snooty caravan site owner might be oblivious to her numerous charms.

We hopped from the cab and ambled into the office. The walls were adorned with ornate certificates and awards and I'm sure we looked terrified when the manager came out from behind the counter and peered out of the window, but when he exclaimed, 'My God, is that a milk float? What a coincidence! I'm trying to buy one of those,' we began to relax. Once again the gods of chance had delivered us to the right place.

The Oakdown caravan site proved to be so environmentally savvy that they had pictures of David Bellamy hidden in various bushes with information about all the local wildlife. A milk float to help move around all the caravans stored on the site was the next part of their plan to become totally carbon neutral. Electric vehicles have zero emissions (if the electricity comes from renewable resources), not to mention being a great deal quieter than a tractor or Land Rover for early morning activities.

We were ushered to a pitch with two 16-amp charging posts next to a bright orange digger that turned out to be very handy for putting out the washing. It didn't take Pras long to get the charger humming and for us to put the tents up before indulging in a nice cup of tea in the warm evening sun. The manager, Alasdair, stayed for a chat and we began explaining the intricacies of milk floats to the latest milk-float enthusiast we'd managed to stumble upon. When he later referred to us as milk-float 'aficionados', I allowed myself a satisfied grin. If only the 'experts' could see us now.

14
Sidmouth to Shaldon

33 miles

IAN

We lingered at Oakdown, taking the next day off, which was a much-needed tonic. Dan and I managed to lose our tempers with one another and cleared the air somewhat through the medium of brief outbursts of fury. We made another lazy start the following day and my only concession to getting on with it on that pleasant sunny morning occurred when I came to my senses and shaved off my goatee beard at long last. Time to stop looking like an IT contractor, and that's always something to celebrate.

We were now well over halfway into the journey and had time to catch our breath. Talking or otherwise distracting Dan while he was driving was probably not a good idea and so we took the opportunity to have a proper chat after our heated exchanges. Dan was in reflective mood.

'In terms of how I'm feeling, being able to stop and reflect is interesting because it makes you realize that we're living in a very unusual way,' he said. 'Even though we're travelling slowly, the days have been hectic. There's always been so much to do and none of us has had time to think about what it is that we're actually doing.

'I'm feeling slightly uneasy, slightly perturbed. It's almost as if, in the float, we're entering an odd world, but I'm wondering whether we're entering the real world and the one we live in normally is the unreal one. Everything just feels richer and I'm finding that very difficult to adjust to.'

When we set off again later that day, we are happy people. The sun was out and here we were trundling our way through Devon, the last but one county of our journey.

We travelled along the A3052 towards Exeter and came to the top of Trow Hill, which overlooks Sidmouth, rather quicker than I thought we would, which is a pretty crap thing for an official map reader – particularly one who's familiar with the area – to admit.

I was probably put off by the fact we were in Devon, and our day off had left me in an over-reflective mood. Devon is a county of which I have very few fond memories, and perhaps it would have been better to keep busy rather than sink into a seemingly limitless pit of introspection. Perhaps I should just choose my geographical location more carefully next time I take a day off – I was, after all, the navigator – but the fact remained that this particular corner of Devon was one I studiously avoided on the whole. I should explain why.

When I was twelve, I lived in a caravan park quite near here. The van itself was OK, but we had gas lighting in it, and a chemical toilet in a little shack outside. The drafty outhouse was preferable, however, to the privy inside, which was, of all things, an electric convenience. Quite why the only electrical appliance in the caravan was a toilet I cannot recall, but the whole mechanism gave me the willies – a benign pan of blue fluid was at least responsible for a comforting plop, rather than the soft thud and the ensuing whirring of the one inside. I still remember being quite excited at the promise of being moved to a newer van with those most modern of conveniences, the flush toilet and proper electrical appliances.

Our family spent most of our time in Devon living in caravans on various sites. The sole permanent building we did rent turned out to have an insane landlady and a troublesome poltergeist who turned the lights on and off, moved furniture about and even came to sit on my bed one night. The most problematic resident of the flat was, however, a rat the size of a family car. It lived under the floorboards and we could hear it climbing up underneath the stairs every night. After a few weeks of things that went bump in the night, we worked out that the rat was progressively chewing his way, night by night, through the floor into the kitchen. My father actually sat up one night with a twelve-bore shotgun across his lap in case the thing broke through and managed to topple the heavy enamelled bread bin that my mother had placed over the ever-widening hole. Thank God it didn't, because the house was so rickety, he would have taken half the floor and wall out.

As if these memories of destitution and misery weren't enough, Devon still held some unpleasant surprises for my father. Many years later, he suffered an aneurism in a north Devon lay-by – which served at least to explain what he thought was his irrational hatred of Barnstaple – and then died in Exeter hospital about a week later. I carefully recounted all of this to the guys, not in order to bum them out but just to explain why I'm not at home with the whole concept of Devon and why I really couldn't wait to leave. Unfortunately, it's a very large county, although the bit we lived in – east Devon – is only a small part of it. Exeter would be the turning point for me.

To deny that Devon is pretty is pointless. It's a beautiful county full to the brim of photo opportunities – a fact that would not be lost on anyone standing at the top of Trow Hill. The patchwork of fields and woods laid out before us was stunning. Dark green coniferous plantations topped some of the hills, their straight edges bordering on fields, some of grass, some of freshly ploughed red sandstone soil, some filled with golden hay. Hedges delineated these fields like lead strips in a stained glass window. The distance between Devon and Heaven is not really that far – something with which my father would probably concur.

Trow Hill turned out to be long and steep in places, but according to the map, it was the gentlest way down. Even then, the brake linings became a trifle warm, the distinct aroma of burning becoming evident as we neared the bottom. We decided not to go into Sidmouth but to push on to Exeter, where we were to meet Kim, down for another spot of sound recording for the radio.

Just outside Exeter, we stopped to check our tyres, as we were aware that they might be a little soft, and a good job we did. Two of the tyres were effectively half flat and the others weren't that far behind. We pumped them up, set off again and immediately noticed the difference. That gave us hope that, with harder tyres, we would get a few more miles out of each charge where it mattered most – on the hilliest part of the journey.

Our plan was to pick up Kim at Sowton Services on the M5, do a quick photo shoot for the local paper, the *Express and Echo*, and then swing round to the south of the city and make it out onto the coast road to Dawlish, all without hitting a trunk road or motorway and studiously avoiding the city centre. As we lumbered down a long gentle incline to the flood plain that surrounds Exeter, we knew we were late. Actually, we were always late, but this time it was a couple of hours and not the fashionable thirty minutes we usually managed. Negotiating the busy motorway junction round-about turned out to be a doddle, unexpectedly – it's a fast and furious affair but I issued explicit instructions to Dan to prevent us from heading up the M5 to Taunton.

Kim was waiting for us, sitting on a hummock like a pixie, and she greeted us in good spirits, despite our lateness. The man from the *Express and Echo* turned up to take our photo. His creative bent on the world of local newspaper photography was to do away with the wide-angle, close-up gurning and waving beloved of lesser newspapers, and being a little stiff from sitting on our arses for miles, it was a relief not to have to contort our bodies into interesting shapes for tomorrow's paper. Instead, he elected to get out his very long telephoto lens. Prasanth started to giggle.

'Man, that's like an 800mm lens or something.'

'You're not wrong,' I responded. 'He could shoot a couple of deer in Plymouth from here with that.'

In order to fit us all in, he had to retreat farther and farther away – so far, in fact, that we couldn't hear what he was asking us to do.

'If he gets any farther away, he's going to have to phone us up,' reasoned Pras.

He finished quite quickly. We semaphored our goodbyes and went back to the service station. This was our first look at a service area in the context of our mission. It seemed an odd affront to the whole concept of slow travel to be there at all, but one should always know one's enemy. We had claimed our parking space as infiltrators into the world of the svelte, streamlined transport system of the future. And what a dump it was.

It's curious to note that when the UK's first motorway service area opened, at Watford Gap in 1959, it quickly became the height of fashion – not least because the quality of the food and service was quite unlike anything else available at the time in Britain. The Beatles were frequent visitors to Watford Gap, as were a trail of other pop, rock and early TV celebrities. It was the motorways, after all, that made driving a van to gigs up and down the country feasible all of a sudden. Jimi Hendrix famously thought that Blue Boar – the company that ran Watford Gap – must have been a chic London club, because so many of his contemporaries in the music scene of the 1960s raved about it so much.

It wasn't to last. Service was pared down to self-service in short order on the grounds of expense, and service station food evolved into its present parlous state. In 1977, Roy Harper wrote a song called 'Watford Gap' for his album 'Bullinamingvase'. It contained the priceless couplet, 'Watford Gap, Watford Gap, a plate of grease and a load of crap.' The track was curiously omitted from subsequent pressings. The fact that a director of Blue Boar was on the board of Harper's record company, EMI, could, of course, be pure coincidence.

Sowton Services is not really any different from any other service area. Chiefly, it seems to be a place where desperation hangs in the air like a virus. It feeds off your malformed brainwaves, which have been modified by the ever-so-slightly perceptible oscillation of banks of strip lighting and a persistent subsonic hum. This air of overwhelming despondency is carefully managed to put you into a hypnogogic state in which you will not notice the ludicrous price of your cappuccino.

Motorway service areas were the first facet of the glamour of driving at high speed to fade. Now, with the environment near the top of the political agenda, we wondered how long it would be before the whole unsustainable culture of driving like a maniac would come crashing down around our ears. It was just as well, then, that in a search around Sowton Industrial Estate for our next charge, we came across the Exeter offices of the Environment Agency, the government body charged with implementing environmental policy in Britain.

We were struck by the rich irony of asking the Environment Agency for a charge and what we thought would be the inevitable lack of willingness to help us out. Government agencies tend to play it by the book and we had abandoned the book long ago when we clambered into our milk float and decided to drive it across England. There were bound to be health and safety considerations, official policies on the matter, protocols and procedures to follow. It was certain to be a nightmare of triplicate proportions to get civil servants with one hand tied behind their backs to give us a hand. We thought we'd give it a go, though. We were longing for a 'no' as absolutely no one we had been able to engage and reason with had yet turned us down, and an official rejection would have been accepted for its novelty value above all else.

'It strikes me we're just going out of our way to find people who will reject us,' I said to Prasanth as we walked up to the reception of the Environment Agency.

Pras agreed.

'This is turning out to be just like Michael Moore going into Wal Mart.'

After explaining ourselves in a shambolic fashion to the receptionist, we were guided to the back door of the Agency. As soon as we approached the glass screen that marked the enquiries counter – and it's worth mentioning that our travelling circus included Kim holding a microphone and Prasanth filming – several people ducked out of shot in the office behind. That's never good news. Ignoring the camera-shy occupiers of the cubicles, we pressed on regardless. Dan opened the bidding.

'We are,' he stated with absolute conviction, 'Three Men in a Float. We're travelling across England from farthest east to farthest west in an electric milk float. And we're looking for a charge and we couldn't help but notice that you are the Environmental Agency.'

'Environment Agency,' said the woman at the counter, who turned to be called Wendy. 'Not environmental. The only "mentals" are the people working here.'

'Whoops,' said Dan, laughing. 'That's a bit embarrass-ing. Well, we thought there can be nowhere better in the whole of England to charge an electric milk float – can you help?'

Wendy pointed to a man who was desperately trying to hide behind a cubicle screen. 'I've got to check with that man on the phone. If you could just . . . '

'All we need is a cooker socket,' Dan interrupted, trying to fill in as many details as possible.

'Our cooker is gas,' said Wendy.

Unperturbed, Dan pressed on, 'Or a 16-amp socket or a 32-amp – with access to the fuse box.'

'And wireless internet,' I added frivolously.

'And I'll have a cup of coffee,' said Kim, making an unex-pected entry into the arena of unreasonable requests.

We watched as Wendy went to talk to the unnamed man on the phone.

'Looks like that phone call has suddenly got more impor-tant,' observed Pras.

After a moment, Wendy came back with some mixed news. 'We do have an external plug socket, but we can't give you access to the fuse box.'

We glossed over this, quite certain that they didn't want to know what Prasanth's danger rating for the job was. Wendy came out of the office and walked us around to the other side of the building. She wasn't sure where this socket was and we spent a while with her, hunting around the car park for what was in all likelihood an anonymous looking box.

After nipping back to reception to make some phone calls, Wendy eventually located the socket and we all stood around waiting for Prasanth to electrocute himself. So no change there, then. As he had to wire into the socket live, I awarded him a seven out of ten danger rating, making some allowance for the proximity of the Royal Devon and Exeter Hospital.

Dan came around with the float and some free goodies – some hemp bags and tiny sun hats – from the Agency, who had just celebrated, if that's the right word, World Environment Week or some such. Raising awareness of the issues was part of the work of the Environment Agency and we did talk briefly with their Head of Corporate Affairs – PR man to you and me – about the state we're in, but it's fair to say that he wouldn't be drawn into a debate wearing his Corporate Affairs hat. He was there to put over the work of the Agency in a favourable and compelling light, not to offer his own take on government policy or the events and attitudes that shaped them.

Our swift top-up accomplished, we headed out of Exeter on the A379 along the estuary of the River Exe towards Dawlish. This part of the journey was pretty level, the countryside was beautiful and our spirits were high. On that stretch of the journey, we contributed in a small way to diverting attention briefly from the culture of the petrolhead – a monomaniacal obsession with speed and wanton horsepower – when we turned off into the tiny village of Starcross. Several young women were having a pint outside a pub when a pimped-up, modded hot-hatch full of hormonal young men approached from the other direction. The car was one of those you feel has had so much loving care poured into it – running-board style lights, ultra-violet fluorescent tubes, spoilers and tinted windscreens adorned the specially lowered chassis while bewildering bass lines pumped out of the in-car stereo system as the car slowed down to a crawl to impress the ladies. But just before this vision came into these particular ladies' view, a 1958 Morrisons dairy delivery vehicle bearing the legend 'Three Men in a Float' came from the other direction and completely spoiled their approach. The cheers were for us. The hot-hatch skulked away. We had won some kind of tournament. Apparently.

Victorious, we made our way to Dawlish Warren, where I thought we might find somewhere to stay. We took a look at the signs for the holiday parks and dismissed each one out of hand. It was Burton Bradstock all over again – wholesale camping. We had contracted such vile moods at that utterly dreadful site back in Dorset, we didn't feel like repeating the experience. We knew we had to have a site of a certain size in order to find enough power to charge the float, but these places were too big, too Disney for us. Most of all, they had absolutely no regard for where they were located. Once on one of those parks, you could be absolutely anywhere. Night life, food and beer were all provided on site and there was little in the way of local flavour on offer. What's more, even if you sought it out, you would find that the character of the village had been completely overrun by these monstrous holiday parks. We pressed on. I suggested that we tried to make it to Teignmouth down the coast, which I remembered as a little more conservative and old school.

Dawlish marks the end of the Exe Estuary and the coast road started to take us up and down the hills a bit. The terrain was getting steadily more taxing and we found some testing inclines on the way to Teignmouth, but no nice campsites. Crossing over the River Teign on a long, low old bridge, which, although we could see it from some distance, we had difficulty finding, we had unparalleled views up and down the river. We also had a more disturbing view – that of the other side. The hill through the village of Shaldon on the south side of the Teign was incredible, unlike anything else we had seen so far in our trip. It gave me butterflies in my stomach and I started to feel ill. I wasn't sure that we'd make it. The normally laconic Dan actually gasped, either in awe or fear, I'm not sure which.

However, that very morning, Alasdair had pointed out that milk floats were built to carry up to two tons of milk bottles, and so had a lot of torque in an astonishingly low gear, which was useful not only for dairy delivery and pulling around luggage on a caravan park, but also for hills. We crawled up Shaldon Hill no slower than we had crawled up any other hill so far. Indeed, we were good for anything up to one in seven, or even one in five, which is quite an ascent. Typically, we didn't know exactly which model we had bought, so anything we encountered in between those gradients was largely a matter of faith. It took us a long time and lights flicked out one after the other on the dashboard battery meter, but we made it to the top in the end.

We were looking for some kind of campsite and, sure enough, the turning for Ocean View Holiday Park appeared. While we were congratulating ourselves and The Mighty One on her performance in the face of overwhelming odds, we couldn't help but notice that the unoccupied pitches were at least another 100 feet up.

Dan parked on a vicious incline opposite reception as the rest of us tumbled out of the cab to look for someone who could help. Failure to find a high-powered pitch between here and the bottom of whatever hill lay beyond was not an option. A note on the door of reception told us to go to the site entertainments centre, bar and club opposite to book in.

To the strains of 'Don't Stop Me Now' by Queen, we made our way into the bar. A couple of camp entertainments officers were doing a dance routine that was incredibly gauche. In their defence, it was the last children's hour of the holiday week and they were all being pumped up into a frenzy just in time for bed. Kids were running around like crazy, they were screaming, shouting and just having an absolutely superb time. Parents were sitting well back, nursing lagers and white wine spritzers, their terrifyingly knackered faces a portent of the arguments due in the car back home tomorrow.

There's nothing like the forced jollity and plastered smile of a campsite children's entertainer to put your life sharply in focus. You either want to run from the room onto the high balcony beyond and throw yourself into the void, or you count yourself lucky that it isn't you up there, robbed of your shot at fame and compulsively looking through TV listings magazines for the next variation of *X Factor* or Louis Walsh's *Smashed Dignity Showcase* to come on air to give it one more go.

After about five minutes of this maddening tripe, someone came along to escort our shattered minds out of the building and into reception. I was delighted to note that the float was still there and hadn't rolled backwards down the incline 200 feet to the beach. Another potential problem awaited us in reception – a gigantic, panoramic fish tank. Prasanth started to look a little sheepish, so I stood in front of as many of the fish as I could while we booked our pitch. After we explained our exact requirements to the man in reception, he decided that the very top of the site would be the best place for us to practise our electrical sorcery. As Pras filmed the whole spectacle, a small, round angry child came into reception and said, 'Don't film me or I'll break your camera in half – I'm warning you.'

We drove up to the top field and parked up. We had an absolutely amazing, uncluttered view along the coast to Teignmouth and beyond. It felt like being parked on top of a mountain. The lights were coming on in the landscape below us. Tiny lights winked on and off on ships moored out in the English Channel. It was absolutely perfect and every-where felt downhill from here.

15

Shaldon to Burgh Island

44 miles

DAN

At 9 a.m. Pras was up and busy making coffee. As this meant he hadn't actually ingested any yet, I decided not to attempt to speak to him. Before we'd set out from Lowestoft he'd warned me about a dark side in his character that usually emerged if he hadn't had enough caffeine. Apparently, his addiction had begun when he was a mere six years old. I hadn't seen his dark side yet, and didn't particularly want to, so I tiptoed off quietly to the shower block to try to wash myself back into life.

I returned to The Mighty One an hour later, after thrashing around under a half-hearted, but scalding, shower to find things slowly being packed away. Pras had clearly drunk enough caffeine and I joined him in dismantling our two-man tent. Tents and I have never really got on very well and I was reminded of this fact when I managed to break two of the bendy tent poles by simply pulling them carefully out of the space-age material that had kept us relatively warm the previous night. I stood there for a while, wondering how I should break the news to Ian that I'd broken his tent, the one I'd spurned at the start of the trip in favour of sleeping on the back of the float. The Mighty One had proved herself to be wonderful in so many ways but she was certainly not much of a bed, especially since we'd given Chris Yates's son Alex our Hypnos mattress after discovering he was six inches too tall for his previous one. So despite my earlier misgivings I'd had to admit that the extra tent had proved a worthy addition to our bedraggled belongings. Ian took the news reasonably well.

'Well, you and Pras are sleeping in it, so it doesn't bother me,' he said, laughing his head off. I turned to Pras to offer an apology and he just collapsed in hysterics, too. That was the end of the tent. We screwed it up and chucked it in the chest on the back of the float and began rolling cigarettes.

At that moment my phone buzzed. It proved to be a voicemail message from Brother Daniel at Buckfast Abbey. I'd obviously missed the call while I was in the shower.

'Hello Dan, it's Brother Daniel here. We're very much looking forward to meeting you all later on. We've put a charging point out for your milk float at the back of the Abbey, and your rooms are all ready for you, so please give me a ring to let me know when you think you'll arrive. God bless you.'

The prospect of spending the night in a monastery might not be everyone's idea of a fun-packed time. To me, though, becoming a monk was surely the ultimate way of slowing down, and it seemed an appropriate place for us to stop on our meandering journey. Ian and Pras were far less intrigued by the idea than I was. Pras is inherently suspicious of organized religion and I think it would be fair to say that Ian felt the same way. I, on the other hand, was looking forward to it enormously. Monks and monasteries have always really appealed to me, although I'm aware that they appeal to me in the way things sometimes do when I have absolutely no idea of what they actually entail. When I was at college in Alton in Hampshire in the 1990s I'd visited Alton Abbey, along with a coachload of other students. Alton, like Buckfast, is a Benedictine monastery. I can't remember exactly why we went but looking back, sixteen years on, I think that visit had quite a profound affect on me.

We were told to bring food to give to the monks at Alton, and were amazed by the way they had rejected the values of the outside world. One man we met that day made a particular impression. He was American and used to work on Wall Street. He'd amassed enough money to buy a large house and drive a red Ferrari, all of which he'd given away so he could become a monk and live in a monastery in the crap town I was desperate to get away from. Like most people of my age, becoming rich, living in a big house and driving impressive cars were all things I wanted to feature in my future very much indeed. I was utterly dumbfounded about why he would give up 'everything' for 'nothing'. I am one of Thatcher's children after all, and 'greed is good', in the words of Wall Street's Gordon Gecko, was being roundly touted at the time as the new moral base on which humanity would supposedly be perfected. Now I remember that day very fondly as the first time in my life I came across the idea that there's more to life than money. I don't remember the visit leaving any lasting impression on me about God, but it certainly gave me a perspective I've come to revel in wholeheartedly.

After that, I think I may have idealized the monastic life as being more about philosophic reflection than worshipping God, but in medieval times monasteries were certainly places where sanctuary was given to those who didn't 'fit in' with the prevailing values of the day. My friend, writer and editor of *The Idler*, Tom Hodgkinson, has spent a great deal of time researching this period and he told me that the monasteries of the medieval world gave us many of the things we rely on. Monks routinely took in the dispossessed and the poor and helped care for those cast adrift from respectable society. I learned recently that, through beer, medieval monks invented a welfare state. Catholic holidays were so numerous and gave the people so much time off (compared to the pathetic number of bank holidays we have today) that this is where the phrase 'Merry England' comes from. The monasteries would brew beer to sell on the numerous feast days and the money generated was spent on looking after people who were too old or infirm to work. When the Reformation began and the monasteries were sacked and burned, these waifs and strays had nowhere to go and just roamed the land, ultimately bound for Protestant workhouses, where they were treated like criminals rather than simply in need of care.

Hermits are part of the tradition of retreat, and I've always found the idea of slowing down and escaping the modern world a very attractive one. Clearly, the monastic life is taking this idea of retreat to its extreme, but I was hoping to learn something from the monks and bring some essence of their reflective way of life into my own.

All of this put a spring in my step, and I anticipated an evening of conversation with wise and learned men as we set out on a blissful sunny June day, heading in land towards Buckfast.

We took a few wrong turnings and ended up shuttling up and down tiny rural lanes that popped up and over seemingly lost railway lines. The charge was being decimated by the hills but we struggled on through, even though some of the roads were barely wider than The Mighty One herself. I kept turning to Ian with raised eyebrows as the road filled with pot holes and got narrower and narrower still. I was convinced we were heading for the bottom of a random track and a muddy field rather than Buckfast Abbey but the gravel and potholes gave way to tarmac and our speed picked up again. It was soon after that a driver in a white van recognized us from one of our local newspaper appearances and yelled out, 'I've seen the Three Men in a Float!' as we ambled along, which cheered us all no end. Then we stumbled on a pub called the Tally Ho! and decided to stop for lunch and take a long look at the map.

It turned out that we'd missed lunch but the landlord offered to make us a few sandwiches while Pras successfully persuaded him to give us an hour's charge. We emerged a few hours later, blinking in the bright sunlight, and drifted the remaining eight miles slowly towards the Abbey. Brother Daniel had given me directions to avoid the 'public' face of the Abbey, so that we could arrive via the industrial estate behind it. As instructed, we followed a convoluted driveway along a river that was banked by picturesque thickets of daisies on one side and pallets of general industrial detritus on the other, and found our way into the Abbey grounds. Brother Daniel was waiting to greet us, wearing his brown cassock and in classic monk pose. He pointed to a white wall with an outdoor plug socket that he'd clearly had installed for our visit. We pulled up right by it.

Such generosity took me aback slightly but we soon learned that hospitality to travellers is one of the hallmarks of the St Benedictine Order. We were quite late arriving and he explained that dinner would be served in an hour, which gave him limited time to show us to our rooms for the night. The three of us, being male, were allowed to stay in the same building as the monks themselves while Kim, being female, had to make do with the visitors lodgings a few yards away.

We were shown our rooms briefly before Brother Daniel

had to dash off to sing vespers in the Abbey church before dinner – 'The new Abbot says we're not very good, so we need as much practice as we can get.' Each room had a name. I got St Etheldra, Ian had St Peter and Pras was allocated St John, while the room bearing the name St Jerome remained empty, which seemed appropriate enough.

We skulked around outside the door of the refectory at seven, the appointed hour for dinner. I felt like a naughty schoolboy and couldn't get rid of a nervous giggle that seems to alight in my head whenever I find myself around any kind of humourless pomp and ceremony. Eventually, Pras and I pushed Ian through the door and followed sheepishly behind. Talking over dinner is forbidden at Buckfast Abbey, so the three of us walked up to the counter silently, and helped ourselves to ham, soup, vegetables and potatoes before a smiling monk appeared and explained in a whisper where we should sit. I think we'd have found the three places set aside for us without any help, though, seeing as each one had a little card bearing an illustration of a milk float.

Dinner in that echoing hall was a strange and curious experience. All you could hear was the sound of cutlery touching plates, occasional coughing and sneezing, and the rasping echo of chairs moving on the cobbled stone floor. Very quickly, I found myself enveloped by a terrible sense of foreboding. I felt as though the silence and the atmosphere of the room was drowning something vital inside me. The crushing weight of it felt tangible. I looked over to Pras and Ian, who seemed to have finished eating, and gestured to them that I was rather keen to leave. We all walked out very slowly and respectfully but the moment we'd closed the door behind us we skipped off – talking over each other in garbled desperate voices as though we'd been suffocating in the absence of the air of jokes and laughter.

We met up with Kim and decided to walk in the gardens to try to draw in some natural inspiration but I felt immediately and totally overwhelmed by fear. Sitting on a bench looking towards the Abbey, I mentioned my feelings to Pras and he agreed.

'I know! It feels so horrible here, doesn't it? There's something in this place that makes me feel so dark, I can't believe it. Brother Daniel is so friendly but this place . . . it feels cursed.'

Ian felt something too, but seemed less surprised. I felt so strange that I suggested we get our bags and do a runner. Kim looked at us all, grinned, and began shaking her head.

'We can't do that, it's not fair,' objected Ian, reasonably, considering the trouble the monks had taken to make us feel at home.

'Yes we can,' replied Pras with a steely determination I'd never seen in him before. 'This place is fucking weird.'

In retrospect, such a physical reaction to the Abbey is odd, not to mention rather rude and ungracious, but at the time there was no doubt in my mind that we should leave immediately. I couldn't bear the prospect of staying there overnight. It felt so cold, empty and desolate, despite the incredibly generous and welcoming Brother Daniel. I found this contrast unfathomable. I had no doubt about his genuine desire to make us feel at ease but it felt like we'd walked onto the set of *The Wicker Man*. I'd have put it down to simple paranoia if it had just been me, but Pras clearly felt something was wrong. We were so in-synch that at one point he leant over to me and said, 'Where's Christopher Lee? I keep expecting him to appear from the bushes.'

I went for a walk around the 'Garden of the Senses' to try to collect myself but everything around me seemed tainted by some kind of nervous fear. Pras was all for leaving there and then but we settled for heading up the road for a drink in a nearby pub, and the relief we felt on walking through the industrial estate and back down by the river was palpable. My state of mind had changed my perception of the Abbey and it's surroundings completely. We'd seen two enormous silver tanker lorries with 'Buckfast' emblazoned on the sides just behind the Abbey building. This is where the Buckfast Tonic drink that has caused so many problems in Scotland comes from. There have even been calls from politicians, notably Helen Liddell the former Secretary of State for Scotland, for 'Buckie', as it's known in Scotland, to be banned because of it's popularity with under age drinkers. Jack McConnell, Scotland's first minister, went on to describe it in the *Scotsman* as 'a seriously bad drink' pointing out that simply being seen carrying it was a 'badge of pride' among 'those involved in anti social behaviour'. Seeing the tankers parked up behind the Abbey made me wonder whether we'd stumbled on the kind of seemingly respectable hideout so popular with villains in James Bond movies.

Pras and I calmed down a little while we were out having a few beers. When we returned a few hours later, I started feeling rather guilty because by then I'd decided that it was, of course, very rude even to have contemplated doing a runner. So when I climbed into bed, wincing at the sight of so many crucifixes all over the room, I picked up the copy of *The Rules of St Benedict* that lay on my bedside table. This was the book they literally lived by and I decided to be as open-minded as I could while leafing through it.

Reading that book was the best thing I could have done in the circumstances. It focused the unknown, fearful and daunted air I'd felt all around me since arriving into something I could pin down and engage with. Fear, it seemed, was the order of that day and all other days spent in a St Benedictine monastery.

I should point out that despite a few brief snatches of conversation with Brother Daniel and a few of the others, we hadn't been able to interview any of the monks. Interviews were forbidden unless we'd cleared it with the Abbot first and no one was prepared to speak without his permission. But we were not interested in the official party line of the monastery. We wanted to find out why these men had chosen to live such an austere life. The rules stated that the Abbot is 'believed to hold the place of Christ in the monastery, since he is addressed by a title of Christ'. This perhaps explained why the monks we'd seen appeared to be so in awe, and fearful, of him. A few pages further on the rules outlined the subservience of all monks to the Abbot in even greater detail, in a way that rather left the door open for him to abuse his position – 'Obey the orders of the Abbot unreservedly, even if his own conduct – which God forbid – be at odds with what he says.' We'd spotted the newly appointed Abbot earlier, scuttling about in a rather daft-looking frock with penetrating eyes focused behind small glasses. All the brothers had seemed terrified of him. The rules also explained that the monks 'no longer live by their own judgment . . . they walk according to another's decisions and directions, choosing to live in monasteries and to have an Abbot over them'. If that wasn't subservient enough it went on to explain that they should 'live in fear of judgment day and have a great horror of hell . . . Day by day remind yourself that you are going to die.' Unbelievably, it got even more depressing – 'We absolutely condemn in all places any vulgarity and gossip and talk leading to laughter . . .' In utter disbelief, I began reading the steps to humility. 'The first step of humility, then, is that a man keeps the *fear*

of God always *before his eyes* and never forgets it. He must constantly remember everything God has commanded, keeping
in mind that all who despise God will burn in hell for their
sins . . . While he guards himself at every moment from sins
and vices of thought and tongue, of hand or foot, of self-will
or bodily desire, let him recall that he is always seen by God
in heaven, that his actions everywhere are in God's sight and
are reported by angels every hour.'

Every hour eh? Well that must take a hell (sorry) of a lot
of angels. It was all completely absurd and I was about to
throw the small red book on the floor in disgust, but I'd
promised myself to be open-minded and I was only 33 pages
into a 96-page book, so I decided to keep going just to
see how bad it got. The opening line of Chapter 48 read
'Idleness is the enemy of the soul.' At that point I growled
with anger. I was enraged. In my view, the only hope you
have of getting anywhere near to understanding your soul is
through idleness!

During your life you may have wondered why those who
seek to control the minds of others are so afraid of people
being 'idle' or 'doing nothing'. You see words such as
'layabout', 'work-shy', 'scrounger' in the newspapers all the
time, while government speeches from every political party
seem to be peppered with hateful rhetoric on those who dare
to be 'lazy'. It's little known that Hitler made 'idlers' wear a
black triangle on their clothes at all times to point them out,
along with Jews, homosexuals and every other group in society that didn't fit in with his murderous ideology. It seems to
me that every power structure of any kind that has ever
existed in humanity has been completely united on this one
single point. People should under no circumstances be
allowed to be idle. They must all be made to work. It makes
you wonder why they're so afraid of people lazing about

doing nothing, especially monks in monasteries, come to think of it, because no one has ever been anywhere near as idle as God. According to the Old Testament, he worked for six days and then decided to rest forever. Now that's a work ethic I admire. Aren't Christians supposed to believe that they were made in God's image? In which case why are all Christians (and governments of predominantly Christian countries) so obsessed with making us all work so hard? Why is it that those 'doing nothing' have always been so feared by people with power? I think it's because of what you're actually doing when you're doing nothing. If you think about it for a moment, when you're doing nothing, you are doing something. You're thinking and large power structures have never liked it when large groups of people have the time to stop and think. People who have time to stop and think start questioning those who lead them. People with time to think are liable to try to change things.

One of the few things we had managed to find out from Brother Daniel was how regimented the monk's time is and how busy they are kept for all hours of the day. It turns out that St Benedictine monks were among the first people to turn their backs on 'natural time' in the days before clocks became widespread, in favour of a new rigid linear structure, signalled by a series of bells, that enabled them to be more efficient and do more work.

Combine that obsessive work ethic with the state of fear they're supposed to constantly subject themselves to and you start to see these monks as powerless victims rather than reflective and learned men. I began to see them as ghosts haunting the Abbey rather than men living within it. I'm not sure how seriously these St Benedictine monks take *The Rules of St Benedict* because we weren't allowed to speak to any of them about it, but I was totally horrified by what I'd read in its pages. My idea of monastic life had been totally destroyed.

The next morning I woke in a more relaxed mood, having successfully punctured the bubble of fear I'd been trapped in the day before. It was my thirty-second birthday and it began much better than I could have hoped when Wilf sang 'Happy Birthday' for the first time down the phone to me at 7.05 a.m.

We left the Abbey grounds very quickly, all of us keen to get away from that dark place. Our rooms had envelopes so we could make a donation for being put up for the night. I was going to, but then Pras pointed out a large painting called 'Crossing the Brook' by a certain Mr Turner in the hallway and we concluded that they probably didn't really need the money. We all thanked Brother Daniel and shook him warmly by the hand as we left. I wondered whether we could get away with kidnapping him so we could spend the rest of the trip trying to undo the brainwashing he'd sub-jected himself to for the last twenty-nine years, but decided against it in the end. I felt sad for him that we hadn't been able to ask the kinds of questions that could have changed our view of his home. I imagine the reluctance of the Abbey to talk to the press came from being stung by people like us in the past, but this lack of engagement left us with the impression of how things appeared rather than the way it feels to them. No doubt they will feel this portrayal of their order and way of life is unfair – it's probably the very thing they are trying to protect themselves from – but it's how it was and how it felt to us when we were there.

I felt incredibly disillusioned but that is often the case when you discover the truth about the things and the people you project your admiration onto. As we drove away, I couldn't help thinking that if *The Rules of St Benedict* had been written by a man running a cult in California today, instead of by a 'St' in fifth- and sixth-century Italy, he'd have been gunned down by the CIA or chucked in prison by now.

(A few months later the reluctance of the Abbey seniors to speak, and perhaps our instinctive feelings of creepiness about the place, were explained when two of the Abbey's former monks were found guilty of abusing children. Paul Couch was sentenced to ten years and nine months in August and William Manahan, a former Prior known as 'Daddy Prior' was given a fifteen-month prison term in November.)

The world famous Burgh Island Hotel seemed a more attractive place to spend my birthday and so, after nearly getting caught up with a couple of Cornish swingers while scoffing a large and excellent carvery lunch in a pub on the edge of Buckfast (and bidding farewell to Kim – we planned to meet her in Penzance a week later should we get that far), we charged off towards the coast, aiming for mid-afternoon cocktails.

The Burgh Island Hotel, off Bigbury on Sea, was always going to be a highlight of the trip, and after Buckfast we needed a lift more than ever. The hotel is an art deco masterpiece, run by Deborah Clark. It's accessible by 'sea tractor', or boat at high tide. In the 1920s the hotel was a favourite haunt of Agatha Christie, who wrote *Murder under the Sun* while staying there. Noël Coward found it a home from home and, later, the Beatles used it as a bolthole to hide from overzealous fans. Winston Churchill is said to have met US President Eisenhower there to discuss secret operations in the run-up to the D-Day landings.

When we first spotted the island in the distance from the top of a hill in the village of Bigbury, I asked Pras what he made of it.

'You mean that's the hotel? Fuck-ing-hell!' He burst out laughing. 'No way! That's amazing!'

After getting a great deal of friendly attention from car-loads of teenagers on their way back from the beach, and having had to back up a few times on the narrow coastal road to let other vehicles pass, we parked The Mighty One in Deborah's space in a gated car park by the beach. We were soon accosted by a couple of the hotel's drivers, who looked like burly ex-SAS types. They were rather amused that we'd turned up in a milk float.

'You don't exactly believe in slumming it, do you?' one of them shouted as we were driven across the sand on the back of a trailer to the hotel.

Although we were not dressed for the occasion, we were welcomed warmly by Gary the barman, an *Idler* subscriber and creator of delicious and dastardly cocktails, and rather suspiciously by the hotel manager. After being shown to our beautiful and luxurious rooms, we headed down to the Pilchard Inn, a small pub on the island, as the tide chased away the holidaymakers, leaving us cut off as the air grew colder and an evening breeze began to stiffen.

Imagining we would not be able to eat in the hotel's restaurant because we didn't have the right kit, we put the thought of food out of our minds, only to find a table for three, with a red and white checked tablecloth and yellow flowers, laid out in the far corner of the Pilchard Inn. We would dine in style after all. Adopting Homer Simpson's wine-ordering technique – selecting the second cheapest bottle on the menu – turned out to be a good idea and we ended up polishing off four bottles between us during our second fabulous meal of the day. We drank on late into the night, and were regaled with stories of pirates and murder on the high seas by the hard-partying staff. Before becoming so popular with the élite of the 1920s, Burgh Island was a favoured home for smugglers, one of whom was shot by customs men on the steps of the inn itself.

I hobbled back to my room well after midnight and harrumphed onto the beautiful and spacious bed. Outside, waves crashed on the rocks below and I realized that for the first time in the entire trip, we'd been parted from our brave electric chariot. Perhaps we should have attempted to get her across but as it was she was spending the night in relative luxury herself. No doubt she was holding her own among the brash and exotic vehicles in the hotel's mainland car park.

16

Burgh Island to Landrake

32 miles

IAN

We had Dan to thank for arranging our free stay in the art deco magnificence of Burgh Island and what a treat that was. We awoke in a room facing the coastline of South Devon as the last waves retreated from the sandy causeway. Living just off the mainland on a tidal island has its own rhythm, a pace probably well understood by the monks who used to count this as their spiritual haven. In the modern world this tempo of life, forever at the mercy of the tide, could be regarded as an inconvenience, but to stay on an island like Burgh you just have to accept it as immutable fact. Once you have, it becomes a thing to celebrate and you find that surrendering to nature opens up another world. You can't go anywhere because the tide is in, so you make the most of staying where you are. It forces your hand. It's as if the act of making such a compromise is in itself the inspirational first step towards living a richer life.

Prasanth and I watched as the causeway gradually cleared and the hotel's Range Rovers began winding their way across the sand and back on missions to and from the mainland. From our vantage point on the balcony, even the intertwining tyre marks of four-wheel drives took on an aesthetic charm of their own.

Our room was gorgeous, furnished with genuine period pieces from the 1930s, including a fabulous art deco dressing table and a reproduction Bush radio. I was impressed with the attention to detail and care that had been taken over the tiniest finial and the most incidental of ornamentation. It was the real deal, and if this passage ends up in one of their brochures, so be it. It is richly deserved.

Whether the rich are so deserving is another question entirely. The uncompromising grandeur of the Burgh Island Hotel doesn't come cheap. The hotel is a commercial concern and the costs of providing such luxury, on top of the costs of keeping a world-class piece of architectural heritage in good health, must be considerable. The guests pay for all of this and, in effect, you could argue that the hotel is continuing in exactly the way that its original developers intended and that if it were to be run along different lines – say as a heritage attraction – it would inevitably be starved of funds somewhere along the way and quickly be lost to the ravages of time. It would also end up full of cheap guff, such as context boards and multimedia presentations, that would seek to bring it back to life while killing it stone dead. At least this way, when the revolution comes, it'll be a well-maintained wall for the toffs to line up against. That's a joke by the way, you know, like Plymouth Aquarium.

Halfway though the morning, we made our way across the long causeway to be reunited with our steed. Since we'd been separated by high tide as well as the ineffable whiff of luxury, The Mighty One had not been charged the night before, and Prasanth quickly looked into the charging possibilities while Dan and I shuffled to and fro to the beach café to provide him with cup after cup of full-strength coffee.

Fully caffeinated, Pras located a junction box in the parking shelter that ran the full length of one side of the Hotel's mainland car park. It was the only electrical possibility on offer, so it was a relief when, ten minutes later, the charger was humming away and nothing was on fire.

His work done, he adopted what was becoming his second default position, lying under the tarpaulins on the back of the float, dozing fitfully as the breeze flapped the fabric around him. At one point, unaware of the presence of electrical genius under the tarp, Dan started to rummage around for one of his bags, only for Pras to sit bolt upright like a swami interrupted from a particularly far-off astral flight.

'What . . . er wha . . . hey man.'

'I'm just getting my bag – sorry, I didn't know you were there.'

'Oh, I thought you were someone messing around with the charging cable. It's a bit delicate.'

'Really? Oh, OK.' Dan laughed, a little nervously.

'Yeah, you see that?' said Pras, pointing to a strip of copper in the junction box. 'You touch that, you die.'

It's fair to say that Dan found this deeply shocking.

A couple of hours later, we set off to face the ludicrous hills we had driven over to get here from Modbury. Yesterday, in the village Co-op, without any chatter about our strange journey and with the milk float safely out of view, an assistant had come up to me and simply wished us 'good luck' with our endeavour – presumably, because a number of local papers were carrying coverage of our progress. That was really rather nice, especially in this greenest of villages. Modbury had recently made the papers for its outright ban of plastic carrier bags. This time we passed through without stopping, on our way to Plymouth and beyond.

Down here in the allegedly sleepy south-west, Plymouth

was easily the largest city on our route. Home to nearly a quarter of a million souls, it is the second largest urban area in the south-west after Bristol, and a cultural and economic centre for both Devon and Cornwall.

The place is most famous for its long and esteemed nautical history, achieved by virtue of its position at the estuaries of the Plym and Tamar, which together form an exceptionally large natural harbour and this naval prominence continues today. Plymouth is the largest naval base in Western Europe and, beyond tourism, the city's fortunes are heavily influenced by the presence of the Royal Navy at Devonport. Historic maritime sites around Plymouth include the Mayflower Steps on the Barbican, from where the Pilgrim Fathers sailed for the New World in 1620, while the Hoe is the setting for the probably apocryphal story of Sir Francis Drake playing bowls while the Armada sailed up the Channel. Although almost certainly untrue, this story does at least hint at a character flaw in the privateer Drake, who is known to have put personal business before duty on a number of occasions, once leaving his fleet to flounder in disarray while he ransacked the Spanish galleon *Rosario* for his own profit.

As a major naval port, Plymouth was extensively bombed during the Blitz. The attacks were not confined to the port. Much of the city centre was levelled and over a thousand civilians were killed. After the war, the city was rebuilt in the modernist style, which, while not to everyone's taste, does lend it a spacious air with its wide pedestrianised streets.

In Plymouth, we were due to meet up with Stuart Billingshurst, the man who sold us The Mighty One in the first place, and we headed straight for the centre, swinging south at the last minute to navigate our way through the back streets of Stonehouse to Stuart's house in the south-western corner of the city. He had seen us coming and as we parked

The Mighty One he threw a long armoured cable out of an upstairs window. Stuart was an old hand at charging the float. He'd had her for a couple of years, tending to her every electrical need and using her every day to commute to work. As such a seasoned driver of The Mighty One, and therefore privy to her interesting little foibles, we wondered what he thought of our trip.

'I wasn't expecting you to get here quite so quickly,' he told us. 'I had no doubt in my mind that it would be possible, but it's June now and I didn't expect to see you until September. I hadn't taken account of the fact that you would be stealing electricity left, right and centre at all times of the day and night along the way.'

On the float's suitability for shorter trips, he was quite certain, however.

'My wife used the car to get to work, so it was either the float or the bus, and the float turned out to be the more environmentally friendly option – we've got a carbon-neutral energy supplier, so our electricity is green. The fact it goes at 15 miles per hour is neither here nor there. A couple of weeks before I got the float, I used the car to go to work and had the GPS on – the volume of traffic and the traffic lights, meant my average speed was 15 miles per hour anyway. Driving in the float, I would get to the first set of traffic lights, all the cars would rush off when they went green and I would just roll up behind them at the next set, and so on all the way to work. I was doing a steady speed, so I would sometimes actually get to work faster in the float than I would do in the car.'

The other benefit for commuting is that when you are stopped in traffic, you are using no energy at all, unlike all the cars idling around you. About town commuting is as ideal a use for an electric vehicle like ours as the local delivery it was built for — the small distances involved are more or less in keeping with the daily burden of a milk round and the restricted speed is actually a benefit where pedestrians and other vulnerable road users are present. Electric vehicles have, as we found out from Stuart, been considered for more exotic uses, however.

'I do know of somebody who wanted to take the workings of a milk float and use them to power a Land Rover. And the military have played with the idea of a Land Rover that has both the normal diesel engine and batteries in the back — the batteries are so that they can sneak up on the enemy when they're almost in position. There were at least fifty made and I know, through the Land Rover Owners' Club, that at least one of their members has acquired one.'

'I like the idea of electric vehicles, because it's simple. The first cars were not petrol driven. The first cars were electric. Sixty years ago there were more electric than petrol vehicles on the road. The only problem, as you've found out, is charging them — you can't expect people to go to the equivalent of a petrol station in the future and sit around for two hours to charge up their vehicle.'

Stuart's solution is to think in terms of battery exchanges on a garage forecourt, or to find some chemical way of recharging a battery, to bring it into line with the process of filling a tank with petrol.

'There are some conspiracy theories out there that say the technology already exists, but is owned by the car companies, which are, in turn, owned by the petrochemical companies.'

Those petrol companies more or less control most of the market in terms of transport, surely, so what hope is there for the electric car in the future? Did Stuart think that most people would be driving battery-powered vehicles any time soon?

'It's feasible that electric vehicles will play a significant role in our transportation needs of the future, but you forget that petrol cars aren't the only cars on the road at the moment. There's diesel engines, which don't just run on diesel. In fact, diesel engines, as invented by Mr Diesel, were around long before diesel fuel. He demonstrated one at the French Exhibition, running on peanut oil.'

This is something of a salient point as we start to come full circle with the idea of bio-diesel. As far as Diesel himself was concerned, bio-diesel was the norm. The last century of heavy oil fuel for diesel engines has been something of an environmentally catastrophic aberration.

Stuart highlighted another environmental aspect of electric vehicles that is often overlooked – their durability.

'Your float is fifty years old and still going because the drive mechanism is very simple. Electric vehicles don't go wrong. There isn't much on them to go wrong because they are only made of a few parts. Car manufacturers make quite a lot of money selling spare parts – new engines, new seals, new this, new that – but there's little to sell in the way of parts for electric vehicles, which affects the profits of the car companies, which in turn affects the profits of the petro-chemical companies. They don't get to sell you the fuel, either.'

If what Stuart says is true, the car that you think you own is merely rented out to you on a lease that automatically expires every time you empty the tank or something breaks.

By this point, we had been at Stuart's for at least two hours, the sky was greying over and time was getting on, so we decided to move on without allowing the charge to complete – it was a trade-off between letting the batteries equalize and potentially driving in the dark, or just going right now and getting into Cornwall in time to camp in the half light.

I have a fairly incomplete knowledge of exactly how Plymouth is structured, and the map wasn't a lot of use on its own, so I blended the ignorance to come up with a halfway decent route out of the city that avoided most of the main roads. Unfortunately, it didn't manage to avoid all the hills, so our charge quickly dropped back to its pre-top-up level. In my defence, we were due to cross over into Cornwall via the Tamar Bridge, the road deck of which is at a height of a hundred feet, so were always going to have to climb a hill of some sort to get into Cornwall.

It's befitting for a county such as Cornwall, which was once at the cutting edge of industrial development, that when the Tamar Bridge was built, it was ahead of its time. In October 1961 the bridge opened to traffic as the first major suspension bridge to be built since the war, and the longest in the United Kingdom. In 2001, structural improvements made it the first suspension bridge in the world to be widened by using cantilevers and the first bridge of any kind in the world to be widened and strengthened without once being closed to traffic.

I always feel a tremor of pride when I cross the Tamar with friends. You don't live somewhere for nearly twenty years without absorbing something from it, and Cornwall has such a strong identity it's impossible not to get involved with it at every level you can. At the highest point of the Tamar Bridge I can confidently assert that not only are you leaving Devon, but also England. Cornwall is British, but only in as much as Wales or Scotland are British. The haggling over its exact constitutional status is not as cut and dried as it may at first appear.

Detractors of the idea of a Cornish nation point out that Cornwall is merely another English county, but it's far murkier than that. It is actually a Duchy, in much the same way as Wales is a Principality, and, coincidentally, the Prince of Wales and the Duke of Cornwall are one and the same man. Historically, the Duchy of Cornwall was similar in administrative and judicial structure to a County Palatine – an autonomous area run, by permission of the sovereign, as a separate country but loyal to the Crown.

The jury is still out, debate is ongoing and there are good legal and constitutional arguments on both sides, but the reason why I regard Cornwall as a separate entity is because of something far less tangible – its sheer presence.

Pottering into the first Cornish town – Saltash, immediately west of the bridge – you don't get much hint of that essential Cornishness. It grows in power the farther west you go. Indeed, I got into a moderate amount of controversy as the co-author of the *Buzz Guide to Cornwall* because of my description of Saltash as a dormitory town for Plymouth and, referring to the Tamar Bridge and Isambard Kingdom Brunel's unique rail bridge next to it, my assertion that the most interesting thing about Saltash is the way out. The thing about Saltash being a dormitory town wasn't intended as an insult; it's just that most people who live in Saltash work or study in Plymouth. It's not exactly a suburb of its Devonian neighbour, but the night life and work opportunities available next door, across the Tamar, mean that Saltash is always going to play second fiddle.

We bypassed Saltash anyway – by which I mean we didn't drive up the high street, even though we saw some of the fringes. We needed to find somewhere to camp for the night and time was moving on. Coming out the other side, we were at last in the country again. This part of Cornwall has a lot in common with Devon in terms of landscape. The hills are buxom affairs with steep climbs that gradually round out towards the top. The valleys are deep, the hills are long and we alternated between the foothills of some moor one moment and almost sea level the next. This was on the A38, a three-lane road that takes all of Cornwall's traffic in and out of Plymouth, in the late rush hour, and while it was not the worst road we had travelled on in terms of the amount of traffic, The Mighty One found the hills challenging.

A few miles out of Saltash, we came upon a campsite, drove in and were immediately halted by a red and white barrier of the sort you would expect to find in a supermarket car park. A bungalow by the barrier was the only place in evidence where a reception area might be located, so I followed various arrows around the building to a side porch, where a mobile number was displayed for late arrivals. The mobile number rang and rang. I'm sure I heard it ringing inside, beyond the veil of net curtains, so I tried the doorbell. Nobody answered. I walked around a bit, walked back, and saw someone inside. More importantly, he saw that I had seen him. He looked a little disgruntled but opened the door.

'Yes?' he said in a way that I can't bring myself to describe as friendly.

'Hello,' I replied. 'Do you have any electric pitches?'

'What, for that?' he asked, pointing at the milk float. He clearly wasn't expecting to see such a thing parked on his pristine tarmac drive.

'Er . . .'

Just at that point, Dan wandered over.

'What amperage are your electric pitches?' he asked, reflecting the conversation we had been having on and off in the float for the last two weeks.

'No, we're full,' said our man, and pointed in a generally westward and specifically off his caravan park direction. 'There's another site just up by Landrake.'

I was taken aback by the abruptness, but tried to rescue my dignity by asking a question that hinted at some local knowledge and gave him a chance to redeem himself by actually being helpful. 'Is that Dolbeare Holiday Park?'

'Look, I don't know, it's up there, by Landrake.' Just fuck off, will you? You're making my life really complicated with all your specific questions. We agreed that was the subtext and left his stupid campsite, with its ASDA car park barrier and dairyphobic prejudice, and repaired to a local lay-by, where we discussed the possibilities.

We agreed to go for Dolbeare Holiday Park, purely on the basis that I dimly remembered once designing their website when I worked for a company that did that kind of thing. They didn't know me from Adam. I'd never visited or met the owners, but I remembered that the park seemed to be biggish and set in nice countryside. And it was away from the sea, which made it both cheaper and much less likely to be a tourist tat hole. The problem was that we had a dwindling charge and an epic hill to climb to get to it.

We dawdled up Landrake Hill. It was getting to early evening by now and the midges and flies were swirling about in little random pockets as we climbed the hill. The road wound round a long bend to a height of about 300 feet in less than half a mile – it wasn't so much the steepness but the length that was draining the battery. At the top we managed to turn right, despite heavy and fast traffic travelling the other way. We were still half a mile away from the site and it was still uphill.

We limped into Dolbeare eventually, the light almost gone. The owner was perfectly pleasant and didn't have an irrational fear of milk floats. All was well on our very first night in Cornwall.

17

Landrake to Camelford

48 miles

DAN

We were five hundred miles from Lowestoft, having been on the road for nearly three weeks, and that morning Pras finally got round to getting the stereo in the cab working. Our solar panels on the roof had been powering mobile chargers and Ian's laptop for a few days, so we weren't entirely useless, but I did feel that now we were technologically getting into the swing of things it was a shame our journey was set to end so soon. On the other hand, I was getting thoroughly cheesed off with driving. I'd never expected driving a vintage electric vehicle for four hours a day for twenty-one days to be a greater feat of endurance than entering the Le Mans 24-hour race, but so things were beginning to prove. I was particularly concerned that my 'milkman's arse' affliction might have caused long-lasting nerve damage in the lower reaches of my body because my legs were developing pins and needles with alarming regularity. I decided to look up the incidence of milkmen suffering from deep vein thrombosis when I finally got back home.

Now that we were in Cornwall, whatever happened no one could doubt that our adventure had been a formidable achievement, and the aim of the day was to head for Tintagel – the supposed birthplace of King Arthur. It was one of the places I'd been very keen to visit all along, even though it was miles out of our way. Now we were so close to the end, we decided to throw caution to the wind and head north across the eastern flank of Bodmin Moor.

We left the campsite at the uncharacteristically early hour of 9.15 a.m. and after eight miles stopped in Callington, a small town, hoping to find a cute little café or a gut-wrenchingly awful, but nevertheless brilliant, greasy spoon for a well-earned breakfast. We ended up being the youngest patrons, by about fifty years, of a Co-op café. The fry-up was good, though, although for seemingly the hundredth time Ian asked for tomatoes with his breakfast, hoping to get nice halved grilled ones, only to find, when his plate arrived, he'd been given a dollop of tepid tinned tomato slime. Our departure was delayed by a photographer from the *Cornish Times* who asked us to do circuits of the car park for ten minutes, but at least he had proper equipment, unlike the photographer we'd met on the outskirts of Exeter. Then it was on to Launceston for a midday charge.

Ian knew so much about Cornwall, and had so many memories of living there, that every innocent little question Pras and I asked him as we drove along unleashed a torrent of anecdotes and stories. My favourite is the one about the time two of his friends drove all the way back to Penzance from London during a rain storm in a Volkswagen Beetle that had no windscreen. Apparently, they decided it would be wise to wear bin liners for the duration of the journey. Such anarchic craziness seemed to be the accepted way of doing things in deepest darkest Cornwall.

As Bodmin Moor loomed ahead later that afternoon, it occurred to me that this was a part of the country that might still hold a few secrets for us to discover. If there is anything truly unexplained or mysterious left in Britain, this is where you're most likely to stumble across it. It was then that I hatched a plan that soon had Pras and Ian chortling. Five minutes later we'd all agreed to go on our first 'night journey' to try to find evidence for my favourite modern British mystery – the Beast of Bodmin Moor.

At first glance it may seem absurd to go hunting for pumas in a 1958 electric milk float but we'd already discovered that, when it comes to wildlife, what The Mighty One lacked in speed she more than made up for in stealth. What better mode of transport to use when stalking mythical pumas on the back roads of Bodmin Moor than a quiet electric vehicle? It was decided. After visiting Tintagel we would head back to Bodmin and embark on our first nocturnal ramble to see what beasts we could find.

Before that, though, we wanted to stop for a cream tea. Ten miles outside Launceston, on the A395, a ramshackle, hand-painted sign pointing down someone's driveway offered the fabled heart-attack snack. We were not far from Tintagel and the batteries were holding up well so we pulled in off the road, much to the delight of thirty-seven cars and lorries that had backed up impatiently behind us. I parked and we followed a pathway that led to the backdoor of a small pink house. Not really sure what to do next, I peered in through the window and felt for the handle to see if the door would open. It did and we found ourselves standing in a complete stranger's empty kitchen. I thought how trusting these people must be – we could easily have been up to no good. I then found myself thinking about an old episode of *Tales of the Unexpected* in which such 'innocence' masked a far more sinister truth. It began with a man arriving by train and leaving the station to walk down a road full of guesthouses as the opening credits and that famous tune crackled across the screen. The first few places he tried were full up, because of a conference that he was also attending. Somebody suggested that another house just down the road that used to offer bed and breakfast could be worth a try. The man knocked on the door of this unmarked house and was greeted by a friendly old woman who immediately engaged him in polite conversation. He went to sign the guest book and was surprised to find just two other names, one from January the year before and the other from March two years before that.

The landlady appeared soon after with tea and cakes. She chattered away about her two other guests 'who never seemed to want to leave' and the man found himself quaffing tea politely while she enquired about his profession, how long he would be staying and what time he'd need to be woken in the morning. The man suddenly began to feel incredibly cold and tired and was soon ushered up the stairs to his room. When he got there he found he could barely move his legs but the old woman cajoled him into a bed by the door and began tucking him in tenderly. At this point the camera pulled back to reveal two embalmed corpses wearing make-up in the two other beds in the room. The man, now paralysed with fear and whatever his tea had been poisoned with, fought to remain conscious while the landlady kissed him on his forehead before closing the door behind her and calling out 'goodnight'. As the man lost consciousness and breathed his last in terror, the familiar *Tales of the Unexpected* theme began once again.

When someone eventually appeared in the kitchen of the pink house, I was relieved to see a thoroughly normal looking man who gestured to a table in the garden and told us his wife would come and take our order soon. Ian chose a table next to a red toilet the lid of which was left open so the shrubs planted in the bowl had somewhere to grow, while I mentally relaxed, confident that we were unlikely to be poisoned and kept embalmed in a bed, wearing make-up, beneath a flowery duvet any time soon.

Meanwhile, juggernauts were thundering along the road on the other side of the hedge, a mere five metres from where we sat. The noise was so loud that we had to wait for the traffic to pass throughout our conversation. Had I known at the time that Pras was about to have his first-ever cream tea, I would probably have suggested a more picturesque and authentic location, but Ian was dismissive when discovering the news.

'What do you mean more authentic? Having an English cream tea right next to a dual carriageway is as authentic as you can get! Apart from having an English cream tea next to a dual carriageway in the pouring rain.'

Pras was just surprised we were getting any food. 'I thought it was just tea with cream in it,' he remarked. A few moments later his eyes widened with delight when six scones were placed in front of us, along with a tub of jam and a cauldron of thick, clotted cream. 'Wicked, man!'

I have often thought that cream teas are the ultimate achievement of the English nation. I love the fact that tearooms are synonymous with pensioners, as though the old and infirm, having spent their lives experiencing everything that the world has to offer, have collectively come to the conclusion that nothing is more enjoyable than eating cakes and drinking tea; either that or it's simply a means of voluntary euthanasia, achieved via the ingestion of so much clotted cream.

The tea finished, the scones devoured, we were all left feeling slightly sick. Pras, especially, looked a little green.

'I feel ill. I think I've eaten too much,' he groaned.

'Feeling sick after eating a cream tea means you've had exactly the right amount,' I told him, reassuringly.

The final stretch of the road to Tintagel took in some of the most breathtaking terrain, most of which was peppered with majestic modern windmills. I've never understood how anyone can complain about the sight of such engineering miracles. Anyone campaigning to stop such fantastic renewable energy systems should be made to visit Sellafield or Didcot and imagine power stations like those behind their back gardens instead. No doubt NIMBYs hassled Brunel about his bridges 'ruining' the view.

An hour or so later we arrived at the bottom of the village and Ian guided us to a car park where the path to the famous castle on the coast began. It was by now a perfect summer's evening with warm sun and a light breeze. As we made our way down the gravel path, a woman in a Land Rover called out, 'There are basking sharks in the sea. Have a look when you're down there,' but we were waylaid by an English Heritage information poster. Apparently, a concerted campaign by the locals in the early 1900s to prevent development on the site resulted in Tintagel being the first property acquired by English Heritage. So we doffed our caps to the environmental campaigners of the 1900s and walked slowly down to the steps that led up to the ruin of Tintagel castle itself.

When we arrived at the entrance at 6.05 p.m. on that lovely June evening, we found that the castle was closed. None of us could quite handle this news and I became particularly incensed. How could it be closed so early on such a beautiful summer's day? There was nothing we could do apart from sit looking across the cove and out to sea, listening to the water smack onto the rocks far below and the yelp of seagulls above.

Sunlight hit the northern half the beach and the water appeared to be Caribbean blue, something ascribed to the copper content of the slate that makes up the rocky coastline. We sat there for some time, soaking in the undoubted wildness of the place – the rocks and walkways were all dotted with signs warning of impending geological doom. Despite the sense of wildness, wooden walkways of touristification, like metal braces in a teenaged mouth, almost but not quite managed to hide the natural beauty. You could easily imagine howling winds and mysterious shapes merging in the twilight, but that evening it was all laughing sunbathers and congealed ice creams. A few divers appeared to photograph the basking sharks, which I was alone in not being able to spot. There was much excitement, and the whoop of wildlife enthusiasts echoed up from the beach below.

Sitting there, I couldn't decide whether to return the following morning to see the famous castle – a medieval ruin that stood on top of the supposed Arthurian castle of legend. The view of the surrounding area would be largely the same in full daylight, but it was the spirit of the place that felt most enticing and I was beginning to sense it simply sitting there on the cliff. I decided to settle for the Tintagel of my imagination, seeing as the Arthurian stuff was probably disappointingly fictional anyway. I also thought it was appropriate for our journey to have come all that way only to leave that particular tourist box unticked. I reasoned it would be more fun arriving there with Wilf in a few years' time. It would be more likely to preserve its magic if I looked at it through his blissfully childish eyes.

I once had a Benson-and-Hedges-smoking evangelist art teacher who told his class of bemused thirteen year olds that if you spend your life walking round staring at the pavement looking for 50ps, you might not spot all the £1 coins hidden along with them. I'm not sure I would actually, but sitting on that cliff I began to understand what it was that he meant. Had the castle been open, we wouldn't have stopped and sat on that precipice for so long, and it was so beautiful and calm we'd soon resolved to stay there for as long as we possibly could.

Sadly, this moment of placid reflection was disturbed by the most contemptible kind of traveller the world has ever known. He arrived a little while after we did with what looked like his infirm parents, and immediately dashed off down the hundreds of little steps to the beach, changing this serene spot that was minding its own business as a place of staggering beauty into little more than a spreadsheet he felt compelled to complete. I saw his ugly red T-shirt at the bottom and then he turned and ran all the way back up to the top, taking a moment to look at me breathlessly, with an air of self-congratulation on his face, while puffing through his grinning mouth. His poor parents, meanwhile, humoured him by asking if he had got all the way to the bottom. The imbecile replied in a booming voice that was aimed at everyone within a half mile, 'YES, YOU CAN SEE MY FOOTPRINT DOWN THERE! LOOK! I DID IT!'

Happily, this interruption was short-lived and the three of them soon left. I prayed desperately for him to catch some bizarre and rare life-threatening disease by the time he got back to the car park. He was a 'box ticker' if ever I've seen one, treating this wonderful place as just another vapid experience on his production line of an existence. He was the kind of person who visits the pyramids purely to have his photograph taken next to them so he can show off about it afterwards. I do wonder sometimes whether modern travel is merely an exercise in this kind of grandiose box ticking.

The world certainly seems to have been reduced to a list of places you 'have to see' before you die, as though merely seeing them gives you any kind of insight or experience from which you can learn something meaningful. In some ways, the modern disease of over-consumption is more prevalent in the world of travel than designer shoes. The point seems to be working through the sites of the globe rather than allowing your mind to wallow in a new experience. How often do you see people abroad looking at what they've come to see through a video camera? They're not even really there when they are there! They're just recording a fraction of everything they were too blind to see at the time. Perhaps, when they watch the results at home, some of their trip might begin to make sense.

Travel is the thing we do when we're not at work, but because work has become such an integral part of our lives, some of us approach it as though it was just another job. Modern 'fast' holidays seem to be either an exercise in sight-seeing for the sake of it, or just a simple anaesthetic to take our minds of work. Anaesthetic holidays – lying on a beach for two weeks and drinking too much – have their place. I enjoy them often enough myself, but for some of us, this is the only travel experience we ever get.

By contrast, taking your time to get somewhere allows you to adjust to your destination so that when you arrive you are actually in a different *mental* place. This is something I discovered when travelling to Poland to be best man at my mate Henry's wedding eight years ago. It was my first experience of slow travel. Everyone I knew thought I was mad when I told them I was going to get to Warsaw by train.

When my rail trip began to go wrong, I had a few doubts myself but soon these 'disasters' began to turn my concept of what it actually means to travel on its head. An IRA terror-

ist decided to fire a mortar rocket at MI5 the morning my
Eurostar was due to leave. Consequently, my train was rather
late, I missed all my connections and found myself stranded
in Cologne station at midnight reading *The Day of the Jackal*
while being stalked by the world's worst pickpocket.
Fortunately, I managed to talk myself onto a train to Berlin
via Hamburg, and awoke at dawn, in an uncomfortable seat,
to see a horizon peppered with cranes beneath an orange
glow. From Berlin I caught a connection to Warsaw, and as
the train rolled into Poland, it passed through fields where
stout men were dragging their heels behind horse-drawn
ploughs and stations filled with men wearing 'Fast Tony'
style grey suits. I chatted to a soldier on the run from
Germany, gave an impromptu English lesson to a mother and
her ten-year-old-son and even shared my carriage with a
goat. I'd read that the stretch of the line we were travelling on
formed part of Jonathan Harker's journey into Transylvania
in Bram Stoker's *Dracula*, and the view from the window had
hardly changed since so many Jews snatched a glimpse of it
on their way to the death camps during the Second World
War, which gave the thick woodland an air of menace. My
expedition was altering my state of mind because the relative
slowness of rail travel was giving me time to acclimatize to
my surroundings.

I arrived in Warsaw somewhat bleary eyed after a thirty-
hour journey, six hours later than planned. The station was
the kind of brutal concrete communist Lubyanka that awoke
fear and suspicion in my middle-class eyes, despite the smiles
and friendliness all around me. I hailed a taxi and, as we drove
through the new developments of Warsaw, found myself
once again among the trappings of Western life, lurid signs
for Coca-Cola and McDonalds jostling for position with
Sony and Holiday Inn.

At my luxury hotel, which was filled with Western businessmen, I immediately bumped into a friend who was also attending the wedding. He'd been in London just five hours earlier, having, more sensibly in his eyes, chosen to fly. He laughed at my dishevelled appearance and told me how eccentric I had become. But standing in the lobby of that hotel, I could see that he wasn't really in Poland. Not really. He was in a building of the kind he saw everyday at home. He had travelled through a wormhole that began in a taxi outside his flat, took him to an aeroplane in which he was entertained by his favourite television shows, and delivered him in another taxi to this Western hotel. He had no conception of the country he had entered. Neither, perhaps, did I, but at least I had the grace to be aware of that fact. From that moment, I began to understand that all the things that make travel so wonderful have gradually been extracted from the process in the name of ease and convenience. We've become so obsessed with travel being easy and quick that we're in danger of forgetting what it actually means. Well to hell with ease and convenience, I want to *live* instead.

This ease of travel could also account for our lack of respect for the environment and the planet generally. Our ability to 'conquer it' by being able to visit anywhere we like at will could be the very thing that hides what we are looking for when we arrive. As well as restoring the magic of travel, taking a more meandering approach might result in us having more respect for the places we visit. And bearing in mind the energy crisis that Clive warned us about, it seems our addiction to the unhealthy 'fast' kind of travel will be far too expensive for all but the richest people in the world in the not too distant future anyway. In which case, I've seen the future of travel – the future of travel is slow.

We eventually made our way to the car park and, after hanging around staring at scenery for a bit longer, decided to head back towards Bodmin to find a campsite. We ended up in a holiday park called Juliot's Well in Camelford, and immediately began to boost the batteries for our night on the prowl. At eleven, we crept out into the darkness and I explained to my companions why I hadn't, entirely, been joking when I'd suggested we might find ourselves a puma.

In case you're of the view that those who claim to have spotted pumas in the British countryside are the kinds of people who believe in the Loch Ness monster, the evidence for big cats living in Britain is more compelling than you think. My personal view echoes that of Defra (Department for Environment, Food and Rural Affairs). While Defra will happily go on record as saying that the Loch Ness Monster is a load of old tosh, one of their spokesmen pointed out in 1991 that 'Defra are not denying that there are big cats out there'. There are many theories about these mysterious cats. Some believe they are a modern interpretation of the 'black dogs' mentioned throughout British history all over the country, and by, among others, William Cobbett in his travel book *Rural Rides*, published in 1830. In the case of pumas living in the British countryside, the most widely accepted theory relates to the 'Dangerous Animals Act' of 1976. Prior to that, people in Britain were allowed to keep big cats as pets, but with this new legislation came the need for registration and expensive permits for anyone wanting to keep such animals at home. Instead of paying these expensive fees, giving the animals to a zoo, or having them put down by a vet, many people released them into the wild. Some people will have you believe that these released cats adapted well to their new environment and mated.

Rather than get caught up in whether big cats do live in the wild in Britain or not, which is impossible to ascertain without proof, it is surely reasonable to see whether they *could* exist in Britain, and if they could, explain why they remain so elusive. Britain certainly has the perfect habitat for pumas, if that's what they are. Scotland, Cornwall, Devon and Dorset provide plenty of food, bearing in mind the number of deer, sheep and game that live in the countryside. But surely someone would have been able to track and film such creatures if they did exist in Britain? Well, that depends on whom you ask.

Hugh Miles knows more than most when it comes to filming the rarest animals on the planet. He is one of the few people on Earth to have tracked and filmed the snow leopard and has spent years in the wilds of South America filming pumas. His camera work has appeared in some of the most well-known wildlife programmes of the last thirty years, including *Life on Earth*, *The Private Life of Plants*, *Life in the Freezer*, *The Living Planet*, *Silent Roar: Searching for the Snow Leopard*, *Cheetah Story*, *Puma: Lion of the Andes* and even *A Passion For Angling*, the seminal eighties BBC fishing documentary series narrated by Bernard Cribbins and co-presented by a certain Chris Yates. I met Hugh one afternoon a few years ago when he came with Chris and I to watch Southampton FC. He told me a few interesting stories about the way big cats behave in the wild, and his thoughts on whether pumas could really be living in Britain. Apparently, when he spent months alone filming them out in the Andes, Hugh began to sense when pumas were nearby, even though he rarely saw them until they were very close – close enough at one point for him to wake up in the jungle to find a female puma breathing over his face. The fact he wasn't eaten proves that he'd managed to get closer to them in the wild than most have attempted before or since. News that Hugh is in tune with a 'sixth sense' might sound a little far-fetched but I don't know anyone with enough experience in this field to disagree with him. Hugh told me that over the years he has learned how to tell when a puma is watching him, and he hasn't sensed them only in the remotest parts of the Andes. As a keen fisherman, he often finds himself in isolated places in the British countryside at night, and on more than one occasion he's felt the sensation that he attributes to a puma. Conclusive? Perhaps not, but undeniably compelling when coming from a man as experienced with pumas as Hugh Miles.

But if big cats are living among us, surely we'd have discovered them by now? To answer that, Hugh mentioned another story, this time about his involvement in filming a leopard that was being moved from one safari park in South Africa to another. The convoy of support vehicles, and the one carrying the leopard, had to pass through the suburbs of Johannesburg and, to cut a long story short, the vehicle carrying the leopard crashed and the animal escaped. Suburbia was not exactly the ideal place for a wild cat to be on the loose, so they warned local people not to leave their homes and installed traps all over the area in the hope that they might catch it overnight. The next morning they were very disappointed not to have caught the leopard they'd lost, but rather surprised to find that they'd caught seven other big cats instead. Unbeknownt to the locals, these cats had been living in their midst for some time. That proves big cats are very well adept at hiding from human beings, even in built-up areas, so perhaps it's not surprising that no one has been able to get conclusive footage of them living in the wildest parts of Britain.

However, if the idea of such creatures living in Britain still seems too outlandish, consider the story of the man attacked by a large black cat in his back garden in Sydenham, a few miles south from where I live near Peckham in south London. According to the BBC, 'Anthony Holder said a six-foot long black animal pounced, knocked him to the ground, then mauled him with its claws for about thirty seconds. He said, "I am six foot and weigh fifteen stone and it was considerably stronger and bigger than me. The thing was huge" . . . he was scratched all over his body and suffered swelling and bruising to his hand and the back of his head . . . The Metropolitan Police . . . have warned people not to approach the animal and keep pets inside.'

When I'd finished telling Pras and Ian these anecdotes, they suddenly became rather concerned that we might actually come across something.

'I wouldn't fancy my chances driving around a safari park in The Mighty One. These fibre-glass doors aren't exactly protective,' Ian pointed out. 'If we do find a puma, there's a good chance we might get eaten. I don't want to be eaten, Dan.'

'I think we should go back to the campsite now,' Pras added seriously.

As it was, we didn't get very far on our search anyway. We'd used the lights briefly before, but in the pitch-black rural night they were about as effective as two million people marching to protest against an illegal war. We buzzed along for a while but the illumination was so feeble I drove straight into a hedge.

For any would-be David Attenboroughs out there, on the verge of buying a fleet of vintage milk floats, I have to tell you that they are not the ideal puma-stalking vehicles after all.

18
Camelford to Carnon Downs

49 miles

IAN

After a slightly draughty night in the tent, we surfaced in time to make our way into Camelford for a spot of lunch. It's interesting how our grip on time was now so loosened that we'd started to get up ready for some coffee-based faffing about and lunch. To be fair on ourselves, it's a measure also of the sheer inconveniences of life on the road – you must dismantle your temporary home, unpack the coffee pot, kettle and stove, then pack them up again when you've used them, pack away the tents, and tie everything down with luggage straps under the tarpaulin. I challenge anyone to do all that in under six hours. It's only because we've become so efficient that we can do it in less than, say, five.

Camelford hasn't strayed far beyond the main road it grew up on. Finding a place to eat was therefore a breeze, but that was after we'd been into a curious pub along the way, tempted by the promise of a hearty lunch, as advertised on the blackboards outside. Walking in through a side door of the Darlington Inn, we were immediately confronted by a carpet so insanely gaudy it made the focus of my eyes alternate between all the different wavelengths of light reflected from it. As a consequence, just looking at the floor was like going to a disco. We hobbled our way through with half a mind to cling onto the furniture as the carpet was jumping about so much, and came into the bar, which was rammed. This was clearly where the best beer in town was to be found, judging by the lengthy queue on a Wednesday lunchtime. And then, to a man – and I don't recall seeing any women in there – the entire pub turned around and looked at us as if we were three pumas off the moor. We followed suit and looked at one another, turned around and walked out, leaving them to their beers. Fortunately, we found the Four Seasons café across the road and had a rather lovely and proper Cornish lunch of pasties and chips.

After that feast, we continued on our way via a little back road out of Camelford towards the town of Bodmin. After that, we were going on towards the Eden Project – one of the few fixed points on our journey. We'd arranged it in advance, knowing that we would need to cross the central mass of Cornwall to get from Tintagel in the north to the south coast at some point, and it seemed like an interesting place to go.

The road from Camelford ran downhill alongside the River Camel and our progress to Bodmin was quite swift and light on the battery, which was a welcome relief. Having made such a detour to get to Tintagel, we needed to have another big day of travel to get back on track, and the Eden Project would otherwise have been right at the limit of our reach. From Bodmin we had to cross Hensbarrow Downs to get to Eden, but if that's a little too Ordnance Survey for you, I'll give you their local name – the Cornish Alps.

They're not called that for nothing, but it's because of their appearance rather than their height that the name has been coined. This area of Cornwall is the home of the local china clay industry and the alpine peaks are the eerily beautiful, roughly conical slag heaps of white spoil that has been left over from quarrying activities. Once you get close to them, you realize that they really ought to call the place 'the Cornish Moon', because it is one of the most surreal landscapes anywhere in the world.

The industry has declined somewhat over the years, but the spoil tips remain and on a clear day you can see them from miles around. Some of the old clay pits have been flooded, their white bases lending the water an odd blue-green appearance in the bright sunshine. But this hint at a lush tropical beach is deceptive. Very little grows or lives in these desert-like conditions.

We negotiated our way through a number of large villages that had the unmistakable look of mining communities – mostly smartly presented granite cottages with slate roofs, and one or two larger houses. Some village shops were surviving, scratching a living of some kind, I suppose, with a particular proliferation of butchers – at least, I hoped they were butchers. The signs above a couple of shops had the phrase 'meat surgeons' painted on them. Perhaps the shops are still there because these villages are just large enough to support independent traders but too small to be considered worth the while of the large supermarket chains.

Eventually, we turned off the road and followed some labyrinthine lanes, turning left here, right there, left again, until we came to a roundabout in the middle of nowhere and a large sign that told us we had arrived at our destination. I rang Ben Foster – my contact there – and he had some unexpected news. Apparently, a team from MTV had suddenly turned up to do some filming, so we were asked to wait in the car park while he sorted them out. By the time Ben arrived, we had spotted the MTV crew and they had spotted us, and before we knew it, we'd agreed to help them with some kind of link from our milk float. It turned out that the cameraman used to be a milkman and once had his very own Mighty One. What are the chances of that?

Ben interrupted the media whore luvvie-fest that had broken out in the Eden Project car park, and directed us to the electricity supply. We trundled off around some service roads and eventually found the correct building, but then faced an interesting problem. The woman who came out to help us was French and, although her grasp of English was far better than my phrase-book French, she was, curiously, unable to talk about electrical installations with any great confidence. She put us in touch with some techies, who guided us around the warren of buildings, discussing electrical possibilities. A likely looking socket housing attached to a corrugated steel wall raised our hopes, and we took some time carefully opening the thing up, only to find that there was absolutely nothing inside it. Luckily, we found another one around the corner of the same building, which served our needs.

The Eden Project is many things – an educational environmental charity that doesn't preach at you, Cornwall's boldest tourist attraction and host to the two largest greenhouses – at Eden they call them biomes – in the world. If you can, imagine a futuristic conservatory 200 metres long, 100 metres wide and 55 metres high, a greenhouse made out of an enormous piece of stretched bubblewrap where each air pocket is 9 metres wide, and a building that is high enough to hold the Tower of London or eleven double-decker buses arranged vertically. Imagine all that and then fill it with tropical plants. Better than that, make it a more or less self-sustaining habitat with crashing waterfalls, ponds, tropical birds and geckos. Then you still wouldn't be prepared for the sheer scale of Eden. And that's without adding the world's second largest conservatory next door to it to house those plant species you would normally find in the desert.

We got the guided tour from Ben, first of the desert, then the tropical biome: The tropical biome was very warm indeed. Prasanth compared it to Chennai in India, one of the warmest places on Earth. It was full of plants and trees that you might find in the rainforest, particularly those with which man has some kind of relationship. An umbrella plant, a shrubbish tree you would congratulate yourself for coaxing to a height of five feet in your centrally heated living room, here had reached its full height of about twenty-five feet. There were palms of a similar stature, bamboos and a large wild banana tree. I could identify those four without too much problem but, being something of an idiot when it comes to gardening, I hadn't a clue about the thousands upon thousands of others arranged throughout the biome. Some large artworks, mostly by local artists, were being used as shorthand explanations of ecological concepts and, like the guiding principles of Eden itself, these were refreshingly non-po-faced or pretentious.

We spent an hour or so in the biomes and emerged to a cooling breeze that felt, after the intense heat and humidity, like a Swedish plunge pool.

In my opinion, the tropical biome is one of the most magnificent structures ever built, not only because of its laudable purpose, which is to educate visitors in an entertaining way about the importance of plants, but also because of its sheer architectural gall. The best engineers, architects and project managers have made a superb job of presenting Eden as a modern, sustainable attraction that propels the image of ecology away from men with beards and oversized hemp jumpers and into the twenty-first century.

'We're an educational charity, but we're also a pragmatic educational charity,' says Gus Grand, who, because of her association with one of Eden's events – the Sexy Green Car Show, which we have unfortunately just missed by days – has been singled out to talk to us. 'And we try to start from where people are rather than where we think they ought to be.'

'There is, for example, a huge disconnect between the enormous problem of climate change and what you can do. But what you can do is DIY. If we all insulated our houses, used energy efficient appliances, turned electronics off, rather than leave them on standby, drive more efficient cars, we can do a lot about our own carbon emissions, leaving the politicians to argue about policy.'

Dan asked Gus whether there was something, anything, that wasn't being said on the subject of climate change.

'Well, yes there is,' said Gus. 'I think that climate change is a big opportunity to fix a whole lot of stuff that should be fixed anyway. The big thing about climate change is that it doesn't create any new problems, but it does turn up the volume on all the problems we already had – world poverty, health, inequity, all these kind of problems. What climate change does is give us a spur to fix all these other things. The world wasn't designed this way, it grew this way since the industrial revolution, and if we are going to overcome climate change, our generation is going to have to design the world the way we'd like it to be. I think that makes it a tremendously exciting time to be alive.'

We hooked up with the MTV crew and did our link. Rob Petit, the presenter, ran alongside us in our float while we introduced a track of Dan's choosing by the Foo Fighters. If I managed to sound terribly insincere as I said 'Learning to Fly', it's because I don't really have any love for the band or their stupid track. As a reprisal, I determined to play Van Halen during their long spandex phase all the way to Land's End.

Leaving Eden with a topped-up battery, we headed off towards St Austell to the south, whizzing down a precipitous hill into the town and emerging unscathed from the one-way system on the other side. We were now approaching Truro and the Cornish Riviera, but before we could get there we had about another fifteen miles of rather featureless three-lane carriageway to traverse. Coming into Cornwall, I had changed tack on choice of highway, guiding us along a lot of A roads, and for a very good reason – they tended to have been constructed using cuttings and embankments, which flattened out the terrain. As long as we didn't go on the holiday routes on a Saturday, the traffic on these roads was a lot lighter than we were used to. Unfortunately, they all look the same.

We rose out of St Austell on to the A390 Polgooth bypass, a steep and unforgiving hill that was followed by another. As we slowed to our traditional slug's pace, a beaten-up car of the kind we had become used to seeing in Cornwall, over-took us with a friendly toot of the horn and then pulled in a hundred yards up the road. The driver got out of the car and came running towards us, waving a scrap of paper. As we caught up with him, he handed it to Prasanth, shouted something I couldn't quite catch about St Austell and ran back to his car, speeding off in a puff of rather black exhaust fumes.

The note, scrawled in red, had an address, a phone number and an open invitation to come and see him and his partner for a charge on our way back through St Austell. You are, sir, an excellent chap, and even though we had no plans to drive the fucking thing back east, your little red note, your unsolicited kindness, cheered us all up enormously. What an absolutely fabulous day.

To compensate for the featureless road, we took some village detours on our long way to Truro. The grandest of these was Tresillian, where the wide tidal River Fal runs parallel to the road for almost a mile. On the opposite bank, mature broad-leaved trees grow down to the edge, their boughs occasionally dipping into the river. On my original plan for our route, we were going to cross this river, via the King Harry ferry, much farther downstream, where it is both narrower and much deeper – so deep, in fact, that ocean liners, tankers and cargo ships go to rust in peace there at the end of their useful life. Knowing what I know now, I thank my lucky stars that I didn't take us there. The King Harry ferry lies in a very steep wooded valley and we would have had to be towed out the other side.

On the long hill that winds around an extended left-hand bend towards Truro, yet another tailback formed and a certain amount of aggression was in evidence in the rear-view mirror. As we reached the top of the hill overlooking Cornwall's only cathedral city, I had to stop myself warning Dan and Prasanth of what I think of the place. I used to live about ten miles to the south-west in the large, by Cornish standards, town of Falmouth. As a former Falmothian, I harbour an instinctive loathing of Truro, which most Falmothians feel takes itself a little too seriously.

Once, on the train from Falmouth to Truro, I bought my day-return ticket from the guard and he replied, 'Ah, a day return to the Metropolis,' with a little conspiratorial wink. I knew then he was from Falmouth. The trouble is, as their city is the administrative centre of Cornwall, the seat of the diocese and the county's biggest shopping attraction, some Truronians seem to believe they live somewhere special, and it just isn't. Truro is too small, but has a self-image of being much bigger than it is. It's really neither here nor there. Apart from the proliferation of surf and pasty shops, it is also distinctly un-Cornish and seems to exist merely to give its occupants a feeling of superiority, purely based on its status as a city and the fact that there's a branch of Debenhams there. Get over yourselves.

I kept the lid on all of this to give Prasanth and Dan a chance to find some aspect of the place I'd overlooked. We went there with the intention of finding a charge and somewhere to stay, but it was late and most of the shops had closed, save for the odd chippy and Chinese restaurant. We parked up in the car park and Pras surveyed the toilet block and lamp posts for electrical inspiration. For the first time on our trip we witnessed some beered up bar-turds kicking some things in on the other side of the car park, and it made us feel a bit nervous. A sense of humour becomes progressively less useful as a defence mechanism the drunker your opponent becomes. Dan and I went for a walk up the main pedestrianised area.

'This place is so homogenous, we could be anywhere,' said Dan, pointing to a string of brand-name shops that lined the precinct.

'Well, this *is* basically the high street,' I felt obliged to mention, against my Trurophobic instincts. In its defence, most of these brand-name shops are absent from other town centres in Cornwall and, while I like towns to have distinctive retail outlets that have some regard to where they are, if you want to go shopping for brands or take up a special offer or sale at a particular outlet, Truro does at least save you from a long trek to Plymouth.

'I know,' Dan responded, 'but it's so dull. It's awful.'

I knew Truro well enough to know that unless we could

find a willing B&B landlady to let us unplug her cooker from the mains, our only real hope of a charge was to be found on the other side of town, where a couple of big-shed retail estates were located. We were really looking for food and shelter. A walk through to a road where I knew of a couple of lodging houses revealed a lot of 'no vacancy' boards, and we quickly became dispirited enough to abandon our mission and head back to the float.

The batteries were very low, so we had to turn to our default escape plan – find a campsite and charge up there, by hook-up or crook-up. The nearest one was on our route through to the west at Carnon Downs, about four miles away.

Through the boring Georgian streets of Truro we made our way out of the town, up a long hill and on to the Falmouth road. After a short downhill stretch, the road went uphill again and then followed a long windy terrace through woods for the rest of the way.

Just before the tiny hamlet of Playing Place, we dropped down to the fabled 20 per cent – the charge at which we were supposed to stop in case we damaged the batteries, but we had no choice but to carry on. Fortunately, it was just another mile up a straighter and much gentler hill.

We limped into Carnon Downs caravan park and phoned the late arrivals number posted in the window of a rather smart reception block. Superficially, this place resembled Oakdown, near Sidmouth. It had also won a number of awards over the last few years, and had an environmental angle to it. Maybe we had fallen on our feet again.

When I phoned Simon, the owner of Carnon Downs caravan park, I may have neglected to mention the nature of our vehicle to him. As he got out of his car to deal with us, he almost fell over laughing.

'Oh, so you want an electric pitch, then,' he said. 'Would that be to charge up your milk float, boys?'

'You've rumbled us,' I answered, holding out my hand to shake.

'I think this is absolutely brilliant,' said Simon, reading the 'Lowestoft to Land's End in 21 Days' sign on the side of the float. 'That's no problem. What do you need?'

19

Carnon Downs to Lizard Town

32 miles

DAN

After sailing along so effortlessly throughout the trip, our charging tactics finally backfired barely fifty miles from the end. Simon was prepared to let us unplug a caravan overnight to get a charge but The Mighty One was so excited in such salubrious surroundings that after forty-five minutes she'd blown a fuse. We'd tried another charging point – by rather presumptuously unplugging another empty caravan – but she blew that one out as well, so we decided to stop in case we got sued. Forty-five minutes of power wasn't very much but it was probably enough to get us to a charge somewhere else the following morning.

Having packed everything away the next day, Pras discovered that the connectors inside the cab had come loose, so instead of increasing our power, that forty-five minute charge had actually depleted it. We were now stranded, unless Simon could be persuaded to come to our aid. An hour later, we plucked up the courage to explain that we'd already blown two of his fuses before asking if we could have a go at blowing a few more. Considering the damage we'd done, his patience and kindness were a surprise, especially when he refused to let us pay anything to compensate him for the trouble we'd caused, or even for our pitch for the night. Meanwhile, Pras had crawled into the undergrowth beneath a static caravan that was powered by a B20 charging post (that's a 20-volt plug with B wiring, come on, keep up) and wriggled out again, having connected up, convinced that it would do the trick. Sure enough, at three o'clock, with full batteries, we set off for our penultimate stop and Britain's most southerly place – Lizard Point.

Of the many embarrassments we suffered, the worst two occurred within half an hour of leaving Carnon Downs. We came to the bottom of a hill and had soon caught up with a cyclist as we went up it. Full of bravado, I indicated to over-take but as I did so the cyclist decided to push himself on and an agonizing stand-off began. Well, it was agonizing for me. Should I give way and fall back or hammer on, hoping to get past, regardless of the train of cars behind me that couldn't overtake me until I had done one or the other? A few dozen angry horn blasts made up my mind for me and The Mighty One skulked back behind the cyclist, who pulled, gradually, away.

Far worse humiliation was to come, though. I spotted Ian swatting at his face and saw that a bee was in the cab with us, but we were going too slowly for the insect. It flew out of the open door and proceeded to buzz off ahead. It's a sad state of affairs when your vehicle gets overtaken by a sodding bumblebee. Perhaps it was simply repelled by the sound of Van Halen in spandex blaring out of the speakers. (I'd wager that must have been the first time a milk float has trundled along to the accompaniment of Led Zeppelin, The Cult and David Lee Roth.)

After a pit stop in Helston at Ian's obliging in-laws, we meandered down the bit of Cornwall that looks like the heel of Britain on a weather map. Once we'd passed the miles of razor wire on the edge of HMS *Seahawk*, the landscape became pleasingly barren and wild. Whenever the road ahead was clear enough, I surveyed the horizon, looking for pumas.

We soon came upon another exciting, but closed, Cornish attraction – Goonhilly Satellite Earth Station. Goonhilly is home to the world's first parabolic satellite communications antenna, which came into service in 1962 to connect with Telstar, the first communications satellite put up in space. Between them, they managed the first live transatlantic TV broadcast between Britain and the USA on 11 July 1962. President Kennedy was supposed to make a landmark televised speech but he wasn't ready, so footage from a baseball game was shown instead. The big dish – just under 30 metres in diameter and weighing in at 1,100 tons – was nicknamed 'Arthur' and was soon followed by 'Merlin' and 'Guinevere'. In 2008, Arthur will be decommissioned but as it has now become a grade II listed structure, you'll be able to see it not working there for ever more. Goonhilly also has a web café with one of the world's fastest internet connections – 100 megabits per second, according to the press release, if you're into that sort of thing, and if you're interested in Goonhilly, it's fair to say that you probably are. Needless to say, they run Apple computers rather than PCs.

It was while driving down to Lizard Point from the downs of Goonhilly that I stumbled on what I thought at the time was a truly brilliant idea. The blustery, empty and evocative environment began to feel like the perfect finale to our journey and I suddenly couldn't see any point in bothering going down to Land's End. What better way to end an adventure celebrating the joys of the journey than by getting within a stone's throw of your destination only to say, 'Oh sod it, let's just go home.'

There had been a few occasions on the trip when I'd suggested things to Ian and Pras that may have seemed a little odd – Buckfast Abbey springs to mind – and they'd largely humoured me, but this time they weren't going to budge.

'No. That would just be stupid,' replied Ian.

'Really, really stupid,' agreed Pras.

Perhaps it was just my 'milkman's arse' affliction repeating on me, but having ploughed our way through the foliage of narrow roads and parked up in a youth hostel car park an hour later, I was totally convinced that Lizard Point should be our last port of call as we surveyed the ragged coastline. But seeing as neither Pras nor Ian could drive, it didn't seem fair to force the issue. Whatever happened after that, though, my mind was clear. Lizard Point was where my journey reached its spiritual end.

It certainly put the question of tourist 'landmarks' in perspective. Here was a place I'd never heard of before that no doubt thousands of tourists have hurtled past in their quest to have a photo taken at a signpost at Land's End. There was no development to speak of – a few ramshackle old huts selling bizarre old tat (closed when we arrived at 8 p.m.) – a few wild flowers and a bad-tempered coastline marked by rather pathetic safety barriers. Lizard Point didn't seem to exist in the world of health and safety. It was perfect. Evocative, powerful, merciless – if the ridge of rocks stretching out into the sea was anything to go by – terrifying, awe-inspiring, desolate and surprising all at the same time. I couldn't imagine saying the same about the theme park and pasty shop encrusted Land's End. Lowestoft had been an appropriate damp squib but this was the blockbuster finale I'd been looking for.

We were all transfixed by the wind and cauldron of currents converging on the rocks below as the sun began to set.

Lizard Point is so-called because in Cornish 'lizard' (lys-ardh) means 'court on a height' presumably because of a now forgotten dwelling where the village of Lizard now lies. I prefer the apocryphal origin though, the one that attributes the name to the rocks that seem to clamber out into the sea like the spine and limbs of a giant lizard. It's certainly the kind of place that doesn't need a blue plaque to tell you about its past though, because you can feel its history trying to pull you over the edge. Geologically speaking, it's the oldest place in the country.

We met an old lady on the cliff, looking almost as chiselled as the rock itself. She seemed delighted by the expressions of wonder on all our faces.

'Oh yes,' she said, reading our minds. 'The coast should always be left alone.' Nodding wisely, she plodded off down the path.

A bit farther along the coastline, we spotted a dilapidated lifeboat ramp that we learned later was still in use. I began to imagine how desolate this place must seem from the sea. In the days before the far-off lands of the 'New World' were discovered in 1492, to the people of this land, this really was the end of the earth.

As we made our way slowly back to the car park, I couldn't help thinking that whenever we go abroad these days we seem desperate to read as many guidebooks as we can lay our hands on to discover 'local' knowledge, but we seem oblivious to the insight we have for our own land. I'm not saying there's nothing to be gained from travelling abroad but there's certainly nothing quite like spending some quality time getting re-acquainted with an old and much-treasured friend.

It's certainly worth forgetting about the places you 'have' to see and exploring those that lie between the sights instead. For every Land's End there's a Lizard Point; it's just a question of having enough time to discover it and being able to avoid the pull of the popularly mundane. But don't be fooled into thinking all these undiscovered 'landmarks' will make it easy for you by rigidly staying in the same place. A slow tour of Britain is a tour of the people you have the time to meet, just as much as the land itself. We found quite a few of these 'landmarks' perching on barstools, lounging by roaring fires in pubs, and crawling under milk floats looking for wonky wheels. Others were living in a university hall of residence, a monastery, or caravan parks. A few were serving behind bars and one was trying his damnedest to keep ASBO kids from going anywhere near them. We even found one, God help us, in a branch of Tesco. Our journey quickly became a tour of these living, breathing 'landmarks' that even the most up-to-date guidebook could never hope to contain – not that those you would discover on a similar journey could ever be the same as those we found, anyway. And that's the point for me.

I made it back to The Mighty One first and was almost run over by a couple of bored lads doing 'donoughts' in old cars in the gravel car park. In one of the cars, a small dog lying on the shelf above the back seat was barking furiously. It was utterly bizarre. Perhaps living in such a barren and remote place had a detrimental effect on your state of mind.

It was nearly dark when we returned to the small village three-quarters of a mile inland from Lizard Point. There was only one candidate for a bed for the night – a pub and B&B called The Tophouse. Inside, it seemed the kind of boozer where you want to curl up by a fire and drink frothing pints of local ale but, let's be honest, those kinds of pubs tend to have rather basic overnight accommodation. Happily for us, the owners had just spent a fortune on renovating the guest rooms, so we were greeted by flashy chrome fittings rather than upholstery that smelt of cat's piss.

We tucked into the first of many pints of Guinness, as thick mist rolled into the village, and the pictures of lifeboat crews over the ages adorning the walls began to haunt us all. The smiling faces seemed to call you to the rocks of so many tragedies, and we couldn't help but wonder how anyone could be so selfless and brave. Why is it that so many people living along Britain's coast consider themselves wardens of the most treacherous seas? Throughout the evening, as we talked about our adventure and the people we'd met along the way, those lifeboat crews hauled themselves into our collective imagination. We decided that their selflessness was the ultimate act of community.

One of the main reasons our trip was supposed to be 'impossible' was because no one we spoke to at the start believed we'd find enough people who would be prepared to help us along the way. These days everyone is supposed to be far too insular, far too self-obsessed to do anything other than look out for themselves – or as Gordon the former milkman and current warehouse manager at Morrisons in Diss put it, 'It's not like the old days.' Our experience, and The Tophouse's photographs of lifeboat crews from the distant past up to the present day, proved this sentiment to be totally untrue.

Sitting in a corner of the pub, we tried to make sense of our journey and came to the conclusion that driving around the country in a 1958 milk float was essentially little more than an excuse to meet and start talking to complete strangers. Our odd vehicle was just a password that enabled us to side step any cynicism we might otherwise have encountered. After all, you'd have to be a bit hard-hearted to be suspicious of three grinning buffoons crossing England in a milk float. But the way the people we'd met seemed to revel in not having to be suspicious for once while they were in our company was a genuine joy to behold. In our entire trip you could count on one hand the number of people who'd refused our cries for help and even those who did refuse usually had a good reason and sent us in the direction of someone who could help. It's almost as if today the entire country feels it has to cover itself with the thermal underwear of cynicism, even though it's about as natural to us as wearing a hair shirt. Why we all drape ourselves in this mindset is beyond me, but perhaps it's to do with the pace of life to which most of us are yoked – or maybe it's just something about milk floats. If that's the case and our milk float could make so many different people abandon their reticence and suspicions every time we bobbled up the road, then The Mighty One truly is mighty indeed.

All the people we met, regardless of their financial or social standing, were largely indifferent to the comings and goings of the ego-driven classes – the politicians, advertisers and media outlets that all vie for our collective attention (and before you say it, I'm well aware of our place among them). We watched no television and read no newspapers throughout the entire trip. We hardly spoke a word about politics, terrorism, bird flu, or whatever latest paranoia the Government is desperate to inflame, all the while we were on the road, but nonetheless we stumbled upon stories of great significance, which those with power still don't seem to have quite grasped – the idea that climate change is actually an opportunity to fix a whole host of socio-economic and cultural problems from Gus at the Eden Project, the possibility of clean, efficient transport from Stuart in Plymouth, and peak oil and the use of renewable energy sources from Clive, who, don't forget, works in Didcot power station. We heard a great deal about the environment, about sustainability and the merits of our 'green' vintage electric milk float.

In fact, everyone we met congratulated us on the 'eco' credentials of our trip, even though it wasn't a badge we revelled in ourselves. Of all the things I learned, it was really quite sobering to discover that the answer to our future environmental and energy problems can essentially be solved by renewable energy and an updated version of the same technology that has been around in the building of milk floats since as far back as 1958. I can't imagine you could have got as far as Lizard Point from Lowestoft in many cars of the same era.

But despite spending three weeks travelling a distance you could cover in an hour on a plane, or twenty-four hours in a car, the over-riding feeling about our journey when we were sinking pints in The Tophouse was that, somehow, we'd still managed to rush it. When it came to slow travel, it felt as though we had a great deal to learn.

Halfway into the trip I'd got in the car with James, my brother-in-law, to go to buy a few cans of beer, and the sensation of being in a normal car going at 35 miles per hour felt like being stuck on a roller-coaster. I'd already become so used to driving around slowly that the 'normal' pace of transportation felt absurd. Everything outside the window lost focus and became nothing but a blur, so I found myself ignoring it. The stereo drowned out the noise of the engine and everything outside along with it. My body soon accustomed itself to the sensation of speed and the comforts of a modern car, but the absence of the world I'd reacquainted myself with as we sped along felt real and profound. It was a curious and lurid sensation, as though my head had been placed in a rather flashy and exciting environment but I had a niggling feeling it was little more than burying that same head in slightly exotic sand. I spent a lot of time wondering what it would be like to get back into the swing of 'normal' life once our journey was at an end. I'd now come to the conclusion that our trip had been a window on what is actually a 'normal' pace of life and we'd have to go back to ignoring everything we'd started to value and respect from inside our slow, inconvenient and uncomfortable electric float when we rejoined the 'normal' modern world.

Of course, you should be very wary of coming to huge ideological conclusions when coming to the end of such a life-affirming journey, but I felt as though something inside me had shifted. I felt as though I needed to find a much slower pace of life. Although, it must be said, my life was not exactly *hectic* in the first place.

When it comes to the question of our energy future and the effects of climate change, it might seem counter-intuitive to believe that for the first time in history the future is about to slow us all down rather than speed us up – but big changes in our energy supplies suggest the way we live is about to change radically. Perhaps we have reached the point where 'progress' can finally be unchained from its obsession with greater speed and the accumulation of more and more financial wealth and allowed to settle down into being more about the quality of all our lives instead. I think it's time to stop seeing the changes on the horizon as unassailable problems and to think of them as an opportunity to live in a more relaxed and happier way.

More important for our little journey, though, was the answer to the question we'd posed ourselves back in the pub when we were writing on that beer mat. Is it *really* possible to love travel and the planet at the same time?

Well, I think we'll leave you to answer that.

20

Lizard Town to Land's End

39 miles

IAN

It is 1987 and I am hitchhiking my way around the Royal Naval Air Station at Culdrose in west Cornwall. Even then, in those days before global paranoia and some fellow called Al-Qaeda, hitchhiking was a very good way of drawing unwanted attention to yourself and, sure enough, a police car pulls up from out of nowhere. There are two types of police around here – the plain vanilla conventional coppers of the Devon and Cornwall Constabulary and the Ministry of Defence Police, who are known to one and all as the MoD Plod. The MoD Plod patrol the estates of married quarters that are dotted around Culdrose's nearest town, Helston, and, as far as I know, have no authority once they are off Ministry property.

Anyway, it's not the MoD Plod, which is a bit disappointing because they tend to stop for hitchhikers and offer you a lift in any direction as long as it's away from the air base. I have instead been apprehended by the local constabulary. They start to ask me questions, the sort they have no right to expect an answer to but which, for the sake of an easy life and avoiding confrontation, I answer. The formalities over, I gently enquire why I have been stopped.

'We find there's often a reason for someone we haven't seen before suddenly popping up,' says the copper. 'People come down to Cornwall for all sorts of reasons, but one of them is to run away. They run away from a drug addiction, from bad debts, from their wives and husbands and, occasionally, from us.'

Satisfied that I'm not an escaped convict, or wanted in three counties for grand larceny, the police get back in their car and drive off the way they came.

The incident stuck with me for many years because there is more than a smidgen of truth in it. Cornwall represents something very comforting to those in trouble, perhaps because almost anyone who has anything to say about the county has a happy childhood holiday memory that focuses the mind on lazy summer days by the sea. When you hit rock bottom, the bleary, colour-saturated memory of happy times could prove to be the perfect escape; while not actually leaving the troubles behind, you are able simply to dissociate from them.

Cornwall is, in its own way, dissociated anyway – cast adrift from industrial England in the nineteenth century with the wholesale closure of its tin mines; part of Britain but, as Cornish Nationalists believe, not part of England; separated by a wide river that runs along its border for all but a few miles; never completely overrun by the Anglo-Saxons, it is less of a county and more of a social, political, geographical and economic island. And, as if to confirm this, even the weather's from the mid Atlantic.

I came to this otherworld in 1985 when it still had the smack of 'West Barbary' about it. That is the pejorative term given to Cornwall by travelling missionaries and those of a metropolitan and dyspeptic disposition, which was subsequently adopted, from the eighteenth century on, as a pet name – something of a badge of honour – by many Cornish writers for their homeland. It has a non-English 'otherness', which grows stronger the farther west you travel, and here we were at its farthest reaches, where its heel and big toe curl themselves into the warm Atlantic waters.

We left the Lizard in bright morning sunshine and retraced our route over the wild wide plateau towards Helston. Lizard Town has an unfussy air about it. It's not really a resort, more of a place to visit, but a few bucket and spade shops and ice-cream parlours are gathered around the green together with a supermarket and the pub. The green – formally called 'The Square' – is used, in typically Cornish rough-and-ready fashion, as a car park. Off this central space, a number of lanes radiate like capillaries to further extremities of the peninsula and down these you will find Ann's 'Famous Pasty Shop', the Post Office and some lean-to shacks that sell ornaments carved from the local rock, serpentine.

We have Queen Victoria and Prince Albert to thank for them. On a yacht cruise in 1846, the couple visited the area and were impressed by the rock's unusual, mottled and scaly appearance – dark green to black, it's marbled through with jagged red, green and white veins and has a very gothic look about it. Their patronage kick started a vibrant industry of carving for architectural and monumental masonry. This little industry's best days are probably behind it now, but you can still purchase a serpentine lighthouse (with a little bulb in it, if you insist) or some other gothic bric-a-brac from one of the shacks.

Serpentine is a rock unlike most others in that it is not formed in the Earth's crust but in part of the mantle, a thick layer of solid and molten rock that starts about twenty miles under Cornwall and goes on for about 1,800 miles. Hot rock rises within this layer and starts to move horizontally and then falls again as it gets nearer to the surface and cools. This movement creates a conveyor belt effect that moves the

Earth's crust along, which in turn causes continental drift. The whole process is perhaps best understood as being like an enormous lava lamp. The Lizard's serpentine is thought to have been formed about 500 million years ago when Cornwall was located just off the west coast of Africa and the movement of continents brought the molten rock very close to the Earth's surface.

I mention all of this because the geodiversity of the Lizard goes some way to explaining its biodiversity – the rare heath plants, the exotic insects, the lush wooded valleys and wild moors are all there because of the geology – and while you can create a nature reserve just about anywhere with the right application of effort and willpower, it is and always will be beyond the means of humans to get back to first principles and actually move bedrock around the globe. As such, these places should be cherished because they are what nurture nature itself.

In Helston, we stop for another charge at my ever-so-obliging in-laws. Once we are done there, we head out towards Penzance via Porthleven, a classic Cornish working harbour town two miles to the south west. In common with most Cornish harbours, the town is like an auditorium, with terraces of houses arranged along the contours, clinging on to the hillsides that look over the haven below. The terraces are connected to one another by granite steps and by roads that zigzag their way up the precipitous inclines. The predominant colours come from the pinkish brown granite and the bright whitewashed rendered walls with their jet-black skirting. If you own a wall on public display in a Cornish village, you keep it looking spick and span all the time.

We trundled through the town along a granite terrace that wound its way towards the harbour. A Wesleyan chapel mingled with a laundrette, some chip shops and electrical retailers. During our time in Cornwall, I was struck by the fact that here is a place where large brands have not yet taken over (except in Truro). I'd never noticed it in all the years I'd lived there, but to have a locally owned electrical appliance shop in what are basically large villages is unheard of in the other places we visited. The streets of your average Cornish town look like the streets of an English town about fifteen years ago – and I'm not saying that's a bad thing, quite the opposite, in fact. Its low population and relative remoteness have not attracted the corporate world and that, once again, adds an 'otherness' to Cornwall.

The harbour is everything you would expect from a picture-postcard Cornish port. It has a couple of pubs, a fishmonger's and some general stores. Small fishing boats bob up and down on the water and a selection of rusting hoists and cranes stand ready for landing catches and cargo. Although there are small fishing harbours on the Lizard, Porthleven is Britain's most southerly port – the distinction being that a port specifically has facilities for unloading and loading cargo, whereas a harbour is about taking refuge or mooring your boat.

Once through Porthleven, we rejoined the main road, which took a generally downward course to Penzance, our destination for the night, where we were due to pick up the Lady from Radio 4, who wanted to record the last leg of our journey.

In the manner of a firework display, you should always save the best until the very end and I, or rather Cornwall, had a treat for Dan and Prasanth, neither of whom had ever set foot in the county before. I had mentioned St Michael's Mount to them and they may well have seen picture postcards and scenic photos of it, if not on the way through Cornwall, then at some time before the journey. However, nothing can prepare you for seeing the real thing for the first time. The reason why it takes such a great picture for a postcard is, perversely, the fact that you simply cannot capture the whole of its magnificence in two dimensions. Maybe you could hint at its stature by displaying film of it on a massive surround-sound cinema installation located in a wind tunnel with airborne psychedelic drugs helpfully provided in which to marinate your sensory inputs, but I doubt it, and if you're that desperate you may as well spend thirty quid on a rail ticket and go and see it for real.

The Mount, as it's known locally, sits about four hundred yards off the coast at Marazion and is connected to the mainland at low tide by a causeway. It dominates the land and seascape by virtue of the brute force of its sheer physical presence. It has the same visual effect as an aircraft carrier would moored in a boating lake. You just can't keep your eyes off it.

The pyramid-shaped island rises steeply to over two hundred feet, yet is barely more than twenty acres in size. At the top stand a castle, a priory and its own parish church. An oxygen cylinder would be handy as the path is so precipitous, it's no wonder that fishermen saw a vision of St Michael at its summit in the fifth century.

It's likely that, before post-glacial sea levels rose for the last time – around five thousand years ago – the area around the Mount was wooded, which would explain the Cornish name for it, Carrack Looz en Cooz, which means literally 'the grey rock in the wood'. Old Cornish tales tell of the legendary lost land of Lyonesse, which was believed to extend as far as the Scilly Isles, nearly thirty miles to the west of Land's End, and, to add weight to the legends, which may be a version of folk memories passed down through oral tradition, fragments of a fossilized forest have been found nearby in the bay.

Legend has been integral to the Mount ever since. Indeed, the story of St Michael's Mount is the story of Cornwall and also, partly, of Britain, and a few of its highlights are worth recounting here.

The island may well be one of the oldest recorded locations in the whole of Western Europe if it is, as postulated, the Mictis noted by Pliny the Elder in *Naturalis Historia* as well as the Ictis of Diodorus Siculus's *Bibliotheca Historica*. Both of these authors had access to the records of the geographer Pytheas, who visited the Mount at some point between 330 and 320 BC, as part of his circumnavigation of the British Isles, on the Cornish leg of which he decided to undertake a study of the production of tin. Paraphrasing Pytheas' account from the fourth century BC, Diodorus writes in his *Bibliotheca*:

'The inhabitants of that part of Britain called Belerion or the Land's End from their intercourse with foreign merchants, are civilised in their manner of life. They prepare the tin, working very carefully the earth in which it is produced . . . Here then the merchants buy the tin from the natives and carry it over to Gaul, and after travelling overland for about thirty days, they finally bring their loads on horses to the mouth of the Rhône.'

Pytheas is also important because he records the name that the Cornish gave themselves – and eventually, after it was mangled by the Greeks and Romans in the customary way, gave to the entire nation, as well as a royal yacht, a goddess and a medium-sized building society. He noted that the people of Cornwall referred to themselves as 'the Pretani'. This eventually became Britannia under the Romans, and then Britain.

In 1075, following the Norman conquest of 1066, control of the Mount was handed to its French counterpart, Mont St Michel. A church was built there in the twelfth century to act as a priory for the Norman monastery in France. Sixty years later, work on building the castle began.

In 1588, the Mount again played a decisive role in the life of Britain as a whole, when a beacon was lit there, the first to warn of the approach of the Spanish Armada.

Oh, and in 2003, St Michael's Mount, as well as its French counterpart, Mont St Michel, was used as inspiration for the design of Minas Tirith in the first film of Peter Jackson's *Lord of the Rings* trilogy.

We drove along beside a seawall, with the Mount at our left and Marazion Marsh – an area of reed banks and flooded fields – to our right. In Penzance, a large town by Cornish standards, we found Kim at the cab rank outside the railway station. Prasanth transferred to the back of the float and we moved off with Kim in the cab.

The first time we met Kim, she accompanied us to the Bear Inn in Beyton three weeks ago, at the start of our journey. Things could not have been more different. For a start, there was the weather. We were experiencing the latest in a series of bright days with blue skies and a flock of light fluffy fair-weather clouds on high. Back at the Bear, at the absolute nadir of the bank holiday weather, every time any of us walked anywhere, water would squelch and squeeze from our shoes, so dire were the conditions.

Then there was our entire outlook. For the first few days of our mission, we were plagued by the feeling that we weren't going to be able to do it. What started as a kind of niggling doubt gradually evolved into a vague worry. Now, we had almost finished, we knew what we were doing, we knew where to go, what we wanted and how to ask for it. We were almost home.

Talking of home, there had been much talk, before and throughout our journey across England, about how getting to Cornwall was effectively a return home for me. This was strange because I never felt that way. Although I lived in Cornwall for almost twenty years, it was only where I lived, and not really my home. Home is where you feel comfortable, where you are accepted for who you are, where tiny tendrils draw you back when you leave.

I'm not saying it isn't an absolutely wonderful place to be. I don't need to tell anyone that. Whenever I tell people where I used to live, they let out a tiny little sigh. In that sigh is a memory of a wonderful childhood holiday, a mental picture of wide, deep clear water under a blue sky or a *Swallows and Amazons* style vision of a calm river in a steep flooded valley, where the trees come all the way down the slope to the water's edge. My parents, who used to come down to Cornwall from London in the early 1960s, presumably for dirty weekends as well as the lure of the lush scenery, had the same dewy-eyed view of the place. That's the wonder of Cornwall. It inspires that kind of longing. So much so that my father persuaded me – and he was a very persuasive man – to come with him, Mum and my brother Rob, long after my brother and I had officially left home and were comfortable in poverty and living in, of all places, Lowestoft. My dad was a great salesman and so, after a few weeks of soft soap and the use of an old 1970s picture book of Cornwall in which photographs of tiny harbours and sunny cliff tops acted as a brochure for the county, he took it upon himself not to let it go until I capitulated. He was so good, the realization took years to dawn on me that I had never really decided to go to Cornwall; I'd merely agreed to do so.

Somewhere *en route* once again from east to west it suddenly occurred to me that that was the real story here. The last time I travelled from Lowestoft to Cornwall, it was not wholly on my own terms. It was also in a Morris Marina with a broken leaf spring, so it's a toss-up which journey was the more comfortable – three weeks on a mobile park bench or a quick moonlit flit in British Leyland's contribution to the late 1970s. You can imagine my surprise when, after all the propaganda about the Cornish Riviera, the sub-tropical gardens and the gulf stream, I arrived just as it started to snow heavily. I then spent a miserable winter having asthma attacks in a pine chalet that was so cold and damp that you had to dry out the bed sheets every night with a hairdryer.

The one thing that Cornwall told me about itself in the two decades I was there was that it is the lobster pot at the end of the world. On the whole, people come and they do not leave. You probably stand a better statistical chance of getting out if you are born there and are actually Cornish. You take that Cornishness with you and in that you are like generations of economic migrants before you. The world's metal ore mines are full of people with Cornish names, such as Trevithick, Pascoe and Pengelly, a result of the collapse of the tin-mining industry in the nineteenth century. Taking your roots with you wherever you go strikes me as an important part of the concept of home. For my part, my parents were Londoners, and my grandfather was brought up in a street very near to where I live. A little road a hundred yards from his home, known as Vince Street, is only a ten-minute bus ride away. I am at home in London. There is no 'going back' to Cornwall. I am not Cornish.

We had just one more place to go to finish our penultimate day – the tiny village of Madron, just to the north-west of Penzance. We were going there for a specific reason – to stay with my brother Rob, his partner Diane and their family.

My big brother Rob is an electrician, musician and photographer, and as well as looking forward to seeing him, I was wondering how he would get along with Prasanth, our very own electrician, sound and pictures guy. If a refreshing ability to cackle in the face of adversity was anything to go by, I thought, they should get on like a house on fire, even without all 'the tech stuff' as Pras calls it. We were greeted by Di with what I hope she won't mind me describing as a big silly grin, closely followed by my nephew, Luke, wearing a good-sized smile himself. It was fantastic to see them.

'Wow, you're here. Rob's just popped out, he'll be back soon.'

We settled down for lashings of hot tea and pizza. Dan suggested that we should hook up immediately, but I thought it might be better to wait until the electrician of the house arrived back, which was just me being over-sensitive. He would have probably been fine about it. Rob got back eventually and it was great to catch up. It was the first time we'd seen one another for at least a year, so we chatted for a while in the kitchen, the seat of family discussion the world over.

Rob showed Pras the fuse box and the two giggled in the hallway as if they were sharing secret electrician's jokes. The charge sorted, we sat down, drank more tea and talked long into the night about family, floats and just saying, 'Sod it, I'm in control of my own destiny.'

After a sound night's sleep on the lounge floor, I awoke to the realization that this was going to be the last day. Today we would complete our lunatic mission to go from one side of the country to the other in an electric milk float. Today would be the end of our journey.

The true traveller – and I think that's what all three of us had succeeded in becoming on this trip – longs to depart on new journeys, but never really wants to arrive, and so it was with us. The end is never really the destination – the journey is the purpose – but the last moments of a trip are always overtaken by the prosaic everyday preoccupations of real life.

We were all distracted by whether we needed to get some milk; whether we had actually locked the back door several weeks ago, and what we would have for tea tomorrow night. Real life has a way of making its tiresome presence felt.

We were all sad that it was nearly over but I was still keen to cling to the last leg of the journey and looked out some things to do on the way that might make a defining moment, raise an eyebrow of surprise, or simply put off the inevitable. It was rather like having a fantastic meal and hoping to round it off with an apocalyptically wonderful After Eight mint. We had seen so much beauty these last few weeks, met such kindness and warmth, experienced joy, despair and all the other defining emotions, following all of that was going to be exceedingly hard.

At the same time, in spite of our run of magical realism over the last few weeks, this mission had also assumed the mantle of normality, as if it was a perfectly rational thing to do. All we had to do now, on our last day, was shake off that run-of-the-mill feeling and go out in a blaze of non-conforming glory. While the Chinese proverb states that 'even a journey of a thousand miles starts with a single step' or, in our case, 'the turning for the A146 to Beccles', the Japanese proverb has it that 'when you have completed 95 per cent of your journey, you are only halfway there'. Our problem seemed to be that somewhere in our minds we had already finished and were now attempting to give it, in the clichéd jargon of football commentators, 110 per cent.

Before we got going, we loafed around the house for a few hours, putting off our departure. The float had attracted a bit of attention from the kids in the houses around – the children of neighbours – and it was fitting to take Luke and some of the others on little drives up and down the close.

Unable to hold off any longer, we had to make the final

push, the last day on the float, all the way to Land's End, only about ten or eleven miles west. So we left.

I finally realized that forcing the issue was not the answer. Serendipity had been our guide so far and if anything was going to happen, it should occur in the way that it had done all the way down from Lowestoft. Today I would simply get us on the right roads for Land's End.

So we passed by possibly the most interesting part of Cornwall, West Penwith, wherein the spirit of West Barbary truly resides. We passed up the opportunity to go and see Madron Well, with its votive rags hung on trees in hope of a cure for the sick – the idea being that as the fabric rots away, so does the illness (the last time I was there, a number of the rags appeared to be made out of synthetic fabrics, so condemning their owners to a lifetime of sickness). We also drove past the magical Boscawen-Un stone circle, Carn Kenidjack and Woon Gumpus, names that end-to-end walker John Hillaby likened to the sound of an incantation.

We failed also to meet any of the artists, craftsmen and alternative lifestylers for whom Penwith is rightfully a magnet. We preferred to keep our own quiet company – Dan, Pras, The Mighty One and I. We closed ranks and barely noticed the outside world again. Indeed, I can barely remember even our trusty Lady From Radio 4 in the cab – she must have been there, but all I can see is Dan and Prasanth. We had become utterly disconnected and may as well have been in a fast car bombing down the motorway. Our arrival was going to be purely symbolic.

On we ploughed, as slow as you like, to our own anti-climactic end point, the less than truly magnificent Land's End.

We arrived a little earlier than planned, a rich irony given that it took us three weeks to get somewhere even a couple of cyclists could manage in a week. At the entrance to the car park, we were given our final reward – the benefit of free parking is extended for all end-to-enders apparently, a saving of £3 for a six-hundred-mile journey.

We were keen to get as close to 'the end' as possible. Could we park by the famous sign, we enquired.

'No, you can't get down there by road,' the man in the booth replied.

We park up, but immediately find somewhere a bit nearer, so elect to drive on to the 'disabled vehicle' parking spot, reasoning that, as far as vehicles go, ours is about as disabled as you can get. As we arrive, we all notice a pair of blue 32-amp sockets screwed to the fencepost. At last, we think, the gods of serendipity are giving us a final sign. We park again, right in front of the post. The float falls silent and there is a tangible lull in the chatter. I close up my laptop with its Ordnance Survey map of southern England still displaying the bottom left-hand corner of Britain. We have arrived. Job done. But we can't resist the lure of that big blue plug. Prasanth gets out his electric multimeter claw to test the socket. We open it up and find that it is pointing to the sky and, as a consequence, is full of water. It's as dead as the fencepost it's screwed to.

'Just as well,' says Pras. 'It wouldn't be very safe if it was live,' which strikes me as a touching nod to Health and Safety – there's a first time for everything, after all. Maybe after thirty-two charges of varying degrees of danger, Pras was a reformed character and would play it strictly by the book from here on in.

We mill around, a little like we did in Lowestoft, not sure what to do next. We eventually decide to go right to the end and come back for the float if we can get it any nearer. We are nothing if not completists. We set off in the direction of the most westerly point on mainland Cornwall, or England, if you insist.

Before we go, however, there is still the question of a charge – we can't just leave the float here. We have to get it back to Penzance so that it can be loaded onto the back of a truck and taken home. For one last time, we go off in search of electricity.

'Let's do it for old time's sake,' says Dan.

We quickly locate the Land's End information centre and they put a call in to the duty manager, Keith. We explain our predicament, but here we are conscious that it probably doesn't sound that strange to him.

Sure enough, Keith sorts out an outside socket for us and while Prasanth performs his last bespoke electrical installation of the trip, Keith relates some tales of silliness roughly on a par with our own.

'There was a man who travelled from end to end in a swimming pool on the back of a lorry. Claimed he had swum all the way, but he didn't really, did he? Then there was someone on a portable toilet seat. And a guy came from John O'Groats carrying a door, another was walking backwards. We've seen them all, really. I don't think we've seen a milk float before, though.'

Suddenly it dawns upon us that after our few weeks of classic English eccentricity, we have arrived at a spot where this kind of thing is perfectly normal. For even if you've not come here in a consciously wacky manner as we and thousands of others have, everyone here has come out of their way to visit, purely to witness what one of the four cardinal points of the country really looks like.

It turns out that it isn't much to write home about. The journey was what was really important. We charged up, cracked open a bottle of champagne and some packs of cheese balls and then turned the float around to go home.

Acknowledgments

We really wouldn't have got very far with *Three Men in a Float* without either a very long extension lead or the assistance and support of all the following lovely people, arranged here in an east to west fashion, because that's how we do things around here.

John and Janet in Lowestoft, Matt at the King's Head in Bungay and Gordon the ex-milkman at Morrisons in Diss. Johnny and Juliette at the Bear Inn, Lucy and the team at B&Q in Bury St Edmunds, Shelley, Ali, Bobbledy Bob and Fran in Moulton.

Ed Cumming in Cambridge, Jason and the staff of Newey and Eyre in Cambridge.

Graeme at Thermo King in Houghton Regis on the out-skirts of Dunstable.

John Myatt again and his son. Paul in Hitchin, Shane at Top Wok and Kath and Mac in Princes Risborough. Peter Keen and Hypnos Beds, Clive Burke in Dorchester upon Thames, John, Sarah, Coco, Boots and Harry Lloyd. John and Sheila and John Berry at The Cooper's Arms in Pewsey, Pat Shelley, Phil Harding and Keith Moon – the Patron Saint of milk floats in Salisbury, Chris Yates and Tescos in Blandford Forum. Rowland's Wait campsite in Bere Regis, the Axminster Carpet Factory, Alisdair and the staff at the Oakdown caravan and campsite in Sidmouth and the Environment Agency in Exeter. Ocean View campsite in Shaldon, the landlord of the Tally Ho! At Littlehempston, somewhere deep in the Devon countryside. Brother Daniel and all the monks at Buckfast Abbey, Deborah Clark, Gary and the rest of the staff at the Burgh Island Hotel. Stuart Billingshurst in Plymouth (and in many other places, at the end of his customer support phone line).

Ian at the Polbeare Campsite near Landrake in Cornwall, Juliot's Well holiday park in Camelford, Ben and Gus at the Eden Project and Rob Petit and the crew from MTV Flux.

Simon at Carnon Downs Caravan Park. Anne and Gordon Oaten in Helston, Clare and Bev at The Tophouse in Lizard Town. Rob Vince and Diane Adey in Madron and, finally, Keith at Land's End.

Many thanks to Nitin, who let us use his yard in South London and for helping Dan fend off the man they found urinating on The Mighty One – a thinly-veiled pretext for seeing if there was anything worth nicking inside. He also provided many things that would have been useful in an emergency, had one occurred.

And, of course, to Prasanth, provider of rare services indeed.

Finally, to Kate, Freya, Rachel and Wilf who continue to put up with our absurd behaviour. Next time it's Monte Carlo or Bust.